Robert J. Kus, RN, PhD
Editor

Spirituality and Chemical Dependency

Pre-publication
REVIEWS,
COMMENTARIES,
EVALUATIONS . . .

"**R**eading this book has been both educative and refreshing; educative in the sense that the book opened my eyes to numerous gaps in my own "traditional" approach and in strengthening my intuition and feeling that there is at least one more component to the study of addictive behaviors: the spiritual aspect . . . This is an aspect that remains virtually unstudied and was ignored for a long time. It was refreshing in the sense that the philosophical as well as practical approach outlined does not pathologise. It seems that the "Remarriage" of body-mind-and-spirit influences our everyday lives, especially chemical dependent persons. The book's orientation toward the scientific study of the spiritual may improve our understanding of the addictive behaviors and our ability to prevent and treat these enduring problems."

Yaakov Moab, PhD
Director, Methadone Treatment Center
Tel-Aviv, Jaffa and Hadera, Israel

"**S**ome people have a misconception that recovery from alcoholism or other chemical dependencies consists of only abstinence. Those who are most familiar with these conditions know that abstinence is indeed a "sine qua non" for recovery, but it is only a beginning. Abstinence without substantive characterological changes results in the "dry drunk syndrome."

The various personality changes that are essential for quality recovery can all be subsumed under "spirituality." Spirituality is thus what makes the difference between being "dry" or "clean" and "sober." However, there is much confusion about what comprises spirituality. Some people identify spirituality with religion, and while religion has much to offer in spirituality, it is also possible to be very spiritual while being an avowed atheist.

Dr. Kus has presented several perspectives on spirituality. Like a ray of light which is refracted by a prism into its various components, spirituality is indeed "all of the above." Anyone interested in recovery, whether a person struggling to free himself from any of the addictive conditions or to maintain recovery, and certainly those who in any capacity minister to the needs of a recovering person or codependents, will gain a great deal of insight into this essential ingredient in recovery. *Spirituality and Chemical Dependency* is a "must read" for all those who provide services to the people in recovery from any of the many addictive conditions."

Abraham J. Twerski, MD
Founder and Medical Director,
Gateway Rehabilitation Center;
Associate Professor of Psychiatry,
University of Pittsburgh School
of Medicine

More pre-publication
REVIEWS, COMMENTARIES, EVALUATIONS . . .

"**A**ny edited work, even on the topic of spirituality, invites the question, "What's in it for me?" Such volumes offer variety: the reader searches less for a unified theme than for practical insights.

This book wanders widely. Three of its thirteen essays focus on gay and lesbian experience, offering useful suggestions for therapists unfamiliar or uncomfortable with this population. Chapters on art therapy and music therapy offer practical directions as well as hortatory encouragement. Five pieces subject seven of A.A.'s Twelve Steps to varying levels of analysis.

The strongest essays are by Father James Royce and Sisters Letty Marie Close and Mary Gene Kinney. Royce offers a comprehensive interpretation of his "spiritual progression" chart. Anchored in a classic tradition of spirituality, he applies ancient wisdom to the modern phenomenon of addiction, demonstrating that we need not so much "a new understanding of spirituality" as an honest appreciation of what spirituality's story actually offers.

Kinney and Close's unfolding of A.A.'s Steps Eight and Nine har-bors many riches, helpful equally to clinicians and to members of Twelve-Step fellowships working that program. In an era too ready to see self as victim, Kinney and Close gently urge the embrace of responsibility. In the midst of a literature of self-laudatory recovery porn, they suggest change and openness to further change, especially in the difficult area of deep attitudes. Making amends, they remind, must go beyond saying "I'm sorry."

Both articles, Royce's and that by Kinney and Close, will irritate some and provoke discussion by others. But those genuinely seeking to live spiritually will recognize in them the resonance of helpful truth."

Ernest Kurtz, PhD
Adjunct Research Scientist,
Center for Self-Help Research,
University of Michigan

More pre-publication
REVIEWS, COMMENTARIES, EVALUATIONS . . .

"**S**pirituality and Chemical Dependency by Robert Kus is a collection of thoughtful essays that proves that there is still room for another good book about recovery. Reading these essays is nourishing in the same way attending a good 12-Step meeting is: each writer here brings the richness of their personal experience to the familiar steps, gifting the reader with fresh wonder at the perennial wisdom contained in this Program."

Mary Hayes-Grieco, BA
Author, The Kitchen Mystic
and the 1995 calendar Spiritual
Lessons Hidden in Everyday Life

"**T**his book will be of value both to the pastor and the chemical dependency treatment provider. It helps reinforce the crucial links between spirituality and recovery.

The need for a broader view of spirituality is addressed in chapters on new understandings of spirituality and new definitions of God or a Higher Power. The spiritual needs of alcoholics and addicts are addressed all through the book, as are those of abuse survivors, gays, lesbians, Native Americans, and HIV positive people. The roles of music and art in exploring and expanding spirituality are explained, and examples are given. Chapters describe several of the steps, and the roles that clergy can play in facilitating recovery.

This book's great value is all of the alternatives it opens to the reader for new and different ways to experience God, as we understand God or as we don't understand God. The variety of contents encourage exploration and change in a spirit of "take what you want and leave the rest."

John A. Mac Dougall, D. Min.
Supervisor of Spiritual Care
Hazelden Foundation
Center City, MN

Harrington Park Press

Spirituality
and
Chemical Dependency

Spirituality
and
Chemical Dependency

Robert J. Kus, RN, PhD
Editor

Spirituality and Chemical Dependency, edited by Robert J. Kus, was simultaneously issued by The Haworth Press, Inc., under the same title, as a special issue of *Journal of Chemical Dependency Treatment*, Volume 5, Number 2, 1995, Dana Finnegan, Editor.

Harrington Park Press
An Imprint of
The Haworth Press, Inc.
New York •London

1-56023-069-X

Published by

Harrington Park Press, 10 Alice Street, Binghamton, NY 13904-1580 USA

Harrington Park Press is an imprint of The Haworth Press, Inc., 10 Alice Street, Binghamton, NY 13904-1580 USA.

Spirituality and Chemical Dependency has also been published as *Journal of Chemical Dependency Treatment*, Volume 5, Number 2 1995.

© 1995 by The Haworth Press, Inc. All rights reserved. No part of this work may be reproduced or utilized in any form or by any means, electronic or mechanical, including photocopying, microfilm and recording, or by any information storage and retrieval system, without permission in writing from the publisher. Printed in the United States of America.

The development, preparation, and publication of this work has been undertaken with great care. However, the publisher, employees, editors, and agents of The Haworth Press and all imprints of The Haworth Press, Inc., including The Haworth Medical Press and Pharmaceutical Products Press, are not responsible for any errors contained herein or for consequences that may ensue from use of materials or information contained in this work. Opinions expressed by the author(s) are not necessarily those of The Haworth Press, Inc.

Library of Congress Cataloging-in-Publication Data

Spirituality and chemical dependency/Robert J. Kus, editor.
     p. cm.
     "Has also been published as Journal of chemical dependency treatment, volume 5, number 2, 1995"–T.p. verso.
     Includes bibliographical references and index.
     ISBN 1-56024-745-2 (THP : alk. paper). -- ISBN 1-56023-069-X (HPP : alk. paper)
     1. Twelve-step programs--Religious aspects. 2. Recovering addicts--Religious life. 3. Substance abuse--Religious aspects. I. Kus, Robert J.
BJ1596.S735 1995   95-19607
291.1'783229–dc20   CIP

To my friend
Dave Erickson in the Big Sky Country
who could teach us all a thing or two about spirituality!

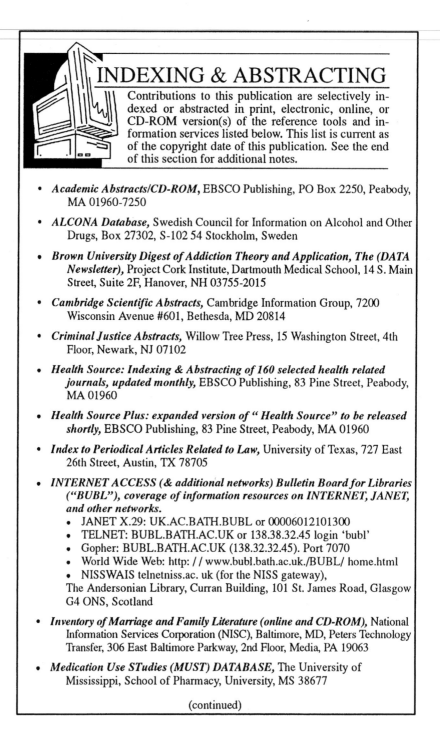

INDEXING & ABSTRACTING

Contributions to this publication are selectively indexed or abstracted in print, electronic, online, or CD-ROM version(s) of the reference tools and information services listed below. This list is current as of the copyright date of this publication. See the end of this section for additional notes.

- *Academic Abstracts/CD-ROM,* EBSCO Publishing, PO Box 2250, Peabody, MA 01960-7250

- *ALCONA Database,* Swedish Council for Information on Alcohol and Other Drugs, Box 27302, S-102 54 Stockholm, Sweden

- *Brown University Digest of Addiction Theory and Application, The (DATA Newsletter),* Project Cork Institute, Dartmouth Medical School, 14 S. Main Street, Suite 2F, Hanover, NH 03755-2015

- *Cambridge Scientific Abstracts,* Cambridge Information Group, 7200 Wisconsin Avenue #601, Bethesda, MD 20814

- *Criminal Justice Abstracts,* Willow Tree Press, 15 Washington Street, 4th Floor, Newark, NJ 07102

- *Health Source: Indexing & Abstracting of 160 selected health related journals, updated monthly,* EBSCO Publishing, 83 Pine Street, Peabody, MA 01960

- *Health Source Plus: expanded version of " Health Source" to be released shortly,* EBSCO Publishing, 83 Pine Street, Peabody, MA 01960

- *Index to Periodical Articles Related to Law,* University of Texas, 727 East 26th Street, Austin, TX 78705

- *INTERNET ACCESS (& additional networks) Bulletin Board for Libraries ("BUBL"), coverage of information resources on INTERNET, JANET, and other networks.*
  - JANET X.29: UK.AC.BATH.BUBL or 00006012101300
  - TELNET: BUBL.BATH.AC.UK or 138.38.32.45 login 'bubl'
  - Gopher: BUBL.BATH.AC.UK (138.32.32.45). Port 7070
  - World Wide Web: http: / / www.bubl.bath.ac.uk./BUBL/ home.html
  - NISSWAIS telnetniss.ac. uk (for the NISS gateway),
  The Andersonian Library, Curran Building, 101 St. James Road, Glasgow G4 ONS, Scotland

- *Inventory of Marriage and Family Literature (online and CD-ROM),* National Information Services Corporation (NISC), Baltimore, MD, Peters Technology Transfer, 306 East Baltimore Parkway, 2nd Floor, Media, PA 19063

- *Medication Use STudies (MUST) DATABASE,* The University of Mississippi, School of Pharmacy, University, MS 38677

(continued)

- *Mental Health Abstracts (online through DIALOG)*, IFI/Plenum Data Company, 3202 Kirkwood Highway, Wilmington, DE 19808

- *NIAAA Alcohol and Alcohol Problems Science Database (ETOH)*, National Institute on Alcohol Abuse and Alcoholism, 1400 Eye Street NW, Suite 600, Washington, DC 20005

- *Referativnyi Zhurnal (Abstracts Journal of the Institute of Scientific Information of the Republic of Russia)*, The Institute of Scientific Information, Baltijskaja ul., 14, Moscow A-219, Republic of Russia

- *Social Work Abstracts*, National Association of Social Workers, 750 First Street NW, 8th Floor, Washington, DC 20002

- *Special Educational Needs Abstracts*, Carfax Information Systems, P.O. Box 25, Abingdon, Oxfordshire OX14 3UE, United Kingdom

- *Violence and Abuse Abstracts: A Review of Current Literature on Interpersonal Violence (VAA)*, Sage Publications, Inc., 2455 Teller Road, Newbury Park, CA 91320

SPECIAL BIBLIOGRAPHIC NOTES

related to special journal issues (separates)
and indexing/abstracting

☐ indexing/abstracting services in this list will also cover material in any "separate" that is co-published simultaneously with Haworth's special thematic journal issue or DocuSerial. Indexing/abstracting usually covers material at the article/chapter level.

☐ monographic co-editions are intended for either non-subscribers or libraries which intend to purchase a second copy for their circulating collections.

☐ monographic co-editions are reported to all jobbers/wholesalers/approval plans. The source journal is listed as the "series" to assist the prevention of duplicate purchasing in the same manner utilized for books-in-series.

☐ to facilitate user/access services all indexing/abstracting services are encouraged to utilize the co-indexing entry note indicated at the bottom of the first page of each article/chapter/contribution.

☐ this is intended to assist a library user of any reference tool (whether print, electronic, online, or CD-ROM) to locate the monographic version if the library has purchased this version but not a subscription to the source journal.

☐ individual articles/chapters in any Haworth publication are also available through the Haworth Document Delivery Services (HDDS).

ALL HARRINGTON PARK PRESS BOOKS
ARE PRINTED ON CERTIFIED
ACID-FREE PAPER

CONTENTS

ABOUT THE EDITOR

Robert J. Kus, RN, PhD, a nurse-sociologist, specializes in gay men's studies and alcohol studies. In addition to studying sobriety in gay American men, Dr. Kus has been conducting cross-cultural gay men's studies in Europe where he has presented over 25 workshops and papers. The author of more than 30 book chapters and journal articles, Dr. Kus has edited *Keys to Caring: Assisting Your Gay and Lesbian Clients* (Alyson, 1990), *Gay Men of Alcoholics Anonymous: First-Hand Accounts* (WinterStar Press, 1990), and *Addiction and Recovery in Gay and Lesbian Persons* (The Haworth Press, Inc., 1995). He is currently studying to become a Roman Catholic priest for the Diocese of Raleigh, North Carolina.

Foreword

Spirituality is normally deductive, *aprioristic,* and imposed. A system for relating to the t(T)ranscendent is proposed and explained. From this system, conclusions are drawn. These conclusions are then applied to the life of the reader or student or person in "spiritual formation." At no point are the religious and spiritual aspirations, fears, concerns and needs of the subject considered. Nor at any point does the teacher, leader, director, or guru pause to ask whether the system which has been imposed has any impact on the subject.

Who, for example, would dream of "evaluation" research on the *Spiritual Exercises* or *Introduction to the Devout Life* or any of the other classics on which spiritual direction is based? Or who would want to test the effectiveness of the newer spirituality of existentialism and psycho-babble? It should be enough, one gathers, to proclaim the spiritual method, and then wait for the expected change to occur. If it doesn't, it is the fault of the subject and not the guru.

Among the many admirable qualities of the essays gathered in this volume is that the spirituality described herein is fundamentally empirical, *aposteriori,* and subject to constant evaluation. Since the very first article in the *Saturday Evening Post* (which I read as a precocious little boy because my father brought the *Post* home every week), I realized that the "twelve steps" were religious but different from the religion I learned in school. Now, a few centuries later, I understand that the spirituality which has been the foundation of dependency treatment ever since is different precisely because its

---

[Haworth co-indexing entry note]: "Foreword." Greeley, Andrew M. Co-published simultaneously in *Journal of Chemical Dependency Treatment* (The Haworth Press, Inc.) Vol. 5, No. 2, 1995, pp. xiii-xiv; and: *Spirituality and Chemical Dependency* (ed: Robert J. Kus) The Haworth Press, Inc., 1995, pp. xiii-xiv, and: *Spirituality and Chemical Dependency* (ed: Robert J. Kus) Harrington Park Press, an imprint of The Haworth Press, Inc., 1995, pp. xiii-xiv. Single or multiple copies of this article are available from The Haworth Document Delivery Service [1-800-342-9678, 9:00 a.m. - 5:00 p.m. (EST)].

© 1995 by The Haworth Press, Inc. All rights reserved.

origin came not from books or sermons but from hard experience–(experience which, of course, was based on the overarching tradition). Further, this spirituality is sustained by constant (if often simple and straightforward) evaluation of success and failure.

Thus, this volume is not merely an exercise in "applied spirituality"–though it is that–it is also an exercise in empirical spirituality and even in evaluated spirituality.

Although rough and ready evaluation is to be found in most of the essays in this volume, I should like to see more systematic evaluation of the sort that those wise in evaluation research perform on government programs. I would also wish that those who engage in other approaches to spirituality learn from the empirical method of the authors of these essays. A retreat master, a mission preacher, a spiritual director should, it seems to me, do a lot of listening before s/he begins to talk, so that the method (whatever it may be) is modified and adjusted to meet the needs and the hungers of those who constitute the "audience." Finally, while I'm not holding my breath, I would hope that such spiritual teachers learn from the authors in this volume that one needs to know after the fact what impact if any the spiritual exercise has had on the audience.

Therefore, I conclude that this collection is not only important for those who must treat chemical dependency, but also for those who one way or another have set themselves up in spiritual roles. On the basis of the evidence, the Holy Spirit (should there be One and whether there is social science as such cannot say) blows whither s(S)he will. She has been known to teach the teachers through the learners and to heal the healers through those being healed. Patently the authors of these essays know that. From them, the rest of us can learn a lot.

Andrew M. Greeley
Grand Beach
Labor Day, 1994

Introduction

Before 1935, a myriad of solutions were tried to deal with the problem of alcoholism. Religion failed. Law failed. Medicine failed. Penology failed. Alcoholism was, in effect, a virtual death sentence.

Then, in 1935, two alcoholic men, meeting in Akron, Ohio, came up with a new approach to the problem of alcoholism: spirituality. From this meeting, Alcoholics Anonymous and other 12-Step groups sprang up and spread over the globe like wildfire, creating one of the most fascinating miracles of the 20th Century–or of any century for that matter.

Because the 12-Step way of life has been the most successful form of treatment for alcoholism and other forms of addiction, and because *all* of the 12-Step way of life can be said to be spiritual, it would be wise to explore how spirituality is used to treat alcoholism and other forms of addiction.

PURPOSE AND STRUCTURE

The purpose of this collection of articles is to share current thinking on how spirituality is used in recovery from alcoholism and other forms of chemical dependency. The spirituality discussed in these articles uses that based on Alcoholics Anonymous and other 12-Step programs. Needless to say, this book is not meant to be an exhaustive collection, but rather, a collection to whet the appetite of the clinician for further research into spirituality and recovery.

[Haworth co-indexing entry note]: "Introduction." Kus, Robert J. Co-published simultaneously in *Journal of Chemical Dependency Treatment* (The Haworth Press, Inc.) Vol. 5, No. 2, 1995, pp. 1-4; and: *Spirituality and Chemical Dependency* (ed: Robert J. Kus) The Haworth Press, Inc., 1995, pp. 1-4; and: *Spirituality and Chemical Dependency* (ed: Robert J. Kus) Harrington Park Press, an imprint of The Haworth Press, Inc., 1995, pp. 1-4. Single or multiple copies of this article are available from The Haworth Document Delivery Service [1-800-342-9678, 9:00 a.m. - 5:00 p.m. (EST)].

© 1995 by The Haworth Press, Inc. All rights reserved.

After sharing some ideas on specific aspects of spirituality in the 12-Step context, the authors answer the ever-important clinical question, "So what?!"–by providing clinical implications.

CONTENT

In "A New Understanding of Spirituality," Fr. Leo Booth offers an understanding of the concept of spirituality as the relationship between mind, body, and emotions which permits spiritual empowerment. He discusses the disempowering effects of the traditional "mind-body-spirit" model of spirituality as well as the negative effects of unhealthy religion. Fr. Leo suggests steps and techniques for reclaiming spiritual empowerment and methods for guiding patients into healthy spirituality.

Fr. James Royce discusses the effects of alcoholism and recovery on alcoholics' spirituality in "The Effects of Alcoholism and Recovery on Spirituality." In addition to presenting his famous *Spiritual Progression Chart,* Fr. Royce discusses the difference between religion and spirituality and what is meant by calling alcoholism a "spiritual disease."

In "Defining God or a Higher Power: The Spiritual Center of Recovery," Drs. Finnegan and McNally discuss some of the ways that addiction affects one's concept of God or a higher power and the ways that recovery helps to change negative conceptions. For many recovering persons, outdated or childhood views of God or a higher power are replaced by more mature conceptions in sobriety, thus facilitating the recovery process.

In "Spiritual Reading as Bibliotherapy," Dr. Rojann Alpers defines the concept of bibliotherapy, reading for self-help or personal growth. Specifically, she focuses on how spiritual reading is critical in the recovery programs of many chemically dependent persons. Finally, Dr. Alpers shares specific literature which many chemically dependent persons have found helpful in their recovery process.

"Self-Examination in Addiction Recovery" contains notes on Steps 4 and 10 and is written by myself. In this article, *The Winter-Star Life Assessment Guide* is introduced as a guide for organizing and completing the 4th Step (making a moral inventory of self), a guide which has successfully been used in Europe and North America by addicts and non-addicts alike.

In "The Clergyperson and the Fifth Step," Fr. Mark Latcovich discusses the dynamics and function of the Fifth Step (admitting to God, self, and another human being the exact nature of one's wrongs) before sharing insights into making clergy referrals to those who request them. Finally, Fr. Latcovich provides clergypersons some helpful hints in assisting in the Fifth Step process.

The next article, "Steps Eight and Nine of Alcoholics Anonymous," is written by two Roman Catholic sisters, Mary Gene Kinney and Letitia Marie Close, who have devoted themselves to working with chemically dependent Catholic nuns. In addition to discussing how people can go about making amends to persons they have harmed, Srs. Kinney and Close share some of the difficulties recovering persons often find in working these steps.

In "Prayer and Meditation in Addiction Recovery," I define prayer and discuss two taxonomies or classification systems of prayer. One is based on purpose, and the other is based on whether or not the prayers are formal (written) or spontaneous. Following this, a discussion of two types of meditation is provided: reflective meditation and centering meditation. A list of popular meditation books used by recovering persons is provided for the clinician.

In "Applied Spirituality: Expressing Love and Service," Mr. Douglas J. King shares his vast experience with the reader. After sharing the stories of four recovering persons and how they apply spirituality in their lives, Mr. King discusses the historical dimensions of applied spirituality in AA. He then shows what types of service activities can be done at various levels of recovery, from the simple emptying of ashtrays for the beginner to sponsorship for the old-timer.

Ms. Mary Ann Miller from The University of Iowa Chemical Dependency Center discusses her work with art therapy in "Spirituality, Art Therapy, and the Chemically Dependent Person." After discussing what art therapy is and how it can enhance the recovering person's program, she shows how this form of therapy is used at Iowa to assist clients to focus more sharply on their own unique spirituality.

In "Music Therapy, Spirituality, and Chemically Dependent Clients," Ms. Joey Walker, also from The University of Iowa, defines music therapy, lists some of the benefits of music therapy, and discusses some of the specific music therapy techniques to deal with spiritual issues. Types of music therapy discussed include lyric analysis, songwriting, playing musical instruments, and doing variety shows. Ms. Walker ends with providing clinicians with valuable tips in this area.

The next article, "Never Too Late: The Spiritual Recovery of an Alcoholic with HIV," is a moving life story of a man who is an HIV+ recovering alcoholic. In addition to sharing his life story and listing some of the special resources available to the HIV+ recovering person, he provides some excellent suggestions for clinicians to help them give top-notch care to their HIV+ clients.

Finally, Dr. Terry Tafoya, a traditional Native American Storyteller, and Mr. Kevin Roeder, a social worker, discuss three minority groups who have very special spiritual needs: gays, lesbians, and Native Americans. In addition to sharing some of the common difficulties each of these groups has experienced as a result of organized religion, the authors share ideas with clinicians to maximize the recovery of the chemically dependent persons in these special populations.

CONTRIBUTORS

Each of the contributors for this collection are fine men and women who have devoted a significant part of their lives to making this a better world by helping those suffering from alcoholism and other forms of chemical addiction recover and maintain their recovery through time. Following the various articles, there is a "Contributors" section which the reader is encouraged to read.

Robert J. Kus, RN, PhD
Wickliffe, Ohio, USA

A New Understanding of Spirituality

Father Leo Booth, MTh, CAC, CEDC

SUMMARY. Father Leo explores a new understanding of spirituality as the relationship between body, mind and emotions which permits spiritual empowerment. He suggests that addictions, depression and other problems are symptoms of a broken relationship within the self. Father Leo discusses the disempowering effects of the traditional "body-mind-spirit" model of spirituality, as well as the negative effects of unhealthy religion, and shows how they contribute to the breakdown of the mental, emotional and physical relationship. Father Leo suggests steps and techniques for reclaiming spiritual empowerment, and effective treatment methods for guiding patients into healthy spirituality. *[Single or multiple copies of this article are available from The Haworth Document Delivery Service: 1-800-342-9678, 9:00 a.m. - 5:00 p.m. (EST).]*

Almost everywhere I go, people come to me confused and frustrated because they can't seem to "get" spiritual. They want me to help them figure out what they're doing wrong that's keeping them

Father Leo Booth is a nationally acclaimed author, educator and trainer in spirituality and recovery from depression, addictions, and low self-esteem. Fr. Leo is a parish priest at St. George's Episcopal Church in Hawthorne, California. He is the author of *When God becomes a drug: Breaking the chains of religious addiction abuse* and *The God game–It's your move: Reclaiming spiritual empowerment.*

Address correspondence to: Spiritual Concepts, 2700 St. Louis Avenue, Long Beach, CA 90806, USA.

[Haworth co-indexing entry note]: "A New Understanding of Spirituality." Booth, Father Leo. Co-published simultaneously in *Journal of Chemical Dependency Treatment* (The Haworth Press, Inc.) Vol. 5, No. 2, 1995, pp. 5-17; and: *Spirituality and Chemical Dependency* (ed: Robert J. Kus) The Haworth Press, Inc., 1995, pp. 5-17; and: *Spirituality and Chemical Dependency* (ed: Robert J. Kus) Harrington Park Press, an imprint of The Haworth Press, Inc., 1995, pp. 5-17. Single or multiple copies of this article are available from The Haworth Document Delivery Service [1-800-342-9678, 9:00 a.m. - 5:00 p.m. (EST)].

© 1995 by The Haworth Press, Inc. All rights reserved.

from feeling spiritual despite all their best efforts: changing religions, reading meditation books, doing service in the community. It's not that they're doing anything wrong, but that often they are being misled by many of the traditional concepts of spirituality. Once they have a different understanding of spirituality, many people are able to appreciate that they are already deeply spiritual.

I define spirituality as the relationship between body, mind and emotions that allows people to be positively and creatively connected to others and the world around them. Spirituality is not "out there" somewhere, on a higher level. Spiritual power is within us; it is manifested in our self-esteem, in our ability to make choices, take responsibility for our lives. Often, childhood messages and experiences cut or weaken the connection between our bodies, minds and emotions so that our ability to access and use our spiritual power is limited.

The relationship within the self of body, mind and emotions shapes the ability to relate to others, and to the spiritual power in the universe. Depression, addictions, compulsive behavior and low self-esteem are symptoms of a broken relationship within the self. They are symptoms of wounded spirituality. When the connection between body, mind and emotions is broken, the ability to respond healthily to life's circumstances is limited. As healers, our task is to help people unite the broken parts of themselves and learn to respond positively and creatively–to say YES to life.

Notice I said nothing about God or religion. That's because we don't have to be religious to be spiritual. We don't have to believe in God to be spiritual. Religion is a set of teachings and concepts about God that can either enhance spiritual growth or damage it. The problems arise when people get stuck with concepts about God which do not offer them healthy means of experiencing God in their lives. One of the most spiritually harmful things I have seen therapists and treatment centers do is hand patients a "spirituality assessment" in which a patient's spirituality is measured by a belief in God, the frequency of prayer and the number of times they think about God during the day, and the amount of service and sacrifice they give.

Spirituality cannot be measured. You can't assess it on a scale of one to ten. You can evaluate the degree of spiritual wounding based on the mental, emotional and physical problems a patient presents. In order to really heal wounded spirituality, it is absolutely essential to discover what someone believes about God, and how those beliefs may have contributed to the breakdown of the mental-emotional-physical relationship. But to measure spirituality in terms of a belief in God only furthers spiritual abuse.

SYMPTOMS OF WOUNDED SPIRITUALITY

- Depression
- Drug/Alcohol Abuse
- Eating disorders (overeating, bulimia, anorexia)
- Perfectionism and overachieving
- Workaholism
- Codependency
- Shame/guilt
- Religious addiction
- Sexual addiction
- Relapse, switched addictions, multiple addictions
- Any symptoms of low self-esteem

SOURCES OF WOUNDED SPIRITUALITY

- Untreated Adult Children of Dysfunctional Families issues (addictions, perfectionism, "looking good" family)
- Unhealthy messages about God and religion
- Negative, shaming messages about expression of feelings
- Taboos about sex; negative messages about sexuality or the body
- Lack of freedom to ask questions, evaluate information
- Physical abuse
- Sexual abuse
- Emotional abuse

In the years following my own treatment for alcoholism, I grew increasingly aware of the devastating effects that an unhealthy use of religion has on spirituality. Most people were raised in some kind of religious setting, even if their parents were devout atheists. And even people who are raised in homes in which there is no religious teaching or exposure are affected by the religious messages which have become ingrained into the fabric of society. Messages or beliefs that people are born sinful or powerless, that women were created secondary or inferior, that the spiritual life involves sacrifice and transcending the physical or material desires all have a common result: they create a sense of powerlessness and subsequent dependency on an outside Fixer/Rescuer. They create a childish, dependent relationship with God in which God does things *for* us or *to* us, but never *with* us. So we never get to discover the spiritual power inherent in a mature, adult relationship with God in which God is a partner, a co-creator, in the choices and actions we take.

THE DIFFERENCE BETWEEN "BODY-MIND-SPIRIT" AND "BODY-MIND-EMOTIONS"

Even people who have not had any formal religious exposure have been affected at some level by the traditional "body-mind-spirit" model of spirituality. I believe this model is responsible for much of the confusion people feel when they try to discover their spirituality. I always see this model drawn as a triangle with nothing in it. This model is damaging on two accounts. First, it fosters the concept of spirituality being a separate place, and needing to transcend the body and mind in order to be spiritual. It leaves emotions out altogether, so it actually breaks us apart. When we are taught that some aspects of ourselves need to be transcended or overcome, we usually disown and abandon those supposedly inferior parts. Thus, this model disconnects us from the source of our spiritual power, and therefore leads to the broken relationship within the self that feeds addictions, depression and compulsive behaviors. Second, it perpetuates the idea that we are spiritually empty and must somehow be filled. A model which does not include the spiritually nurturing richness of human feelings and emotions sets us up to search for something to fill that "hole in the soul." When it teaches us to look outside of ourselves for God's spiritual power, it leads us away from ourselves, and from God.

I believe that God's spiritual power is within us. We do not have to ask God for power. It has always been within us, in the whole range of human potential and ability. God's power is found in our ability to think and evaluate, to feel, to respond. It is housed in the very essence of being human–in our strengths, and in our limitations. It flows through the connection between our bodies, minds and emotions that allows us to respond fully and healthily to other people and the world around us. Negative, shaming messages, painful or abusive experiences can combine to hide that spiritual strength from us, so that we do not know we have it, or never learn how to access it.

When nearly all of our scripture, liturgies, hymns and inspirational writings emphasize the need to attain some ethereal level that will attract God's approval, we become vulnerable to a host of unhealthy attitudes and behaviors. When we feel we must hide, disown or remove some part of ourselves, we do not let ourselves be real. Instead, we fall prey to perfectionism and victim roles, judgmentalism and fear, sexual dysfunction and poor body image, codependency and loss of intimacy–almost all the issues which accompany addictions.

This is why I created a new spiritual model which emphasizes the relationship between body, mind and emotions that permits people to be positive, creative and empowered to take responsibility for their lives. When I talk about responsibility, I don't mean just being accountable for our attitudes and behaviors, although that's important. Spiritual response-*ability* involves our mental, emotional and physical responses to our life experiences. When our spirituality is wounded, we are not able to fully respond to anything. Perhaps we were taught in childhood not to express our feelings–joy, anger, sadness. Maybe we were never allowed to ask questions or examine information given to us by authority figures, so we don't get to use our minds. So we can't see choices, make decisions or take risks. Some people are taught that sex and their bodies are base or dirty, so their sexuality may be hurt, or they end up with a poor body image. This puts them out of touch with their bodies–with the way their bodies respond to feelings and thoughts and physical touch or exercise. All these kinds of things diminish our spiritual connections.

Teachings about religion or spirituality which limit or restrict where and how God is to be found damage us spiritually by cutting us off from the full range of experiences we can have with God. Healthy spirituality allows us to feel just as connected to the world when we successfully complete a project at work as we do when we watch the sunset. Healthy spirituality is to be found not just in an act of kindness and self-sacrifice, but in the moments in which we set our boundaries and say, "No, this is not acceptable."

MOVING FROM SPIRITUAL POWERLESSNESS TO SPIRITUAL EMPOWERMENT

We are most spiritually healthy when we allow ourselves to be real, to be imperfect. As the Skin Horse says in *The Velveteen Rabbit,* the process of becoming real is a lengthy one; it doesn't happen all at once. "You BECOME. That's why it doesn't happen to people who break easily or have sharp edges, or who have to be carefully kept. Generally, by the time you are REAL, most of your hair has been loved off, and your eyes drop out and you get loose in the joints and very shabby. But these things don't matter at all, because once you are REAL, you can't be ugly, except to people who don't understand" (*The Velveteen Rabbit,* pp. 12-13).

This simple passage from a children's fable beautifully defines the key to healthy spirituality, and to a creative partnership with God. And as the Skin Horse says, it's not easy, and often it takes a long time. It involves a willingness to identify our core beliefs about God, for I believe that people become what they believe about God. If they believe in a God who is an angry judge, they will be angry, judging and controlling. If they believe God abhors sex and physical pleasure, they will disown their sexuality, and disconnect from their bodies. If they believe God is their only source of strength and salvation, they will be codependently helpless, waiting for someone else to fix or rescue them, and more importantly, missing the ways in which they are co-creating with God in their lives.

There is a lot of confusion about the difference between the powerlessness of addiction and the corresponding need to let go of control which permits recovery, and spiritual empowerment which puts people in charge of the changes in their lives. This confusion is one of the things I'm most often asked about by patients in treatment centers where I consult, or those who attend my workshops and lectures. Curiously, although the addict self rebelliously resists the idea of powerlessness and giving up control, there seems to be even greater resistance to the concept of self-empowerment. To a majority of the people I talk with, "turning it over" to a Power greater than themselves seems to mean having no role in or responsibility for their own lives. The myths about spirituality and dysfunctional religious messages have given people the idea that powerlessness equals helplessness.

A belief system which emphasizes self-sacrifice, denial of physical needs or desires, constantly focusing on human frailty rather than human strength automatically jeopardizes our ability to use the qualities which I believe are God-given. When I began revising my Spirituality Service for people in recovery, I realized that much of the traditional religious and inspirational literature sows the seeds of powerlessness and codependency. I looked at the text of that staple of comfort, Psalms 23, and suddenly saw a different message: "The Lord is my shepherd. I shall not want." The very language itself implies dependency: we are dumb sheep who must be led, fed, restored. Similarly, I looked at the poem, "Footsteps," which many people in Twelve Step programs use as an example of "turning it over" and the message is the same: God carries us. We do nothing. The same passivity applies to many of the affirmations supposedly used to create self-esteem: "I am a child of God." "I am a precious person." "I deserve love." Nearly everything in our religious and inspirational teachings tells us we are little children who must be guided, fixed, rescued–that if we do something good, God did it for us–we're only capable of making mistakes.

This creates a different kind of unmanageability–the kind which grows from a belief that we have no control over our lives–that we must constantly look to someone who can do it for us. That's what most people really think Step Two means: somehow, we are to be magically restored without doing any footwork. The powerlessness and unmanageability of addiction come from trying to control feelings by escaping or numbing with substances or behaviors–from trying to force things to go our way. But sitting and waiting for a Rescuer to get us a job, pay the rent, take away hunger, fix the relationship–and believing that if those things don't happen it's because some Power didn't want us to have it–creates even greater powerlessness and unmanageability. We end up feeling like children whose parents won't let us have cookies after school.

Real spiritual power comes from what I call a co-creatorship with God–a partnership which signifies equality and balance of power. So many times I hear people say, "God keeps me sober; I don't do anything." This totally denies the decision to enter recovery, the risks taken in opening up to a sponsor or therapist, in attending meetings, in choosing, on a daily basis, not to use alcohol and drugs. This denial of self can lead to chronic depression, switched or multiple addictions, relapse or even suicide.

People who, at their core, believe that God will either "get" them, fix them or rescue them, will then apply this concept to Step Three of the Alcoholics Anonymous Twelve Steps: "Made the decision to turn our will and our lives over to the care of God *as we understood Him*" (*Alcoholics Anonymous*, p. 59). They do not understand that, first of all, Step Three isn't about handing our will and our lives over to a Spiritual Power who is now going to call all the shots. It's about making the decision to change. "Turning it over" does not mean passively waiting for a fixer. It means turning–changing direction. It involves developing a relationship with a support group of guides who can dialogue with us about what action to take to effect that change. This is an adult relationship with God.

When we are children, our parents teach us what to do, when to do it and why. As we mature, we are given more responsibility: we may get to choose what chores we will do in order to receive an allowance, or set our own bedtime, or decide when to study. We are left home alone without supervisors or babysitters. In time, we learn that our choices have consequences, and if we get to be reasonably mature, we even learn to accept those consequences. I have seen so much pain in people who were never allowed to make their own decisions until they grew up or left home. They either become rigid rule-followers, or run totally undisciplined. Yet most of us, to some degree or other, gradually moved from dependency on our parents, from seeing them as omnipotent authorities to human people with strengths and weaknesses.

As a child, I was taught that God would give me everything if I was a good boy. (Not surprisingly, many people find that their childhood images of God get mixed up with those of Santa Claus). As an alcoholic and religious addict, I alternately raged at God for not keeping His promises and beat up on myself for not being good enough to make God keep those promises. As an adult child of God, I do not look to God to do things for me. Just as my parents showed me I had the power to tie my shoes on my own, so I learn from God that I can learn to use the tools God gave me to shape the pattern of my life.

If people believe, at their core, that God should be totally in charge of their lives, they become pawns in some Cosmic chess game, powerlessly waiting to be moved and used. In time, they come to see themselves as objects to be pawned, or given in pledge for something. This can create vulnerability to a life of mindless service and sacrifice in which we are not truly present or real. So when people enter treatment and are told that helping to make coffee or putting away chairs in Twelve Step meetings is going to help them spiritually, this, too, could be spiritually abusive. Yes, there is something to be said for doing service: it provides a means of discipline, a first tentative step away from self-centeredness and into self-esteem. Some people's childhood image of God created a pattern of people-pleasing and caretaking in order to feel valuable and acceptable to God. I would suggest those people *not* do service. Indeed, their service is to themselves, in setting boundaries and discovering their value by learning to share who they really are instead of giving themselves away. Just as I believe people must include themselves when they learn to make amends, I believe people must learn to include themselves when they look for a worthy cause to which to give service and sacrifice.

CREATING SPIRITUAL WHOLENESS IN TREATMENT OR THERAPY

In my book, *The God Game–It's Your Move: Reclaiming Spiritual Empowerment,* I describe more fully the process of identifying unhealthy beliefs and learning to make the spiritually healthy moves which allow us to be co-creators and partners with God. It is a call to action and change issued to all who are involved in the healing of wounded spirituality: individuals, clergy, religions, and the treatment and therapeutic communities.

The task for treatment centers and hospitals is to develop programs which work from the ground up to heal wounded spirituality on all levels. This means making sure your intakes and assessments are as comprehensive as possible when you look for sources of shame and guilt–the chief killers of spirituality. In turn, this may involve providing in-service training to your treatment team on issues such as religious abuse, sexual addiction, the relationship between eating disorders, religious abuse and sexual abuse, codependency and the denial of personal power. As you document symptoms of depression–the impaired concentration, the lethargy, chronic headaches and sleep disturbances, the dysphoria and possible suicidal ideations–you can begin to relate them not only to specific incidents and issues in a patient's life, but to the patient's world-view.

If a patient presents with an overwhelming despair and negativity, ask where the sense of hopelessness came from. Perhaps this patient has been taught that God only answers the prayers of those who pray a certain way, live according to certain rules. Maybe this patient's depression is born of a sense of never being able to be good enough for Mom, Dad or God. Has the patient experienced fluctuations in weight? Look for distorted body image, and behind that, for messages given by religion or through sexual abuse. You cannot treat what you cannot identify, and I have met so many people whose treatment began and ended with just one symptom–the booze, the drugs, the weight, the codependency. Treating only the body or the mind, and leaving the spirit for later may rob the patient of tools needed for total recovery. I consider that many of those I have met who have relapsed time and again, or entered a series of treatment programs for a multiplicity of addictions have been misdiagnosed and mistreated because no one looked at the sources of their mental, emotional and physical pain in one context.

Creating healthy spirituality can be summed up in two words: awareness and action. First, we must become aware: gain insight and information. Then we must take action, which means we must acquire the tools with which to act. So education about the relationship between the mental, emotional and physical is vital to creating a spiritually-based program. The next step is to put into place treatment methods which begin to give the patient tools needed to gain self-empowerment. Part of my work as a consultant is to train the staff; the other part is to work with the patients. I start by giving them cognitive information about addictions, depression, and how the mental, emotional and physical interact to create spirituality. Then I work with both the patients and staff to discover the best tools for changing beliefs and behaviors. I advocate varieties of journaling, drawing, inner-child dialogue and affirmations, because these can be used to address a number of issues. I teach people how to look for ways in which they give away their power. This often means first teaching them that it's all right to question, to analyze and evaluate. I think these are key elements in beginning to reframe old beliefs. When this awareness blossoms, it touches so many dysfunctions: food and substance abuse, codependency, workaholism, sex addiction. If we can see where and how we give ourselves away, give up our power, we can see more clearly what needs to be done to reclaim it.

When we work with people who are struggling to find self-empowerment, it is important to examine their beliefs about God. I believe that people who think of themselves as children of God see themselves as *little* children, toddlers and preschoolers, totally dependent on Mommy or Daddy God to take care of them. They may not recognize that's what they believe, much less how that belief perpetuates powerlessness and self-victimization. They don't realize that this belief clashes with the injunctions they may hear to "grow up and take responsibility." I have found it effective to have people list their favorite inspirational texts, and then take them apart, line by line, looking for messages which imply powerlessness, and those which foster self-power.

The awareness which this creates opens the door to reversing many of the childhood messages which keep people stuck in victimized, child-like dependency. I then suggest they rewrite their favorite passage using language which signifies action, power, change. I recommend having people create affirmations which emphasize *doing* more than *being*: "I love myself" rather than "I am loved."

"I choose power" rather than "I am powerful." When I ask people to look at their concept of God, I want them to notice if they are "turning over their will and their lives" to the care of a Being they believe is supposed to come fix them if they "do the right things." Can they imagine having a Higher Power that they do things with, not who does things for them? Exercises and psychodramas about choice, responsibility and decision-making help move patients away from the helplessness, plant the seeds of self-power.

No matter what specific problems you are treating: alcoholism and substance abuse, eating disorders or codependency, religious abuse or sexual abuse, there are certain key elements which form the foundation of healthy spirituality: Choice, Responsibility, and Action. We are connected mentally, emotionally and physically to the spiritual power within us and outside of us. The stronger our mental, emotional and physical connection, the stronger our links to the spiritual powers available to us.

The most important element is Choice, which provides the vital link to other spiritual powers. We must teach people to move out of black-and-white thinking and learn to see choices. When people are healthy spiritually, they know that they always have choices and are able to use other spiritual tools to help discover what those may be. Being connected mentally, emotionally and physically strengthens spiritual power by allowing people to fully recognize what is going on within them, so that they can more clearly see their choices. They do not stay mired in helplessness and victimization. Yes, they may experience feelings of helplessness, but they are able to move out of them and into active solutions.

This is what I mean by being positive and creative. Positive is not just putting on a Pollyanna happy-face or trying to find something good in a situation. Sometimes, the most positive thing we can do is to acknowledge and feel pain. Instead of denying, minimizing or avoiding pain, or seeing it as a sign of weakness or failure, embracing and walking through pain is one of the most spiritually powerful moves we can make. It is in walking through pain that we often truly "give our prayers feet." I believe that prayer is not just sitting and asking God to do something, or telling God about what's wrong in our lives. Prayer is also the act of seeking and moving through solutions. Being positive and creative is also a sign of true Responsibility–the ability to fully respond mentally, emotionally and physically to any situation. In the response, is action, is movement. Choice, Responsibility and Action are the natural products of the healthy connection among body, mind and emotions. They are tangible proof of healthy spirituality. If you are teaching your patients to develop the ability to make choices, and take active responsibility, you are helping them to reclaim their spiritual power.

REFERENCES

Alcoholics Anonymous. (1986). New York: Alcoholics Anonymous World Services, Inc.

Booth, L. (1994). *The God game–It's your move: Reclaiming spiritual empowerment*. Walpole, NH: Stillpoint Publishing.

Williams, M. (1985). *The Velveteen Rabbit*. New York: Avon Books.

The Effects of Alcoholism
and Recovery on Spirituality

Rev. James E. Royce, SJ, PhD

SUMMARY. The progression of alcoholism as a spiritual disease and the importance of spiritual factors in recovery are depicted in a "dip" chart and exemplified in the case history of an alcoholic clergyman. The difference between religion and spirituality is explained and what is meant by calling alcoholism a spiritual disease. The Twelve Steps of Alcoholics Anonymous are used to illustrate many aspects of spiritual recovery. The article is based on the author's 46 years of experience as a clergyman and psychologist counseling alcoholics and training addiction counselors. *[Single or multiple copies of this article are available from The Haworth Document Delivery Service: 1-800-342-9678, 9:00 a.m. - 5:00 p.m. (EST).]*

Pastor Frank Green is an alcoholic whose story and recovery illustrate the nature of alcoholism (or addiction to any other drug) as a spiritual disease, as well as the difference between spirituality and religion. When still drinking he continued to function as a minister of religion, but his spiritual life was virtually dead. It is practically

Rev. James E. Royce is a Jesuit priest and Professor Emeritus of psychology and Founding Professor of addiction studies at Seattle University. His *Alcohol problems and alcoholism* has won two national awards and is the leading textbook in the field.

Address correspondence to: Rev. James E. Royce, 621 17th Avenue E., Seattle, WA 98112-3919, USA.

[Haworth co-indexing entry note]: "The Effects of Alcoholism and Recovery on Spirituality." Royce, Rev. James E. Co-published simultaneously in *Journal of Chemical Dependency Treatment* (The Haworth Press, Inc.) Vol. 5, No. 2, 1995, pp. 19-37; and: *Spirituality and Chemical Dependency* (ed: Robert J. Kus) The Haworth Press, Inc., 1995, pp. 19-37; and: *Spirituality and Chemical Dependency* (ed: Robert J. Kus) Harrington Park Press, an imprint of The Haworth Press, Inc., 1995, pp. 19-37. Single or multiple copies of this article are available from The Haworth Document Delivery Service [1-800-342-9678, 9:00 a.m. - 5:00 p.m. (EST)].

© 1995 by The Haworth Press, Inc. All rights reserved.

impossible to pray well when either drunk or hung over, and he was often both while people still saw him as Pastor Green.

Like most alcoholics, he started drinking for the usual reasons. As a good pastor he took his parishioners' problems seriously, which often left him physically and emotionally exhausted and needing the relaxation a drink or two could afford him. Only one or two, mind–he never intended to get drunk; after all, he was a man of God. Then there were times when he felt it proper to imitate Christ's ability to mix with common people and have a drink with them, to say nothing of the times when well-meaning parishioners would press him to have another drink because he was so tired and over-worked.

Once he found how relaxing alcohol could be, he found himself keeping a bottle in his room, rationalizing to himself that he could never be one of those skid-row bums. Besides, an alcoholic was one who couldn't quit drinking, whereas he could quit any time he wanted to. This unconscious denial persisted even after he had lost his third pastorate. He wasn't an alcoholic, he just had to be more careful next time. He began feeling resentments against the bishop and anyone who talked about excessive drinking. His bishop transferred him to different parishes three times, but never addressed the real problem by sending him to treatment for his alcoholism.

He still prayed out of habit or because a situation called for it, but he felt no closeness to God. His religion was getting pretty sick, just a formality with no inner spiritual meaning. In fact, he was becoming overwhelmed with guilt feelings, along with indefinable fears and anxieties. He became depressed, confused in his thinking, and utterly lacking in any sense of self-worth. Yet he had vague spiritual desires and groped for spiritual meaning in his life. Now he was drinking just to dull the pain and to escape the problems caused by his drinking. He was about to hit bottom in his spiritual disease of alcoholism.

This is a true story, one of hundreds. But denial is still rampant, not only on the part of the alcoholics themselves, but among family and friends and bosses. The loyal spouse or boss says, "he/she is too intelligent to be an alcoholic" or "he/she is my best worker, when sober." When I approached one pastor about hosting a workshop on alcoholism, he replied, "We don't have that problem in *our* congregation." I knew, however, that while this pastor was on vacation two of his vestrymen, long-time members of Alcoholics Anonymous, had just taken a third member of the vestry to an alcoholism treatment center.

IMPORTANCE FOR THE COUNSELOR

How will knowledge of spirituality help the average counselor in daily work? The total person must be included in the continuum of care if success is to be lasting. We often say that addiction to alcohol or other drugs is a physical, psychological, and *spiritual* illness, but a review of the research questions whether we really believe this (Miller, 1990). A three-year study of 441 patients called the spiritual the most neglected part of therapy (Ryan, 1983). This was borne out by a 1985 report that 91% of patients in treatment centers complained that their spiritual needs were not adequately taken care of. Other research (see Prugh, 1986) indicates that the percentage of success of treatment is in direct proportion to attention to the spiritual aspects of the disease.

These are hard data, facts which a scientific psychologist cannot ignore. The counselor may not consider spiritual values to be important. Regardless of our own biases, a true professional responds to the needs of the client or patient, at least by an intelligent referral. As a psychologist I understand why some psychotherapists are inimical to religion, which to them means either guilt and fear, or soup kitchens, or a revival-meeting emotionalism–"Hallelujah! I got religion! I'm saved!"–which is superficial and short-lived even when sincere. But a true spirituality is also psychologically sound, a facing of the spiritual realities that are in the lives of all of us, even the avowed atheist.

David Powell, a national leader in addiction-counselor training and credentialing, told the National Association of Alcohol and Drug Counselors that "The spiritual dimensions of counseling require a counselor's dedication to quality care with a sense of purpose and mission" (1990). I heard Joseph Kellerman, author of *Alcoholism: A Merry-Go-Round Named Denial*, say that "The general consensus seems to be that the reason for relapse is invariably a spiritual regression" and Peter Bell, President of the National Black

Alcoholism Council, asserts that "spirituality is the major factor in recovery." If you can't face the ultimate questions about the meaning of life, how can you face life without alcohol? All this suggests that we examine alcoholism as a spiritual illness and the spiritual aspects of recovery (Royce, 1985).

My Spiritual Progression Chart (see p. 24), depicting the downward course of alcoholism as a spiritual disease is not theory, or something I imagined. In this spiritual "dip" chart I have attempted to portray what alcoholics and their spouses have told me in over 46 years of working with them, showing the progression of alcoholism as a spiritual disease on the "down" side, and after hitting bottom, the various aspects of their spiritual recovery on the "up" side. It is easy to follow the chart, starting at the upper left corner, when reading the story of Pastor Green.

SPIRITUAL DISEASE

What do we mean by calling alcoholism a spiritual disease? To begin with, health is not the absence of sickness; sickness is a lack of health. To be healthy, "hale and hearty," means to be whole, since hale, from höle, means whole or total–*integer vitae* as the Latin poet sang. Sickness or disease is a defect in this integral functioning, a lack-of-ease, a dysfunction. In this broader sense a broken leg is a disease, an inability to function with ease. So is an allergy, an inability to function with ease regarding strawberries or shellfish.

Addiction, to alcohol or any other drug, is an inability to function with ease regarding that drug. Rather than being at ease, the individual uses the drug obsessively and compulsively. Addiction is basically physiological, but spiritual, too.

But how can a material thing like alcohol affect the spiritual, touch the intangible? Unlike the divine or angelic intellects, human intellect and will must work through the animal or sensory powers that reside in the brain. When alcohol works its toxic harm on brain function, the spiritual powers of the soul are robbed of the instruments through which they normally work. Compare this to the artist, whose capacity for beauty is ultimately spiritual but must express itself through a brush. Knocking the brush out of the painter's hand does not touch his artistry directly, but makes the expression of it impossible, so no beauty results. Alcohol cannot touch our spiritual powers directly, but it knocks out the brain's ability to serve as the sensory instrument of the soul. The result is spiritual dysfunction or disease.

How, then, is the alcoholic spiritually sick? Spiritual here does not mean religion. Although the two should and often do go hand-in-hand, there are people who go to church regularly but are not very spiritual, and there are those who never go near a church who are living intensely spiritual lives. The difference is strikingly illustrated in the case of Pastor Green, whose spiritual life had reached a very low ebb.

I define spiritual as *our capacity to relate to the Infinite.* Just as the stomach relates us to food, and the eye to the visible, so our intellect and will put us in touch with the intelligible and the lovable –the True and the Good. Now the physical or material is always limited, finite: a nice light can be too bright or a nice sound too loud, and we can even get too much chocolate. But the most learned persons have an unlimited capacity for knowledge and are the most curious; they never stop learning. And the hunger of the human heart for love has been celebrated by poets and dramatists for centuries. Our spiritual capacities are unlimited: their object is "to dream the impossible dream," to reach beyond the farthest stars, to seek the ultimate reason for life and the universe. As poet Robert Browning says, "A man's reach should exceed his grasp, or what's a heaven for?" Our capacity for knowing and loving cannot be completely satisfied by anything less than infinite knowability, infinite goodness and beauty. That is what I choose to call God. People can examine whether God as they understand Him fits this definition. Probably it does.

Alcohol impairs the ability of the mind to think and feel right about God. "Dis-ease" means lack-of-ease, discomfort. Spiritual disease means one is not at ease in the presence of their Creator, uncomfortable in God's presence, dysfunctional regarding the Infinite. Certainly that describes the last stage of Pastor Green's disease. He was spiritually bankrupt, although still a member of a religious organization and even a leader in it. His faith had grown so weak that he was on the verge of despair, if not suicide.

The Spiritual Progression Chart
Alcoholism as a SPIRITUAL Disease: Progression and Recovery

Alcohol sedates value system, which gets indifferent, confused

Grandiosity, perfectionism, pride

Intolerance of others: Suspicion, distrust, argues

Religion getting sick: Rigid, arrogant, unrealistic; disenchantment with childish idea of God

Loses interest in life: "Blues"

Guilt feelings, not "at-ease" with God

Stops daily prayer; attends church out of habit or pretense

"Nobodiness"—feels estranged, alienated, lonely

"Weller than Well"—higher levels than believed possible

Unselfish: Goes out to others because God loves them

Deeper relation to God as a loving God

Growth in proper concept of God

Prayer and meditation

Serenity, peace of soul, joy

Increased tolerance of others

Gratitude

Appreciation of spiritual values

Rebirth of ideals

Courage, optimism—new freedom

Promptly admits when wrong

Honesty: Makes amends

Return of self-esteem (God not a rescuer)

24

False ego deflated

Humbly asks God to remove shortcomings

Reconciliation: Personal relationship "at ease" with

God (more than just "dumping garbage")

Forgiveness: Not "why did I?" but "forgive me"

Patience: "One day at a time"

Appreciates possibility of new way of life

Trust: "Thy will be done"

Conversion: "Let go and let God"

Acceptance (surrender—Tiebout)

• Second BOTTOM: "Existential crisis"

Thirst for God examined (hard struggle for some)

Hope dawns: Can be restored to sanity

New faith: "Came to believe"

Vague notion of Higher Power

Honest desire for help

In spiritual fog

• ADMISSION (compliance—Tiebout)

Immaturity, some irresponsibility

Life has no meaning

Anxiety, indefinable fears

Resentments: Angry at God, Hostile to mention of religion, projects fear into concept of God as a tyrant

Moral deterioration: Dishonest, selfish

Loss of faith: Consciously rejects God, unconsciously longs for Him—a "sick love" relation

Remorse: Depression, suicidal thoughts, impaired thinking

Vague spiritual desires

Gropes for spiritual meaning

hits BOTTOM: drinks to cope with problems of drinking

25

Going back to the chart, let us fill in some details from other cases:

- Alcohol in the brain sedates people's scale of values, so they get confused as to what is important and what is not. Indifference creeps in–God isn't really that important anyway.
- From this follows grandiosity, pride. People try to take the place of God in the scheme of things. Chapter 5 in the A.A. big book describes how alcoholics often try to run the whole show, arranging the lights, the scenery, the other actors. When things don't go right, they try even harder. They are trying to play God. Perfectionism becomes the bane of many alcoholics; they drive themselves and everybody else nuts trying to have everything just so–obsessive/compulsives at their worst.
- Intolerance of others grows, since others are imperfect and not up to their standards; they find it hard to be patient with others' defects. Suspicion and distrust of others creeps in; they argue with everybody about every little point . . . on which they are always right, of course.
- The alcoholic's religion is starting to get sick: rigid, arrogant, unrealistic. Their religion is mechanical, shallow. Although unaware of it at the time, their spiritual life is dormant. Alcohol has anesthetized their spiritual values. They are no longer sensitive to what relates them to God. They become disenchanted with their childish ideas of God. If people have distorted ideas of God or feelings toward God, they cannot believe or trust, and hence can never love. The alcoholic mind develops a weird image of God, with a resultant poor relationship.

The trouble is not with God, but with our inadequate and childish concepts–"God as we *don't* understand Him," if you will. Spiritual sickness means distorting our concept of God so we are unable or unwilling to relate to One who should be our best friend. The Anglican clergyman J. B. Phillips (1944) describes much of this in his *Your God is Too Small*. The image of God as a cruel tyrant who won't let us have any fun (like the mother who won't let the three-year-old play with the nice sharp butcher knife), or a far-away abstract principle, or an old gray-beard, male instead of the purely spiritual Source of all perfections female and male, or an egotistical pip-squeak that has to be adored every Sunday to gratify his ego, are more projections of our own problems than sound theology.

- There is a loss of interest in life, which becomes a big blah. The result is frequent bouts with "the blues."
- With things going this way, there are usually feelings of guilt. Anger at God is just one more projection of blame on others. Addicts then feel guilty about that. There is a tendency to blame the clergy or nuns, the church, the pope, or even God. But any member of Alcoholics Anonymous will quickly recognize that as rationalization, the projecting of one's own ills on somebody or something else. It's like blaming the boss, one's spouse, the police, the "system"—anything but the alcohol. There is a feeling of guilt, not because God is unforgiving and cruel, but because alcohol has blinded them to God's infinite mercy and kindness. They are not "at ease" with God.
- Although they don't realize it at the time, many recovered alcoholics have told me that looking back, they see that at one point they gave up the habit of daily prayer. They may continue to go to church, out of habit or pretense. This is what the Harvard psychologist Gordon Allport called external religion, as opposed to internal or, I would say, truly spiritual religion.
- There is a sense of being "nobody"—alienated, estranged from friends, self, and God. No wonder the drinking alcoholic feels lonely!
- Alcoholics exhibit a certain degree of immaturity, once thought to be the cause of alcoholism and now recognized as an effect. They show irresponsibility—alcohol is a "don't give a damn" drug.
- Life begins to be meaningless. "Who cares? Have another drink!"
- But since alcoholics are basically good people, not morally depraved no-good-nicks, there is a sneaking anxiety underneath this bravado; vague, indefinable fears that all is not well.
- This anxiety creates resentments: they are hostile at the very mention of religion, which reminds them of their responsibilities. They are angry at God, because they project their fears into a concept of God as an unreasonable tyrant. They justify,

rationalize, defend, get angry–sure signs that they have a problem. Their professed atheism *may* be just shame and guilt.
- They also report moral deterioration: they become dishonest,
  selfish, perhaps sexually promiscuous. Again, this moral deterioration was once thought to be the cause of alcoholism,
  which was looked upon as moral depravity or bad will. We
  now know that it is largely the result of the addiction, as alcohol has anesthetized their sense of values.
- All this involves some loss of faith, although this varies
  greatly with the individual. I have known alcoholics who in
  their very worst stages never lost their faith. Rarely is faith
  gone entirely.

The alcoholic, perhaps more than others, is a God-seeker. Bill W.
(A.A. co-founder) and Carl Jung and Ernest Kurtz are all in agree-
ment that alcoholics are seeking, not escaping. This is congruent
with the current understanding among alcoholism specialists, which
actually goes back to Tiebout and Jellinek and has been confirmed
by the important longitudinal study by Vaillant (1983) and the psychological research of Milam and others, that most alcoholics do
not drink to sedate psychological problems, but for the lift, the
glow, the positive effects of alcohol. They are not looking for seda-
tion so much as for solace, trying to satisfy the hunger of the heart.
It is not that the world is too much for them, but that it is not
enough. It may be that they are seeking to find in alcohol the answer
to spiritual needs not met in our materialistic culture. One alcoholic
said that human nature has a "God-shaped hole" in it, a vacuum
that only God can fill. Whether they know it or not, in their perfectionism they want nothing less than the Infinite. Bill W. said that
alcoholics "seek God in a bottle"–although all they may get is
addicted to the drug alcohol.

David Stewart, a Ph.D. psychologist and recovering alcoholic,
author of *Thirst for Freedom* (1960), has some very interesting
ideas in his later book *Addicted and Free at the Same Time* (1984)
on how alcoholics tend both to feel rejected and to be rejecting.
Their love affair with God is certainly sick in this way: consciously
they reject God even though unconsciously they are longing for

Him. One alcoholic told me, "I don't believe in God, but I pray to Him a lot."

- There is a vague groping for the spiritual meaning of life. Even professed atheists have vague spiritual desires. And ranting about the hypocrisy of organized religion does not prove there is no God.

- In this state of impaired thinking alcoholics inevitably have guilt feelings, remorse, discouragement, depression, even suicidal thoughts. They have reached bottom. The depression they feel might be compared to the "dark night of the soul" described by the mystics: the cup must be emptied of all that is material before it can be filled with God.

HITTING BOTTOM

"Hitting bottom" can mean different things to different people. To a surgeon it might mean losing his/her license to practice medicine; to a housewife it might mean burning the toast once too often. Certainly it does not always or even usually mean ending up in the gutter as a penniless, brain-damaged skid-row bum. Only about three percent of America's alcoholics fit that stereotype. The others look more like the rest of us, of either sex and of any color or age. I have known full-blown alcoholics 12-years-old, and have a Ph.D. friend who insists that she was an alcoholic at age six. In Pastor Green's case, "bottom" meant a loving intervention (Johnson Institute, 1987) by a small group of concerned parishioners.

More and more we hear talk of "early bottom" or "high bottom" or even "forced bottoms" to indicate that one does not have to reach that last pitiful stage before recovery is possible. Hitting bottom really means acceptance of the fact that people are powerless over alcohol, that their "lives have become unmanageable," to use the wording of the First Step in A.A. It can happen any time in the course of the illness, but it is never easy.

SPIRITUAL RECOVERY

We come now to the right-hand or "up" side of the chart. Note that this side of the chart has more on it than the down side–spiritual recovery is very rich. As one Al-Anon member remarked, "I learned more from his recovery than from his drinking days, e.g., about tolerance of others."

A recent research study reported that 60% of one group said they were atheists while drinking, but all believe in God now that they have been sober for a while. Once there is a real desire for sobriety, when confronted with the choice of God or getting drunk, they choose God. But one often hears, "organized religion failed us when we were drinking, and was no help in getting us sober." Did religion abandon them, or did they leave it? I think it important that organized religion not look on A.A. as competition, but as complementary. A.A. will make one a better Lutheran, or Jew, or Catholic, or Baptist. Many alcoholics who have wandered far from the religion of their childhood need to grope their way back to God out of the alcoholic fog by means of some vague notion of a "Higher Power," and it is a mistake to force more formalized concepts of religion on them too soon. Pushing Jesus at persons newly struggling for sobriety may just drive them away. The A.A. slogan "Easy does it" applies here.

- Hitting bottom means admitting our powerlessness. This is so hard on our ego that the admission may be just a superficial compliance at first. The first three steps of A.A. can be very hard. All this healing takes TIME. I agree with many experienced counselors that it is a mistake to attempt Steps 4 and 5 in early recovery (except as a preliminary test of honesty and growth in stability).
- At first there may be just an honest desire for help. They are confused, need something to believe in. With a new faith, they "come to believe" that there is hope, that they can be restored to sanity. The great psychiatrist Carl Jung felt that alcoholics are unconsciously seeking God and will never find lasting and comfortable sobriety until they find God. To examine this thirst for God can involve a hard struggle for some. The biggest reason is those false images of God from childhood we spoke of earlier. If we are going to let God be our new Manager for lives that have become unmanageable, we have to know God correctly. In order to really trust God one must know more about God than that His last name is "damn." Just common sense tells us that the Creator must have Infinite

Goodness and mercy, yet we don't give God credit for the decency we would expect from a common boor. The proof is how all this changes when one stops drinking. Like the parents who are seen quite differently after their adolescent children mature, God improves greatly when we get sober!

The Great Spirit is wise and loving. Christians believe God shares our human nature. They tell the story of the little girl who was supposed to be asleep upstairs while her parents tried to hold adult conversation. Her mother said, "Go to sleep!" but she hollered down over the bannister, "I'm tired of being up here with just God and my dolly; I want somebody with skin on." That, of course, is the story of Christianity: Incarnation means enfleshment, God taking on human skin.

- Admission gradually becomes acceptance, a term I prefer to Tiebout's *surrender.* How often in open A.A. meetings do we hear Saint Augustine quoted, "There but for the grace of God go I." Here we have a true conversion, a radical personality change which enables one to "let go and let God." After years of being unable to trust anybody or anything, alcoholics can now say, "Thy will be done." Now they can begin to appreciate the possibility of a whole new way of life with spiritual values, a life more God-centered.
- Many will face a "second bottom" later on in sobriety, when the residual brain toxicity has subsided enough to allow them to face an existential crisis. (For most, this probably occurs later than indicated on the chart.) Abstinence alone may not bring a lasting state of peace. New anxiety arises as they begin to face the larger issues of life, ignored during the first crisis of freeing themselves from the addiction by learning just to avoid that first drink one day at a time. "Now that I'm no longer a drunk, who am I?" "What do I really value in life?" Also, doing A.A.'s Step 8 (making a list of persons one has harmed), Step 9 (making amends), and Step 10 (continuing personal inventory) may force them to see that growing up means they have to face responsibility, which makes them uncomfortable.
- Hence the need for patience. They must learn to take up these new tasks one day at a time. That is why some A.A. members

define time as God's way of seeing to it that everything doesn't happen at once; we couldn't take that.

- We now come to realize the true answer to guilt is God's forgiveness, not analyzing why we did something to explain it away but accepting the fact that we are imperfect human beings. One psychology student in a mental health course, referring to yearly confession, said, "The Catholic Church makes you face reality at least once a year." Psychology is good to get rid of false or unrealistic guilt, but it can make you feel guilty about feeling guilty. I believe that real guilt can be relieved only by the infinite mercy of God. The A.A. Fifth Step says, "We admitted to God, to ourselves, and to another human being the exact nature of our wrongs" and when people making this step with me say they have done things so bad even God can't forgive them, I reply, "You flatter yourself: you are finite, God is infinite, you can't possibly commit sins bigger than God's infinite forgiveness."

And forgiveness is more than just "dumping garbage," a phrase often heard around A.A. The psychological value of catharsis was recognized by Aristotle 2,000 years before Freud, but reconciliation involves more than that. True healing means reestablishing a personal relationship, eliminating the spiritual dis-ease, getting "at ease" with God again. God once more becomes a good friend.

There is a lot of practical psychology in the Twelve Steps. Step 5, for example, does not allow one to confess to God solely in the secrecy of the heart. Rather it calls for one to confess out loud to another human being, "somebody with skin on"–reality therapy or authentic encounter, if you will. That is why Step 5 may be even more important than Step 4, making a searching and fearless moral inventory. One person whose Fifth Step I heard said, "I learned more about myself from having to say it out loud to you, than I did writing out the Fourth Step." Incidentally, contrary to what Fr. Ralph Pfau (Father John Doe of the books and tapes) says, the big book *Alcoholics Anonymous* (3rd ed., 1976, p. 74) says it is quite permissible and even recommended to do a Fifth Step in confession if called for by whatever religion one may happen to belong to.

- Being entirely ready for God to remove our shortcomings, as the A.A. Sixth Step suggests, we can then humbly ask God to do so (Step 7). But *humbly* implies deflating our false ego. Perfectionism and grandiosity are classic alcoholic symptoms and the source of many problems (Ackerman, 1989; Adderholt-Elliott, 1989; Kurtz, 1992). Perfectionism stems from pride, an inability to accept our own limitedness. Pride and humility appear often in the writings of Bill W. Humility is the remedy, but humility is much misunderstood. It is simply truth, and the truth is not that you are no good, just that you are not perfect–*Not-God* in the felicitous title of that most scholarly history of A.A. by Kurtz (1991): the story of two million people who discovered they are not God. Much of the Twelve Step program is aimed at humility. You soon learn "Rule 62": *Don't take yourself too seriously.* Kurtz says it is hard to maintain grandiosity in a room where everybody laughs. Humility gives a sense of ease with ourselves, others, and God: we are no longer spiritually diseased–satisfaction guaranteed or your ego back!
- The result of true humility is not a beating down of the person, but a return to a correct Self-esteem, dropping the facade we tried to maintain and drank to avoid admitting. Finding our place on the ladder of reality in faith and trust is a result of accepting our role as not-God. Slavery to the bottle gives way to a new sense of freedom; the power of choice is restored: with God's help, I can choose NOT to drink. Paradoxically, acceptance of our own imperfection can become humility rather than humiliation–a relief rather than a burden: "Thank God, I don't have to do it all alone any more!" The result is a new courage and optimism, when one can say with St. Paul, "I can do all things in Him who strengthens me." For this reason I object to the current phrase "self-help" programs. The whole burden of Chapter 5 of the "Big Book" *Alcoholics Anonymous* is that reliance on self is exactly what got us in trouble, and the answer is to stop playing God. They are really *God*-help programs, not self-help; but if you find that objectionable you can say *Twelve-Step* or *group-support* programs.

As for those psychologists who think that dependence on God is neurotic escape, I suggest that if God is the Supreme Reality, then it is the atheist who is escaping. It is unscientific to ignore a major portion of the universe, the spiritual. To those who are skeptical, I suggest they try it on the off chance that they might connect with something. "What have you got to lose? Act 'as if' and see what happens." Admission of dependence on God need not be taken as neurotic or demeaning. After all, we are dependent on oxygen, but this does not label us all neurotic. One suggestion to a patient struggling with the notion of Higher Power is to "think of whatever it is that enables you to breathe." Some people talk as if dependence on a psychotherapist is all right, but not dependence on the Creator. Actually, some do get addicted to therapy.

On the other hand, this does not mean an immature escaping from responsibility. It is good theology that God helps those who help themselves; God is a good Al-Anon, not an Enabler or Rescuer. I often hear the expression around A.A. meetings "turn it over to God," but that is not what the Third Step says. "To turn our will and our lives over to the *care* of God" means that we still have to do it, but under God's loving care and with Divine help to overcome our powerlessness. Divine providence means using our God-given abilities, not sitting back and leaving it to God.

- Real humility is required by A.A. Steps 8 and 9 which bring a return to honesty by making amends where appropriate, and by Step 10 which says that when wrong we promptly admitted it. As we grow spiritually, pride, perfectionism, and grandiosity are replaced with a genuine humility which makes the person more attractive to others because of comfort with self.
- The new freedom these steps bring generates a rebirth of ideals, a courage and optimism not felt in years.
- Appreciation of spiritual values is growing, as shown in our increased tolerance of others and in our gratitude. In A.A. one hears much talk about gratitude. Members often introduce themselves as grateful alcoholics. Presumably they have a God to thank.
- They exhibit a serenity, a peace of soul and joy they could not have imagined a few years earlier. They find that sobriety is

more than just abstinence, that spirituality is their number one means of coping with stress.

Lasting and joyous sobriety seems inevitably to involve growth in the spiritual life. That is why in Step 11 the A.A. founders "sought through prayer and meditation to increase our conscious contact with God as we understood Him" and their whole lives began to change. By conscious contact with God in prayer one grows in knowledge of a loving God, not one to be feared. Meditation is just thinking quietly in God's presence about some saying or truth or passage from the big book or whatever, and then talking it over with God and trying to see it from God's perspective, which is that of eternity. Prayer is conversation with God, and conversation is a two-way street. We don't pray to inform God, who already knows everything. We pray to dispose ourselves to receive what God sends. In other words, we need to listen.

"Praying *only* for knowledge of His will for us and the power to carry that out" as Step 11 bids, our lives become simpler and set in the path of spiritual *progress*, not *perfection*. One proof, even a test of this, is that relations with others improve. One becomes unselfish when one begins to love others because God loves them and wants us to, not because they are pretty or handsome or rich or fun. Spiritual values have replaced material values.

Is this just pious speculation, or do people really live this way? I deal all the time with people who do—members of A.A. and non-members alike. One mother of five tells me that the first thing she does when she wakes up is to ask God what to do today, then asks God to remove any thoughts that might detract from that. One head counselor reads books on mystical prayer. When Dr. Susan B. Anthony addressed a general audience in our public alcohol information series at Seattle University, ALL of the questions in the second hour were about prayer. One A.A. member, a beautiful black woman, spends a solid 60-minute hour in prayer each morning of her life now; the serenity and depth of her soul shows in her face, even to those who would never guess its source.

- As indicated at the top of the chart, where the heavy line ends up higher than it starts on the down side, they become "weller than well"–better than they were before their illness, or than they would have been had they not found A.A. Psychological research by Mellor (1986) seems to confirm this notion.
- Resentment and anxiety are replaced by serenity, fear by courage, doubt and confusion by wisdom and faith. Recovering persons often develop a deeper relationship with God, now seen as a loving God rather than a cruel tyrant.
- They become unselfish. We use the word *transcend* to mean that we can go beyond the bodily or physical self, in three ways: (a) We can go beyond *selfishness,* beyond personal gain or pleasure, to connect with others. We attain a sense of communion with all other human beings, regardless of physical qualities like color of skin. (b) We can go beyond *immediate* reality to the Supreme Reality. Spiritual is that within us whereby we can relate to God, however we understand the term. Hence we can experience awe, wonder, mystery, the sacred, "the great Beyond" which we cannot see but can relate to in faith and trust and love. (c) But this transcendence comes full circle: having gone *beyond self* toward others and God, we find *a new acceptance of self* as a worthwhile being, a new sense of our own human dignity, as based on more than physical beauty or strength or wealth. One has a new sense of the universe and one's place in it. The spiritual is thus essential to true humanness. Maslow's self-actualization is not complete without realizing the Divine within each of us, our relation to God. If the spiritual includes the capacity to enjoy a beautiful sunset, this sensory experience is ultimately spiritual only if it stimulates one to unite with God in faith and love.

I was shocked when I heard Pastor Green say "I'm glad I'm an alcoholic," until he went on to explain that if he weren't an alcoholic, he would never have joined A.A. and learned how much God loved him and how much he loved God. A.A. spirituality has done more for him and for many clergymen than religion had. He is indeed "weller than well."

REFERENCES

Ackerman, R. (1989). *Perfect daughters*. Deerfield Beach, FL: Health Communications.

Adderholt-Elliott, M. (1989). *Perfectionism: What's bad about being too good?* Minneapolis: Johnson Institute.

Johnson Institute (1987). *How to Use Intervention in Your Professional Practice*. Minneapolis: Johnson Institute.

Kurtz, E. (1991). *Not-God: A history of Alcoholics Anonymous*. Center City, MN: Hazelden.

Kurtz, E. (1992). *The spirituality of imperfection*. New York: Bantam Books.

Mellor, S. et al. (1986). *Psychology Reports, 58,* 411-418.

Miller, W. R. (1990). Spirituality: The silent dimension in addiction research. *Drug and Alcohol Review, 9,* 258-266

Phillips, J. B. (1944). *Your God is too small*. New York: Macmillan.

Powell, D. (1990). Clinical symposium. *The Counselor, 8*(5), 30.

Prugh, T. (1986). Alcohol, spirituality, and recovery. *Alcohol Health and Research World. 10*(2), 28-31, 53-54.

Royce, J. E. (1989). *Alcohol problems and alcoholism*. New York: Macmillan.

Royce, J. E. (1985). Sin or solace? Religious views on alcohol and alcoholism. *Journal of Drug Issues. 15*(1), 51-62

Ryan, S. (1983). *NIAAA Information and News Service,* IFS n. 106, April 1, p. 2; *Alcoholism: The National Magazine,* July/August, 1983, 64.

Stewart, D. (1960). *Thirst for freedom*. Center City, MN: Hazelden.

Stewart, D. (1984). *Addicted and free at the same time*. Toronto: Empathy.

Vaillant, G. (1983). *The natural history of alcoholism*. Cambridge: Harvard University Press.

Defining God or a Higher Power:
The Spiritual Center of Recovery

Dana G. Finnegan, PhD, CAC
Emily B. McNally, PhD, CAC

SUMMARY. One of the central aspects of alcoholic recovery in the Twelve Step model is relying on God or a power greater than oneself. Unfortunately, many persons' conception of God or a higher power is fuzzy, negative, or nonexistent. In this article, Drs. Finnegan and McNally discuss traditional concepts of God which may or may not be helpful, the changing nature of God-conceptions recovery often brings, alternatives to the Twelve Step program of recovery, and clinical implications. *[Single or multiple copies of this article are available from The Haworth Document Delivery Service: 1-800-342-9678, 9:00 a.m. - 5:00 p.m. (EST).]*

INTRODUCTION

Very often, perhaps most times, people who suffer the trauma of alcoholism have already been traumatized before they ever even

Dana G. Finnegan is a certified alcoholism counselor in private practice. She is Co-Director of Discovery Counseling Center, Millburn, NJ and NYC; Co-Founder and current Board Member, National Association of Lesbian and Gay Alcoholism Professionals; a faculty member of the Rutgers Summer Schools of Alcohol and Drug Studies; Co-Author (with Emily B. McNally) of *Dual Identities: Counseling Chemically Dependent Gay Men and Lesbians* (1987), Hazelden.

Emily B. McNally is a licensed psychologist in private practice. She is Co-Director of Discovery Counseling Center, Millburn, NJ and NYC; Co-Founder and current Board Member, National Association of Lesbian and Gay Alcoholism Professionals.

Address correspondence to: Drs. Finnegan and McNally, 708 Greenwich Street #6D, New York, NY 10014.

[Haworth co-indexing entry note]: "Defining God or a Higher Power: The Spiritual Center of Recovery." Finnegan, Dana G., and Emily B. McNally. Co-published simultaneously in *Journal of Chemical Dependency Treatment* (The Haworth Press, Inc.) Vol. 5, No. 2, 1995, pp. 39-48; and: *Spirituality and Chemical Dependency* (ed: Robert J. Kus) The Haworth Press, Inc., 1995, pp. 39-48; and: *Spirituality and Chemical Dependency* (ed: Robert J. Kus) Harrington Park Press, an imprint of The Haworth Press, Inc., 1995, pp. 39-48. Single or multiple copies of this article are available from The Haworth Document Delivery Service [1-800-342-9678, 9:00 a.m. - 5:00 p.m. (EST)].

© 1995 by The Haworth Press, Inc. All rights reserved.

begin to drink (Bean, 1981). Many alcoholics come from dysfunctional (often alcoholic) families in which they were severely neglected or physically, emotionally, and/or sexually abused prior to their alcoholism.

As J. L. Herman (1992) states, trauma survivors' "sense of self is shattered" (p. 61); they are, therefore, at high risk of substance abuse. In alcohol, they seek and may temporarily find solutions for and relief from the terrible pain and devastation wrought by their earlier traumas. Thus, recovering alcoholics often report that initially alcohol made them feel safe; it gave them a sense of connection with themselves and others; it made them feel powerful and in control; it helped them regulate their emotions; it enabled them to emotionally soothe themselves. Many say that alcohol helped them to transcend the misery of their lives and become "whole" and feel one with the universe. It gave them hope and made them feel that life was worth living.

Unfortunately, the destructive effects of alcoholism eventually outweigh and finally obliterate the benefits of alcohol. While alcoholism is a disease which attacks people physically and mentally, perhaps the most devastating attack is on people's spirits—both on their inner sense of self and on their sense of self in relation to others and to a power or spirit greater than themselves. As people's addiction advances, their spiritual selves are ravaged by corrosive self-doubt, denial, alienation and isolation, and fragmentation. They also suffer an essential loss of meaning so that they are left in despair, in "helplessness and isolation [which] are the core experiences of psychological trauma" (Herman, 1992: p. 197).

PURPOSE

The purpose of this article is to explore a process central to recovery from the spiritual trauma of alcoholism—that of defining God or a Higher Power. The article will examine people's cultural and personal histories and contexts for this process, the steps they take to create or find this definition, and the importance of this process and this definition to their recovery. In addition, clinical implications and suggestions will be provided to assist clinicians in helping alcoholic clients on their journey to recovery.

THE PRE-ALCOHOLISM STAGE:
THE CONTEXT OF ADDICTION

Many–perhaps most–actively alcoholic people are ill-equipped to contend with the erosion of and attacks on their spiritual selves which occur in the course of their alcoholism. The large majority of them have grown up with conceptions of God that fail them and/or hinder them as they engage in the tough life search for meaning and safety. Many are raised on "cotton candy" descriptions of God and Heaven–God is an old man with a long white beard in flowing white robes who, like Santa Claus, benignly presides over the world, rewarding those who are "good." Many others are raised on punitive conceptions of the angry old man who judges people according to their wrongdoings, smiting sinners with "His terrible swift sword" and consigning them to Hell if they do not repent and change their ways. Still others are raised on a hybrid view of God– Santa Claus and Doomsayer. Since most alcoholics have been sub- jected to *some* kind of traumatic experience in their younger lives, they are very likely to believe that they are bad, wrong, sinful, defective–and that whatever goes wrong in the life around them is their fault, that somehow they are to blame. It follows, then, that they might respond with beliefs such as–**Since I'm bad, not good, "cotton candy" can't save me**–or–**Hell awaits me because I'm bad. I deserve whatever punishment is meted out to me.** Obviously, childlike and primitive conceptions of this sort will either fail or, at the very least, hinder people in their attempts to find hope and meaning, something worth living for.

THE EFFECTS OF ADDICTION ON FAITH

In the face of the major, on-going trauma of alcoholism, even those people whose faith has been strong and positive and based on mature and realistic principles of belief cannot easily withstand the dramatic pounding of this trauma. And the faith of those who were raised to believe in a "cotton-candy" or a wrathful God tends to crumble in response to the ravages of their alcoholism.

The downward descent into alcoholism is a descent into a hell of loss–loss of faith in a God who cares; loss of connection with any God or power outside of self; loss of connection with others and with self. The world of the self narrows radically to just the self, disconnected, alone, terrified, helpless. Finally, people lose touch with their Selves, with who they are and what they mean. Whatever conception of God remains is of a wrathful, punitive, uncaring, *absent* figure who has turned his face from the suffering alcoholic. The comments of people in recovery about their alcoholic experience bear this out: "I believed that the awful things happening to me were God's punishment of my sins"; "I thought that God hated me"; "I was sure that God had abandoned me"; "I just knew that God couldn't love anyone as terrible as me." Rage, guilt, shame, terror, and despair attack and corrode alcoholics' souls. Many of them simply give up–they reject God outright or passively accept their "deserved punishment." At the same time, however, on some deep level, most suffering alcoholics long for connection with God or Higher Power or something that will give meaning to their lives (Bean, 1981).

This downward spiral continues till people reach the bottom of their experience, till they reach the end of their endurance of their trauma. Something has to give. They come face to face with the devastation of their alcoholism. They encounter their helplessness, their isolation, their despair. They will either die or go crazy or self-destruct–or they will begin their recovery.

RECOVERY: THE UPWARD PATH

When this encounter marks the beginning of recovery, it is usually a transformative experience. Many alcoholics at this point undergo a spiritual conversion, a spiritual turnaround which enables them to begin and hopefully continue their tough and demanding journey of recovery and spiritual development. At some core level, they make a decision to take the risk of living, to take the risk of seeking meaning. Those who have experienced other traumas prior to their alcoholism oftentimes need a lot of help and a lot of work in order to be able to maintain their risk-taking about life.

As Herman (1992) states, "Empowerment and reconnection are the core experiences of recovery" (p. 197). Central to this process of recovery is the need to find sources of power and meaning to restore the annihilated or deeply wounded self. Restoration involves (re)defining and (re)discovering The Power–whatever form that may take–and (re)connecting with that power in ways that give life meaning. As one woman commented, "It was phenomenal. The longer I stayed sober, the more aware I became of a *presence* which seemed to be guiding me. Oh, I don't mean spooky stuff. I just mean that I felt the comfort and strength of a power *which seemed to come from within me* and which felt in some way like it had always been with me though I hadn't known it."

Just what do we mean when we talk about Higher Power or God? We use these terms to refer to that power-force-spirit in the universe which touches the soul and whispers, "Hope!"; which touches the soul and leads it toward the light; which tells the soul to live, even in the face of terrible odds and circumstances; which infuses people's lives with a meaning beyond survival. It is that power which guides people along paths that lead to acceptance, courage, wisdom, and serenity.

On a practical level, especially in the early years of the recovery process, people have to focus on how not to drink, how to take care of themselves, how to structure their life and time, and how to live alcohol-free. On an emotional level, people must struggle with not feeling much of anything or with being overwhelmed by their feelings, with handling mood swings, with controlling their impulses, and/or with managing powerful feelings of rage, guilt, terror, and shame. On a spiritual level, people's central tasks are two-fold: (1) They must let go of the disastrous belief that *they* are the center of the universe, that *they* are "God" (Kurtz, 1979); (2) They must create or find or rediscover a conception of God or a power greater than themselves and establish a "right relationship" with that god or power.

The process that AA describes as coming "to believe in a *power greater than ourselves*" is a slow, difficult, and complex one for many. Central to this process is the task of defining or determining what that power is. Depending, of course, on people's length of sobriety and on the support they find as they proceed on their quest, their conceptions of this *power greater than* may change and hopefully become more positive and meaningful as they progress. But the essential struggle is *what can I–do I–should I–believe in?*

People's answers, of course, are as various as people. If they go to Alcoholics Anonymous (AA), they are exposed to conceptions of God/Higher Power based on and described in language drawn from the Judaeo-Christian heritage. Thus the word "God" (or in one, the pronoun "Him") appears in five of the Twelve Steps (3, 5, 6, 7, 11). But in recognition of the problem that many have in accepting a strict definition or conception of God, people are asked to believe in God *as they understand Him,* thus making possible extremely broad and personalized interpretations of God. It makes room for conceptions ranging from more traditional views of God as creator who is loving, caring, merciful to a Higher Power who may consist of the AA Program or a particular AA group or people's inner selves or nature or a life force or spirit. One AA story has it that one person's sponsor told him he could believe in the radiator as his Higher Power if that was what he was able to believe in and if that would help.

This wide latitude about definitions of God *as people understand him* is not enough for some people. Some women feel extremely alienated by the strongly patriarchal tone and tendencies of the AA program and either do not relate to the program or leave it. Many leave only after having struggled for a long time, changing the word "God" to "Goddess," refusing to say the Lord's Prayer, and changing all the "He's" to "She's." Many of these women redefine God either as the Goddess or as a non-gendered force, power, or spirit and look to women's support groups or groups like Women for Sobriety or groups founded on Charlotte Kasl's (1992) "Sixteen Steps for Discovery and Empowerment" for the help they need to deal with their addiction.

Various other people may either leave AA or not feel comfortable joining it for different reasons. Women (and some men) who have been sexually abused by men often have great trouble with the maleness of the traditional God explicitly and implicitly referred to in the AA program. People who have been physically and/or sexually abused and lesbians, gay men, and bisexuals who have been (and continue to be) abused by a homophobic society often need to define the recipient of their faith either as a Goddess or as a non-gendered power-spirit-force. People of color who have been traumatized by racism often look to the African-American church as the source of meaning in their recovery. Many Latinos/Latinas turn to or turn back to *spiritismus* for spiritual nurturance in recovery. Both groups may avoid traditional AA meetings because they are predominantly white. Native Americans are likely to find their source of meaning and support in their communities and their culture's beliefs, not in mainstream white culture.

As Herman (1992) points out, traumatized people suffer "(a)lterations in (their) systems of meaning" including a "loss of sustaining faith (and a) sense of hopelessness and despair" (p. 121). Their recovery, both spiritual and otherwise, requires that they come to terms with these feelings and define, create, or discover some power greater than themselves that affords hope but is not experienced as being affiliated with the oppressive, destructive power structure in this society.

CLINICAL IMPLICATIONS

Three statements have bearing on the clinical implications of working with chemically dependent people struggling to recover. As Ross V., a member of AA, says, "Religion is for people who are afraid of going to hell; spirituality is for those who have been there" (Kurtz, 1992: p. 15). Bill Wilson writes in his personal correspondence, "We must find some spiritual basis for living, else we die" (Kurtz, 1992: p. 11). And as the "Big Book" of AA states, alcoholism is "an illness which only a spiritual experience will conquer" (*Alcoholics Anonymous*, 1976: p. 44). Although all these statements spring from one source–AA–many other writers agree that survivors of trauma, in this case the trauma of alcoholism, must find some source of existential meaning, some spiritual connection and empowerment in order to continue to survive and to begin to thrive (Bean, 1981; Denzin, 1987a and 1987b; Herman, 1992; Kasl, 1993; Kurtz, 1979; Kurtz and Ketcham, 1992; Twerski, 1990).

It is crucial that treating professionals keep in mind the reality that people need some kind of spiritual meaning in their lives and that alcoholics especially need some type of spiritual experience in order to heal from the trauma of their addiction. But it is equally important that clinicians bear in mind that the definition of *spirituality* must be as broad, as inclusive, and as diverse as possible. In addition, the definitions of God or a *power greater than oneself* must be all-encompassing to allow room for *whatever* beliefs will help people heal. Thus it is critically important that therapists examine their own belief systems and monitor their countertransference in light of those systems. Furthermore, therapists need to make room for very different paths of recovery and spirituality, for very different (and perhaps upsetting to the therapist) ways of defining God or a *power greater than*. The only viable criterion is–does it work for this person? Ultimately, it comes down to the fact that clinicians need to respect and honor clients' choices, their ways of making those choices, and the pace at which they travel on their journey.

How can treating professionals be helpful? Clinicians may need to introduce clients to the spiritual realm, to the concept that spirituality–however one defines it–is an important part of recovery. But therapists must be prepared for and willing to accept clients' rage at God, their bitterness, their cynicism, their rejection of God and see these feelings as inevitable in the face of such trauma. An important task of clinicians is to remain stable and steadfast in the face of such spiritual chaos and despair.

As people begin their recovery journey, AA may be the path they follow. If so, they may need help and reassurance that they don't have to conform and hold a traditional view of God/Higher Power in order to belong or to work the Program. Therapists can provide information about how others define God/Higher Power in non-traditional ways such as a life force, energy, or one's inner voice. In addition, clinicians may need to help clients with the notion that they're "not doing their spirituality right." It is helpful to point out that people's views of God/Higher Power are not fixed, but change over time in relation to people's experiences of their life and recovery processes. Clinicians also need to examine their own beliefs to determine whether they are biased in favor of AA and *against* any other path to sobriety and whether they are biased about conceptions of God. For example, it could be destructive for clinicians to oppose, whether consciously or not, whether subtly or not, people's seeking sobriety by fervently embracing religion. It could be harmful for clinicians to oppose people's seeking recovery through such organizations as Secular Sobriety.

It is also extremely important for therapists to honor women's feminist reactions to the maleness of AA and its patriarchal belief system. Clinicians should not ignore or minimize women's feelings about such matters as the "Our Father" or the constant use of the male pronoun. Many women feel alienated by such language and beliefs and may not go to AA because of it. It is therapists' responsibility to help women find a way to tolerate such language (for example, by changing God to Goddess, He to She) or to help them find viable alternatives.

It is equally important for clinicians not to minimize lesbians' and gay men's mistrust of institutions, including organized groups like AA. Gay people have been traumatized by the homophobia of the power structure and may, therefore, be extremely wary of power–higher or otherwise. For those gay people who wish to, attending AA special interest groups is often helpful (Kus and Latcovich, 1995). For it is there, among real peers, that they may be better able to come to terms with God/Higher Power. Or, if gay clients have been so wounded by homophobia, they may need therapists' support to find their recovery path somewhere else or make their journey a solo one.

Treating professionals also need to be aware of and sensitive to the many different paths other people of different ethnic or cultural or philosophical backgrounds may successfully take. Native Americans may use the sweat lodge as an important tool for recovery. Numerous people, both white and African-American, get and stay sober by following the teachings of Jehovah's Witnesses. Many African-Americans fervently embrace the teachings and spirit of their churches and thereby find God and sobriety. Many women now seek and find sobriety by joining groups which use Charlotte Kasl's (1992) Sixteen Steps for Discovery and Empowerment.

Ultimately, what counts is that clinicians acknowledge the truth that there are many, many ways to find and define God/Higher

Power and many, many paths to recovery. All people, especially those traumatized by alcoholism and perhaps other disasters, need to be encouraged and supported in their search for meaning–for God or a Higher Power or something they can believe in. This search for meaning is what brings empowerment and re-connection–that state in which, as the angel says to Adam and Eve, thou "shalt possess/A Paradise within thee, happier far" (John Milton, *Paradise Lost,* Book XII: ll.586-587).

REFERENCES

Alcoholics Anonymous. (1976). *Alcoholics Anonymous* (3rd ed.). New York: Alcoholics Anonymous World Services, Inc.

Bean, M.H. (1981). Denial and the psychological complications of alcoholism. In M.H. Bean, E.J. Khantzian, J.E. Mack, G.E. Vaillant, & N.E. Zinberg (Eds.), *Dynamic approaches to the understanding and treatment of alcoholism* (pp. 55-96). New York: Free Press (Macmillan).

Courtois, C. (1988). *Healing the incest wound: Adult survivors in therapy.* New York: Norton.

Denzin, N. (1987a). *The alcoholic self.* Beverly Hills: Sage.

_____ . (1987b). *The recovering alcoholic.* Beverly Hills: Sage.

Finnegan, D.G., & McNally, E.B. (1987). *Dual identities: Counseling the chemically dependent gay man and lesbian.* Center City, Minn.: Hazelden.

Herman, J.L. (1992). *Trauma and recovery: The aftermath of violence–from domestic abuse to political terror.* New York: Basic Books.

Kasl, C.D. (1993). *Many roads, one journey: Moving beyond the 12 steps.* New York: HarperCollins.

Kurtz, E. (1979). *Not-God: A history of Alcoholics Anonymous.* Center City, Minn.: Hazelden.

_____ , & Ketcham, K. (1992). *The spirituality of imperfection: Modern wisdom from classic stories.* New York: Bantam.

Kus, R.J., & Latcovich, M.A. (1995). Special interest groups in Alcoholics Anonymous: A focus on gay men's groups. *Journal of Gay & Lesbian Social Services,* 67-82.

McCann, I. L., & Pearlman, L.A. (1990). *Psychological trauma and the adult survivor: Theory, therapy, and transformation.* New York: Brunner/Mazel.

Pharr, S. (1988). *Homophobia: A weapon of sexism.* Little Rock: Chardon Press.

Spiritual Reading as Bibliotherapy

Rojann R. Alpers, PhD, RN

SUMMARY. Spiritual reading is a key ingredient in spiritual growth. In this article Dr. Alpers discusses spiritual bibliotherapy, the methodology of spiritual reading, and the benefits and limitations of spiritual bibliotherapy. In addition, the author gives the reader some concrete examples of spiritual readings which many 12-Steppers have found to be particularly helpful in their journey to wholeness. *[Single or multiple copies of this article are available from The Haworth Document Delivery Service: 1-800-342-9678, 9:00 a.m. - 5:00 p.m. (EST).]*

BACKGROUND

The purpose of this article is to discuss a special type of bibliotherapy, spiritual reading. Spiritual reading is quite often a particularly appropriate activity for chemically dependent persons as the spiritual component is crucial in recovery from addiction. It is no accident that the most effective treatment programs ever devised for treating addiction are Alcoholics Anonymous and other 12-Step pro-

---

Rojann R. Alpers is Assistant Professor in the Harris College of Nursing at Texas Christian University. Dr. Alpers, who specializes in public and maternal-child health, has presented her research findings in maternal/child and alcohol studies in the United States and Europe.

Address correspondence to: Dr. Rojann R. Alpers, 6817 Windcrest, Ft. Worth, TX 76133 USA.

[Haworth co-indexing entry note]: "Spiritual Reading as Bibliotherapy." Alpers, Rojann R. Co-published simultaneously in *Journal of Chemical Dependency Treatment* (The Haworth Press, Inc.) Vol. 5, No. 2, 1995, pp. 49-63; and: *Spirituality and Chemical Dependency* (ed: Robert J. Kus) The Haworth Press, Inc., 1995, pp. 49-63; and: *Spirituality and Chemical Dependency* (ed: Robert J. Kus) Harrington Park Press, an imprint of The Haworth Press, Inc., 1995, pp. 49-63. Single or multiple copies of this article are available from The Haworth Document Delivery Service [1-800-342-9678, 9:00 a.m. - 5:00 p.m. (EST)].

© 1995 by The Haworth Press, Inc. All rights reserved.

49

grams, which are essentially spiritual programs. And a major component of any spiritual journey is spiritual reading.

De Coppens (1980) describes the purpose of spirituality as assisting us to unfold and actualize our faculties, potentialities, and talents which leads us to a fuller, richer, more conscious, creative, and useful life. In addition, de Coppens (1980), Clinebell (1988), and Hovel (1991) all agree that genuine spirituality touches our entire being and affects every dimension, principle, facet and action of our lives. It implies a constant and conscious process of expanding, deepening, and heightening our capacity to know, to love, and to create. Spirituality, according to Heller (1988), is a journey toward integrity–wholeness. It is the "fruit" of human evolution–it is maturity.

It is important to note, however, that spirituality is not identical with religion or religiosity, which provide us with a set of teachings and principles that may help us achieve spirituality. In addition, it is not synonymous with spiritualism which is based on the belief in after-death survival of the soul and our ability to contact souls of the dead. Further, psychic and extrasensory powers are also not spirituality.

SPIRITUAL READING AS BIBLIOTHERAPY

Bibliotherapy too, has many definitions. Russell and Schrodes (1950) identify it as a process of dynamic interaction between the personality of the reader and the literature, an interaction which may be utilized for personality assessment, adjustment, and growth. Stadel (1964) views bibliotherapy as psychology through literature reading that is used to help solve or prevent problems. Kus (1989) defines it as the use of literature of any type, and in any form, for the purpose of self-help or personal growth. And Lundsen (1972) simply states it is the right book to the right person at the right time about the right problem. Bibliotherapy in its most simplistic form is using books to help people.

Bibliotherapy has its roots in ancient times as noted by an epigraph found on the Alexandria Library of around 300 B.C. which reads "Medicine for the Mind." Additionally, the library in Thebes was dedicated to the "Healing of the Soul," and the medieval

Abbey Library in Switzerland carries the inscription "Medicine Chest for the Soul." Throughout history the written and spoken word has been one of the most influential tools to heal troubled souls and to change the human condition. Spiritual bibliotherapy, or spiritual reading, could therefore be defined as reading literature which leads to personal healing, stimulation, growth, insight, and inspiration.

THE METHODOLOGY OF SPIRITUAL READING: THE BIBLIOTHERAPEUTIC PROCESS

The first step in the bibliotherapeutic process is assisting clients to identify their needs. This can be accomplished using a variety of techniques such as observing one-on-one, or group interactions, conferences with other professionals, or interpreting written responses to open-ended questions. It is especially important to note that chemically dependent clients often have issues other than their addictions that also may need to be addressed (e.g., divorce, incest, internalized homophobia, poor self-esteem). The following open-ended questions, suggested by Cornett and Cornett, may prove helpful in assisting clients in identifying their myriad needs.

Starter Questions or Directions:
My biggest problem is?
The things I would change about me are?
My saddest experience is?
Things I do best are?
My three worst fears are?
Decide on three problems you have and put them in order from biggest to smallest.
List all the things you would like to change about yourself and then number them in the order you'd like to change them.
What do you do with your free time?
How would you change your family if you could? (Cornett and Cornett 1980: pp. 21-23).
Thought Completion Exercises:
My home . . . ? My family . . . ? If I could be/do anything . . . ?
If it weren't for . . . ?

Inquire about dreams (Cornett and Cornett, 1980: pp. 23-24).

The second step in bibliotherapy is matching the client with the appropriate materials. It is important to note that a variety of materials may be used in bibliotherapy. These can include but are not limited to books (in total, or selected chapters), magazine/journal articles, audiotapes (for those individuals with literacy or sight difficulties), comic books, movies/films, songs, or poems. Haven't we all read, heard or seen things that touched us, stimulated us, elicited a memory, or made us think of things we had not contemplated previously, or given us new perspectives on old ideas? But of course the question is–where do I get these materials? Several sources may prove helpful.

First, start with your own personal or professional library. Have you read something recently that aided you in thinking about a problem or concern in a new way? Are there favorite authors that you can "always recommend" such as Leo Buscaglia, Catherine Marshall, Norman Vincent Peale, Robert Schuller, Billy Graham, James Dobson, or Robert Fulghum?

Second, go to a local bookstore. A good place to begin is the religion, self-help, psychology and humor sections. Take the time to read the book jacket and then ask one of the store assistants for their impressions. It has been my experience that most book store assistants are voracious readers and often have cogent opinions on most texts.

Third, visit your local college, university and city libraries. Notably, the university library tends toward the more scientific, philosophical materials. However, a number of readable, not so "academically oriented" materials may be available. The local library will tend to have more of the current self-help materials most often seen in the bookstores and discussed on the national television talk shows. Examples of key words which might be helpful in a computer search (or in locating books in a bookstore) are: alcoholism; addictions; AIDS; behavioral therapy; bibliotherapy; children's self-help; codependency; coping; depression; eating disorders; family health; gay studies; group therapy; inspirational works; lesbian studies; men's studies; religion; self-help; sexuality; spirituality; women's studies. Almost any "problem" can be entered into the computer search under "subject" and will yield numerous texts. In addition, most library computers will also search by author's name. Therefore, writings by favorite authors can also be located. Journals can also be searched in a similar fashion by accessing the "periodicals" section of the computer menu.

Additionally, not to be overlooked, are the music and video sections of the library or bookstore (audiovisual therapy). These materials may require more time to locate as a number of city libraries still use a card catalogue for these holdings, or they may simply have a case of videos, records and cassettes. Again, these materials may best be identified and used if they are familiar to you personally, or if your client has mentioned a favorite artist or performer. Agencies such as Hazelden have whole catalogs of just such audiovisual materials for purchase. (Hazelden's number is: (800)-328-9000).

It is of paramount importance to note that simply finding a book which *appears* to match a problem or issue with the reader is insufficient; literary merit must also be considered. Again, Cornett and Cornett (1980) provide a set of criteria by which the appropriateness of the literature can be judged. These criteria are:

(a) Is the book appropriate for the client's reading ability? Are the vocabulary and main ideas of the book understandable? (b) Is the material written at a level that is developmentally appropriate, or is the writing style one that transcends age and would appeal to children and adults alike? (c) Do the major themes in the material match the present needs of the client? (d) Are the characters believable enough for the reader to empathize with their situation, or are they "bigger than life" and therefore, appeal most to fantasy? (e) Does the author/characters involve creative problem-solving? (f) Does this material's format enhance its contents? In other words, is it too long, and does it appropriately use illustrations and pictures? (Cornett and Cornett, 1980, pp. 24-26)

Another criterion is generated by one of the goals of bibliotherapy which is to cause the reader to think about alternative solutions to problems/issues. Therefore, alternative perspectives and their inherent consequences must be explored.

Ideally, the clinician should read and evaluate all materials to be used with the above criteria before recommending them to clients. However, with time always being a scarce resource and with the plethora of materials available, this may not always be realistic.

SPECIFIC SPIRITUAL READINGS

Spiritual reading in the Twelve Step way of life would probably include the following types of reading. These reading materials are available at most libraries and bookstores, with many of them also available on audiotapes. The following types of literature are the most common ones found in 12-Steppers' libraries and in treatment centers.

Daily Meditation Books

Daily meditation books are one of the most popular forms of spiritual reading for persons in the Twelve Step way of life. Some of the more popular meditation guides for recovering persons are the following books published anonymously by Hazelden: *Answers in the Heart: Daily Meditations for Men and Women Recovering from Sex Addiction* (1989); *The Color of Light: Daily Meditations for All of Us Living with AIDS* (1988); *Day by Day: Daily Meditations for Recovering Addicts* (1974); *Each Day a New Beginning* (1984); *The Eye Opener* (n.d.); *In God's Care: Daily Meditations on Spirituality in Recovery* (1991); *Keep It Simple: Daily Meditations for Twelve-Step Beginnings and Renewal* (1989); *The Little Red Book* (1970); *Stools and Bottles* (1970); *Today's Gift: Daily Meditations for Families* (1984); *Touchstones: A Book of Daily Meditations for Men* (1986), and the granddaddy of them all, *Twenty-Four Hours a Day* (1954). Other meditation guides published by Hazelden include: Beattie's *The Language of Letting Go: Daily Meditations on Codependency* (1990); Brady's *Daybreak: Meditations for Women Survivors of Sexual Abuse* (1991); Casey's *Worthy of Love: Meditations on Loving Ourself and Others* (1990); Casey's *If Only I Could Quit: Recovery from Nicotine Addiction* (1989); Cordes' *The Reflecting Pond: Meditations for Self-Discovery* (1988); Dean's *Night Light: A Book of Nighttime Meditations* (1986); Fossum and

Fossum's *The More We Find in Each Other: Meditations for Couples* (1992); L.'s *Inner Harvest: Daily Meditations for Recovery from Eating Disorders* (1990) and L.'s *Food for Thought: Daily Meditations for Overeaters* (1980); Larsen and Hegarty's *Days of Healing, Days of Joy: Daily Meditations for Adult Children* (1989); Limon's *Beginning Again: Beyond the End of Love* (1991); Pitzele's *One More Day: Daily Meditations for the Chronically Ill* (1988); and Roeck's *Look to This Day: Twenty-Four Hours a Day for Everyone* (1978). Other meditation guides include AA's *Daily Reflections: A Book of Reflections by A.A. Members for A.A. Members* (AA, 1990) and Hifler's *A Cherokee Feast of Days: Daily Meditations* (Council Oaks Books, 1992).

INSPIRATIONAL RECOVERY LIFE STORIES

Frequently, solace and comfort are gained from knowing we are not alone in a situation and that others have successfully faced similar problems and dilemmas. Recovery biographies and autobiographies may assist clients to empathize, gain self-awareness, and to envision a successful recovery for themselves. Examples of this type of literature include: *Dr. Bob and the Good Oldtimers* (A.A., 1980); *"Pass it on": The Story of Bill Wilson and How the A.A. Message Reached the World* (AA, 1984); *Bill W.* (Thomsen, 1984); *It Must Be Five O'clock Somewhere* (Cary, 1986); and Welch and Vecsey's *Five O'clock Comes Early: A Young Man's Battle with Alcoholism* (1982).

BIG BOOKS

Most of the 12-Step fellowships have a basic "bible" describing their fellowship. These also contain inspirational stories of men and women who have entered recovery by living the spiritual 12-Step way of life advocated by the fellowship. Because the first of such works, the first edition of *Alcoholics Anonymous,* was printed on heavy paper, these books came to be known as "Big Books." The most famous is, of course, *Alcoholics Anonymous,* 3rd edition (A.A., 1976).

PRAYER BOOKS

Much less commonly used than meditation books are prayer books. These are especially helpful for members who have a difficult time with spontaneous praying or who have a very poor background in praying. An excellent example of such a book is Pittman's *The 12 Step Prayer Book: A Collection of Favorite Prayers and Inspirational Writings* (1990).

GENERAL SPIRITUALITY

Often recovering persons read literature designed to offer them basic information such as notions of God or other higher powers, what spirituality is and is not, and how people like them experience spirituality in recovery. Examples of this type of literature are: AA's *Came to Believe . . . The Spiritual Adventures of A.A. as Experienced by Individual Members* (1973); Bernas' *Practicing Spiritual Reality* (1993); Dollard's *Toward Spirituality: The Inner Journey* (1983); Fields et al.'s *Chop Wood, Carry Water* (1984); Hazelden's *Conscious Contact with a Higher Power* (1985); and Twerski's *Animals and Angels: Spirituality in Recovery* (1990).

STEP GUIDES AND REFLECTIONS

Another common type of spiritual literature is that which offers guidance or reflections on the various steps. Examples of this type of literature would be Farrell's *One Day at a Time: Meditations and Prayers on the Eleventh Step* (1976); Hazelden's *Stairway to Serenity: The Eleventh Step* (1988); Alcoholics Anonymous' *Twelve Steps & Twelve Traditions*; and Kus' *The WinterStar Life Assessment Guide* (1990). Additionally, there are many series of step guides available such as Hazelden's *12 Step Pamphlet Series* and the *Keep It Simple Workbook Collection*.

HISTORICAL LITERATURE OF VARIOUS FELLOWSHIPS

In this category are books written about the early days of the 12-Step movement. Generally these books are read more by persons who have been in the 12-Step way of life and who wish to learn more about the early days of the movement. Examples of this type of literature are: AA's *Alcoholics Anonymous Comes of Age: A Brief History of A.A.* (1957); Mel B.'s *New Wine: The Spiritual Roots of the Twelve Step Miracle* (1991); Darrah's *Sister Ignatia: Angel of Alcoholics Anonymous* (1992); and Kurtz' *Not God: A History of Alcoholics Anonymous* (1979).

SPECIAL POPULATION RECOVERY LITERATURE

In addition to the spiritual literature designed to meet the needs of recovering persons in general, there is also a body of literature designed to meet the needs of special populations in recovery. Examples of this type of literature include: AA's *AA and the Gay/Lesbian Alcoholic* (1989); AA's *Memo to an Inmate Who May be an Alcoholic* (1961); AA's *A Letter to a Woman Alcoholic* (1954) and *A.A. for the Woman* (1968); AA's *Do You Think You're Different?*; Berg's *Alcoholism and Pastoral Ministry: Readings on Recovery* (Guest House, 1989); Bluestone's *The Impaired Nurse* (Hazelden, 1986); Kominars' *Accepting Ourselves: The Twelve-Step Journey of Recovery from Addiction for Gay Men and Lesbians* (Perennial Library, 1989); and Kus' *Gay Men of Alcoholics Anonymous: First-Hand Accounts* (WinterStar Press, 1990).

OTHER READINGS

Besides the common types of spiritual reading mentioned above, many recovering persons find they need to work on a host of issues which are often the result of addiction. For example, many find they need literature to help them work on anger, low self-esteem, resentments, internalized homophobia, stinking thinking, jealousy, and the like. There is a rich treasure trove of literature designed to help persons work though these issues and much of it is available from such sources as Hazelden or Courage to Change (800)-935-8838.

The third step of the bibliotherapy process is implementation. Once you have assisted in matching the person, the need, and the book, guided reading can begin. Guided reading simply means providing the reader with a few examples of the kinds of questions you would like them to think about as they read. Remember, an important aspect of guided reading is to mutually and realistically agree on the time needed to complete the reading. This must include not only the actual reading but also the incubation time required to fully immerse, absorb, contemplate, create, apply, and gain insight from the exercise. This will help give direction and purpose to their reading. Most importantly, keep it simple and focus on the "whys" of the reading rather than on the "whats."

The following is a list of questions which may assist you in giving direction and purpose to your client's reading:

- What is the main theme or point made in this reading?
- What challenges did the main character face?
- How did he/she handle those challenges?
- What pictures come to mind as you read?
- Can you see yourself in this story?
- How is this character like, unlike you?
- How would you have handled the situation in the book?
- What words really stood out for you from this reading?
- How might you use what you read today? Tomorrow? In talking with your family/friends? At work?
- How did this reading make you feel?
- Can you summarize this reading in one sentence?
- What effect has this reading had on you?

As another option, you may suggest some follow-up activities from the reading. These may include initiating and keeping a journal of insights, personal challenges faced and their resolution, a personal annotated bibliography, words or passages that struck a particular chord, feelings associated with the reading, or just "happy thoughts and ideas." Two texts offer suggestions for potential follow-up activities that may be adapted for individuals of all ages. These are Prather's *A Book of Games: A Course in Spiritual Play* (1981) and Rainwater's *You're in Charge: A Guide to Becoming Your Own Therapist* (1979).

The final step to spiritual bibliotherapy is evaluation. Evaluation entails summarizing what has occurred and discussing what has been achieved; what, if any, conclusions have been derived; how the exercise might be improved; what the client needs next; and what the future direction should be. Ideally, this is accomplished at the completion of each reading exercise.

BENEFITS AND LIMITATIONS
OF SPIRITUAL BIBLIOTHERAPY

Positive results from bibliotherapy have been noted by many researchers and writers (Agnes, 1947; Bump, 1990; Cornett & Cornett, 1980; Fisher, 1965; Herminghaus, 1954; Kus; 1989; Livingood, 1961; Martin, 1955; Schulteis, 1969; Smith, 1948; Swift, 1984; Tauran, 1967; Weiss, 1961). Positive changes identified include improved problem-solving ability, values development, increased self-esteem, improved personal and social adjustment, personal enrichment, enhanced creativity, stimulation, personal insight and acceptance of self and others. In addition, improvement in critical thinking, the ability to generate alternatives and self-evaluation have also been noted.

Further, Kus (1989) notes the cost-effectiveness of having, with minimal expenditure, the wealth of information contained in most of these volumes. This information would often otherwise require many hours of in-depth teaching and therapy to acquire. Also, the accessibility of books either from a bookstore or library makes this approach particularly attractive to rural or other more isolated clients. Additionally, this less structured form of therapy allows clients to read and contemplate at their own pace and leisure and in the privacy of their own homes, and it allows clients to return to the (therapy) text as personally desired or needed. Finally, and perhaps most importantly, spiritual reading invites the implementation of the Twelfth Step–share and pass it on.

While the benefits of bibliotherapy are well documented, its success can be limited by both the client and the therapist. First, the therapist's intervention assumes client literacy, but as discussed previously, this may be managed with the use of audiotapes. Second, bibliotherapy may be limited by the clients' readiness to see themselves in a spiritual mirror. And finally, this therapy relies upon the clients' ability to transfer their insights from the reading into their lives. In addition, the therapist's skill in directing the spiritual bibliotherapy, the quality of materials chosen, and the quality of questions asked may all act as limitations if the texts are not thoroughly explored and the therapist is not well prepared.

Clearly, bibliotherapy is recognized as a potentially powerful intervention strategy for people of all ages, and spiritual bibliotherapy can be particularly appropriate for individuals who are chemically dependent and who have embraced the 12-Step program for recovery.

REFERENCES

Alcoholics Anonymous. (1989). *AA and the gay/lesbian alcoholic.* New York: AA World Services, Inc.

Alcoholics Anonymous. (1968). *A.A. for the woman.* New York: AA World Services, Inc.

Alcoholics Anonymous. (1976). *Alcoholics Anonymous,* 3rd edition. New York: AA World Services, Inc.

Alcoholics Anonymous. (1957). *Alcoholics Anonymous comes of age: A brief history of A.A.* New York: AA World Services, Inc.

Alcoholics Anonymous. (1973). *Came to believe . . . The spiritual adventures of A.A. as experienced by individual members.* New York: AA World Services, Inc.

Alcoholics Anonymous. (1990). *Daily reflections: A book of reflections by A.A. members for A.A. members.* New York: AA World Services, Inc.

Alcoholics Anonymous. (1976). *Do you think you're different?* New York: AA World Services, Inc.

Alcoholics Anonymous. (1980). *Dr. Bob and the good oldtimers.* New York: AA World Services, Inc.

Alcoholics Anonymous. (1954). *A letter to a woman alcoholic.* New York: AA World Services, Inc.

Alcoholics Anonymous. (1961). *Memo to an inmate who may be an alcoholic.* New York: AA World Services, Inc.

Alcoholics Anonymous. (1984). *"Pass it on": The story of Bill Wilson and how the A.A. message reached the world.* New York: AA World Services, Inc.

Alcoholics Anonymous. (1981). *Twelve steps and twelve traditions.* New York: AA World Services, Inc.

B., Mel. (1991). *New wine: The spiritual roots of the twelve step miracle.* Center City, MN: Hazelden.

Beattie, M. (1990). *The language of letting go: Daily meditations on codependency.* Center City, MN: Hazelden.

Berg, S. (1989). *Alcoholism and pastoral ministry: Readings on recovery.* Lake Orion, MN: Guest House.

Bernas, E. (1993). *Practicing spiritual reality.* Center City, MN: Hazelden.

Bluestone, B. (1986). *The impaired nurse.* Center City, MN: Hazelden.

Brady, M. (1991). *Daybreak: Meditations for women survivors of sexual abuse.* Center City, MN: Hazelden.

Bump, J. (1990). Innovative bibliotherapy approaches to substance abuse education. *The Arts in Psychotherapy.* 17, 355-362.

Cary, K. (1986). *It must be five o'clock somewhere.* Minneapolis: Comp-Care.

Casey, K. (1989). *If only I could quit: Recovery from nicotine addiction.* Center City, MN: Hazelden.

Casey, K. (1990). *Worthy of love: Meditations on loving ourself and others.* Center City, MN: Hazelden.

Clinebell, J.H. (1988). *Spirit centered wholeness: Beyond the psychology of self.* New York: Edwin Mellen Press.

Cordes, L. (1988). *The reflecting pond: Meditations for self-discovery.* Center City, MN: Hazelden.

Cornett, C.F, Cornett, C.E. (1980). *Bibliotherapy: The right book at the right time.* Bloomington: Phi Delta Kappa Educational Foundation.

Darrah, M.C. (1992). *Sister Ignatia: Angel of Alcoholics Anonymous.* Chicago: Loyola University Press.

De Coppens, P.R. (1980). *The spiritual perspective: Key issues and themes interpreted from the standpoint of spiritual consciousness.* Washington, D.C., University Press of America.

Dean, A.E. (1986). *Night light: A book of nighttime meditations.* Center City, MN: Hazelden.

Dollard, J. (1983). *Toward spirituality: The inner journey.* Center City, MN: Hazelden.

Farrell, J.E. (1976). *One day at a time: Meditations and prayers on the Eleventh Step.* Liguori, MD: Liguori Press.

Fields, R. et al. (1984). *Chop wood, carry water: A guide to finding spiritual fulfillment in everyday life.* Los Angeles: Jeremy P. Tarcher, Inc.

Fossum, M., & Fossum, M. (1992). *The more we find in each other: Meditations for couples.* Center City, MN: Hazelden.

Hazelden. (1989). *Answers in the heart: Daily meditations for men and women recovering from sex addiction.* Center City, MN: Hazelden.

Hazelden. (1988). *The color of light: Daily meditations for all of us living with AIDS.* Center City, MN: Hazelden.

Hazelden. (1985). *Conscious contact with a higher power.* Center City, MN: Hazelden.

Hazelden. (1974). *Day by day: Daily meditations for recovering addicts.* Center City, MN: Hazelden.

Hazelden. (1984). *Each day a new beginning.* Center City, MN: Hazelden.

Hazelden. (n.d.). *The eye opener.* Center City, MN: Hazelden.

Hazelden. (1991). *In God's care: Daily meditations on spirituality in recovery.* Center City, MN: Hazelden.

Hazelden. (1989). *Keep it simple: Daily meditations for Twelve-Step beginnings and renewal.* Center City, MN: Hazelden.

Hazelden. (1970). *The little red book.* Center City, MN: Hazelden.

Hazelden. (1988). *Stairway to serenity: The eleventh step.* Center City, MN: Hazelden.

Hazelden. (1970). *Stools and bottles.* Center City, MN: Hazelden.

Hazelden. (1984). *Today's gift: Daily meditations for families.* Center City, MN: Hazelden.

Hazelden. (1986). *Touchstones: A book of daily meditations for men.* Center City, MN: Hazelden.

Hazelden. (1954). *Twenty-four hours a day.* Center City, MN: Hazelden.

Heller, A. (1988). *General ethics.* New York: Blackwell.

Hifler, J.S. (1992). *A Cherokee feast of days: Daily meditations.* Tulsa, OK: Council Oaks Books.

Kominars, S. (1989). *Accepting ourselves: The Twelve-Step journey of recovery from addiction for gay men and lesbians.* New York: Perennial Library.

Kovel, J. (1991). *History and spirit.* Boston: Beacon Press.

Kurtz, E. (1979). *Not God: A history of Alcoholics Anonymous.* Center City, MN: Hazelden.

Kus, R.J. (1989). Bibliotherapy and gay American men of Alcoholics Anonymous. *Journal of Gay & Lesbian Psychotherapy,* 1:(2), 73-86.

Kus, R.J. (1990). *Gay men of Alcoholics Anonymous: First-hand accounts.* North Liberty, IA: WinterStar Press.

Kus, R.J. (1990). *The WinterStar life assessment guide.* North Liberty, IA: WinterStar Press.

LE, (1990). *Inner harvest: Daily meditations for recovery from eating disorders.* Center City, MN:Hazelden.

LE, (1980). *Food for thought: Daily meditations for overeaters.* Center City, MN: Hazelden.

Larsen, E., & Hegarty, C.L. (1989). *Days of healing, days of joy: Daily meditations for adult children.* Center City, MN: Hazelden.

Limon, W. (1991). *Beginning again: Beyond the end of love.* Center City, MN: Hazelden.

Lundsen, S. (1972). A thinking improvement program through literature. *Elementary English.* April. 505.

Pittman, B. (compiler). (1990). *The 12 step prayer book: A collection of favorite 12 step prayers and inspirational readings.* Seattle: Glen Abbey Books.

Pitzele, S.R. (1988). *One more day: Daily meditations for the chronically ill.* Center City, MN: Hazelden.

Prather, H. (1981). *A book of games: A course in spiritual play.* New York: Doubleday.

Rainwater, J. (1979). *You're in charge: A guide to becoming your own therapist.* New York: Peace Press, Inc.

Roeck, A.L. (1987). *Look to this day: Twenty-four hours a day for everyone.* Center City, MN: Hazelden.

Russell, D., & Shrodes, C. (1950). Contribution of research in bibliotherapy to the language arts program. *School Review,* Sept. 35.

Schulteis, M.A. (1972). *A guide book for bibliotherapy.* San Francisco: Psychotechnic, Inc.

Stadel, A. (1964). Bibliotherapy. *Ohio Schools,* April. 23.

Swift, H.A. (1984). *Program management: A.A. and bibliotherapy.* Center City, MN: Hazelden.

Thompson, R. (1974). *Bill W.* New York: Harper Colophon Books.

Twerski, A.J. (1990). *Animals & angels: Spirituality in recovery.* Center City, MN: Hazelden.

Welch, B., & Vecsey, G. (1982). *Five o'clock comes early: A young man's battle with alcoholism.* New York: William Morrow.

Self-Examination in Addiction Recovery: Notes on Steps 4 and 10

Robert J. Kus RN, PhD

SUMMARY. Self-examination is a critical part of any spiritual journey. In this article, the author explores the two Steps of A.A. devoted to self-examination, Steps 4 and 10. In Step 4, individuals make a searching and fearless moral inventory, while in Step 10, they continue to take a personal inventory and, when wrong, promptly admit it. After offering preliminary notes on the importance of self-examination, Dr. Kus provides a tool for working an organized and thorough Fourth Step, *The WinterStar Life Assessment Guide*. Following notes on the Tenth Step, the author provides clinical implications for those devoted to helping recovering persons. *[Single or multiple copies of this article are available from The Haworth Document Delivery Service: 1-800-342-9678, 9:00 a.m. - 5:00 p.m. (EST).]*

> *Oh God*
> *help me*
> *to believe*
> *the truth about myself*
> *no matter*
> *how beautiful it is!*
> (Wiederkehr, 1991, p. 71)

Robert J. Kus is a nurse-sociologist who specializes in gay men's studies and alcohol studies. A former University of Iowa professor, Dr. Kus is currently studying to become a Roman Catholic priest.

Address correspondence to: Dr. Robert J. Kus, St. Mary Seminary, 28700 Euclid Avenue, Wickliffe, OH 44092-2527 USA.

[Haworth co-indexing entry note]: "Self-Examination in Addiction Recovery: Notes on Steps 4 and 10." Kus, Robert J. Co-published simultaneously in *Journal of Chemical Dependency Treatment* (The Haworth Press, Inc.) Vol. 5, No. 2, 1995, pp. 65-77; and: *Spirituality and Chemical Dependency* (ed: Robert J. Kus) The Haworth Press, Inc., 1995, pp. 65-77; and: *Spirituality and Chemical Dependency* (ed: Robert J. Kus) Harrington Park Press, an imprint of The Haworth Press, Inc., 1995, pp. 65-77. Single or multiple copies of this article are available from The Haworth Document Delivery Service [1-800-342-9678, 9:00 a.m. - 5:00 p.m. (EST)].

© 1995 by The Haworth Press, Inc. All rights reserved.

One of my favorite images of the spiritual life is that of a flower garden. As children, our parents take great pains to cultivate the soil of our spiritual gardens, making the soil pliable and rich. In this garden, they plant flowers to make it beautiful, and they vigilantly watch the garden for the growth of weeds. The "flowers" of the garden are virtues such as kindness, love, hope, faith, and courage; values such as belief in the dignity of all humanity; and behaviors such as doing to others as you would have them do to you. The "weeds" in this garden are such things as selfishness, jealousy, unkindness, and the like.

Parents, teachers, and others, therefore, teach the child to continually examine his or her spiritual garden for the weeds growing there, dig them up, and replace them with flowers. Needless to say, this is a lifelong process.

For still-using chemically dependent persons, their spiritual gardens are often neglected. The flowers of joy and hope and well-being and meaningfulness are choked with the weeds of resentment and self-pity and self-loathing and irresponsibility and estrangement from God and others. Fortunately, the co-founders of AA knew the value of self-examination, and this is reflected in Steps 4 (making a moral inventory) and 10 (continuing to make a moral inventory). By working these steps, individuals learn to weed and replant, weed and replant.

PURPOSE

The purpose of this article is to explore the concept of self-examination in the 12-Step way of life. In particular, I will introduce the *WinterStar Life Assessment Guide* as a concrete tool for self-examination, and will discuss how people go about doing Step Ten, one of the so-called "maintanance" steps. Clinical implications will follow.

STEP FOUR

Step 4 says, "Made a searching and fearless inventory of ourselves" (Alcoholics Anonymous, 1981, p. 6). It is the first of the so-called "action" or "housecleaning" steps, the others being steps 5-9. Unfortunately, of all the steps, this is perhaps the one which produces more procrastination than any other. The procrastination is often due to perfectionism on the part of the recovering person, or it may be due to a lack of understanding of what, exactly, an inventory is.

Some persons confuse an inventory with a history. An analogy might be helpful. Imagine a grocer of 1995. When he takes an inventory of his store, he is concerned about what is on the shelves now, not what was on them in 1940. He wants to know what items need reordering and which need to be discarded. He needs to know if any of them are outdated.

On the other hand, he must know at least something about history. Although it isn't important to the 1995 grocer what was on the shelves in 1940, he does need to know enough history to be able to detect trends or patterns. For example, he needs to know that candy canes seem to sell better in December than in August and that sun tan lotion sells better in the summer months than in the winter. If he does not recognize these trends, he cannot keep his store stocked properly.

Likewise, when individuals do a personal inventory, they need to see what their life is like *today* in terms of negatives as well as the positives. The negatives, called "wrongs" in the the Fifth Step, "defects of character" in the Sixth Step, and "shortcomings" in the Seventh Step, include things such as procrastination, self-pity, unfaithfulness to one's lover or spouse, irresponsible spending, lying, cheating, and the like. Positive aspects of self might include such things as hope, determination, good works, friendliness, and the like. Unfortunately, in early recovery, individuals often feel so bad about themselves, that they have a hard time thinking of good aspects of self. This too may be a source of procrastination in doing Step 4.

Like the grocer who must focus on the here-and-now in doing an inventory, so too must individuals. What one did at age 5 is usually not terribly relevant for a 30 year-old's inventory. However, like the grocer who must do at least some looking back into the past to spot trends and patterns, so, too, must individuals look back enough to recognize patterns of behavior or thinking which may need to be abandoned or modified.

FOURTH STEP GUIDES

There are various sources available for individuals to help them make their Fourth Step. First, there are suggested methods for going about doing a Fourth Step in the "Big Books" of the various 12-Step programs. *Alcoholics Anonymous* (3rd edition), for example, discusses a typical way to work this step (1976, pp. 64-71).

Second, there are many commercial step guides available on the market in both print and video forms. For a complete list of these, the reader may consult stores such as Hazelden (1-800-328-9000).

A third source of help is the individual's sponsor or counselor or 12-Step friends. Often these persons have a particular method which they found helpful.

Finally, many individuals simply rely on their own thinking and use this as the basis for organizing their Fourth Step.

Usually formal guides focus on the relationship and mental health realms and leave many life realms untouched. To correct this, the *WinterStar Life Assessment Guide* was created.

THE WINTERSTAR LIFE ASSESSMENT GUIDE

Background

The *WinterStar Life Assessment Guide* (Kus, 1990) was created by this author to assist members of 12-Step groups to work their Fourth Step in an organized and non-threatening way. It has been successfully used in Europe and the United States by persons not in the 12-Step way of life as well as by 12-Steppers.

Unlike most guides which focus on just a few life realms, this guide invites the user to look at all the major life realms; for alcoholism and other forms of addiction, if allowed to progress, negatively affect all realms of life. The fourteen life realms the *Winter-Star Life Assessment Guide* covers are: physical health; leisure time; finances/spending habits; legal issues; stewardship; celebration rituals; citizenship; friendships; work/school; mental health; general spirituality; applied spirituality or helping others; sexuality; and family relations. Each life realm is listed on a separate page. Under the life realm's name are a series of stimulating questions to help the individual get into the mind-frame of that particular realm. By no means are the questions meant to be exhaustive ones which could be asked about that realm. Two lined columns appear under the questions and are labeled "Strengths" (positives) and "Weaknesses" (negatives).

Because individuals new to the 12-Step way of life are often terribly hard on themselves and can only see the negatives in their lives, this Guide asks them to search hard for their positive qualities, as well as their negative qualities.

Directions

Persons using the *WinterStar Life Assessment Guide* are asked to choose a comfortable place to work on the Guide and to pick a time when they will not be disturbed. They are asked to approach this project as an exciting time, not a fearful one. They are encouraged to be honest and thorough but not compulsive. Trying to be perfectionistic or compulsive leads to frustration and further procrastination. They are asked to stay in the here-and-now rather than dwell in the past too much. After all, it is an inventory, not a history, which is being created. On the other hand, individuals should know enough about the recent past that they can spot patterns or trends which need to be addressed.

In addition to listing their weaknesses, individuals are asked to list their strengths. In fact, it is good to put a positive for every negative if possible. The individual may use more paper than the actual guide has if necessary.

If individuals are not able to complete the Guide at one sitting, they are encouraged to come back later to do so–but not to procrastinate too long. The advice to the procrastinator is important here: "It doesn't have to be perfect; it just has to be done!" Individuals are encouraged to treat themselves when finished for a job well done.

The actual Guide realms and stimulation questions follow.

Physical Health

How is my physical health in general? How is my weight? Am I overweight, underweight, or just about right? How about my nutrition? Do I eat balanced meals? If I've abused food in the past, how am I doing now? Am I avoiding putting harmful substances into my body? How about rest and relaxation? Am I able to sleep without taking sleeping pills? Do I allow time to just relax and rejuvenate myself? How about physical checkups? Do I get an annual checkup? Do I follow medical advice when it's given to me? Take medication only as prescribed? How about exercise in my life? Do I have a healthy plan of exercise or do I overdo or not do at all? How is my grooming and hygiene?

Leisure Time

How satisfied am I with my leisure time in general? How is the variety of my leisure time activities? A wide variety or too little variety? How willing am I to adopt new hobbies or engage in new activities to enrich my life? If I've had trouble in certain places in the past, such as in bars, am I avoiding such places to spend my leisure time? Do I take enough leisure time for good mental health, or am I a workaholic who rarely takes vacations? Or do I take too much time and not work enough? In my leisure, do I try to engage in active pursuits at least some of the time, or do I just do passive things such as watch television? Do I feel refreshed from my leisure time?

Finances/Spending Habits

How are my finances in general? Do I attempt to budget my money? Am I stingy with my money? Generous? Do I give to those less fortunate than me? Am I wasteful with my money? Do I live beyond my means? Am I getting into debt with credit cards? Am I an impulse spender? Do I save regularly? Am I adequately preparing for my old age so I'm not a burden to others? How about insurance? Do I have adequate health, life, home, accident, and car insurance? Am I truly grateful for my finances, or do I constantly wish for more? How do I show my gratitude for my wealth? Do I measure my self-worth in terms of how much money I have? Or do I realize that money does not make the person? If I've had trouble with gambling in the past, is that under control?

Legal Issues

Do I obey laws which I believe in? Do I try to change laws which I believe are unjust? Do I fight for the creation of laws which I think are needed to make this a better world? How prepared am I for death? Do I have a will? Is it up to date? Have I made arrangements for someone to take care of my decisions and affairs if I should become mentally or physically unable to do so? Do I cheat on my income taxes, or do I make a genuine attempt to be honest? How about things that "everybody does?" For example, do I make copies of copyrighted videos even though it is illegal to do so? If I've had legal problems in the past, am I cleaning these up by paying fines or successfully meeting probation requirements?

Stewardship

Stewardship is caring for worldly goods. Usually it refers to caring for others' things. But, since we are all just passing through this world, how we take care of all our possessions and environment can be seen as part of stewardship. What kind of steward am I? How do I care for my physical belongings? Am I rough with them? Or am I gentle? How do I care for my home or apartment? Am I proud to have company over? How about my lawn, garden, or other property? Do I keep my car in good running order? How do I care for these things? Do I support efforts to beautify my neighborhood, community, country? Do I support efforts to preserve the environment for future generations? How do I show I'm a good (or not so good) steward?

Celebration Rituals

Holidays, birthdays, and other special occasions help us put some sparkle in our lives. Holidays mark the seasons in a special way. They take us away from ordinary day-to-day living. Rituals help us celebrate these days and make them special. How am I building my own celebration rituals for holidays? For special occasions such as birthdays? If certain holidays have bad memories for me from my past, how am I changing the negative patterns? Am I adopting new and exciting ways to celebrate them? Or am I simply avoiding them, hoping they'll disappear? If I have no one to share my celebrations with, do I still do something special for myself to make the day special? Am I open to learning new customs? Am I living within my means in celebrating holidays and other special occasions? Or are they becoming too expensive for me? Is sharing myself with others part of my celebration rituals? Do I send cards? Write cheery notes? Give a friend a call? Am I careful to remember the true meaning of various holidays, or do I get lost in the external preparations? Do I share my holidays and special days with those who have no one to share them with?

Citizenship

What kind of citizen am I? Do I keep up-to-date on current issues? Am I registered to vote? Am I up-to-date on what the various candidates stand for? Do I go out and vote? Do I contribute to the candidates and/or party of my choice in terms of time, skills, or money? How am I helping to make my neighborhood a better place? What do I volunteer for in my community? How do I show I'm a solid citizen of the world? Do I keep up-to-date on global issues such as war and peace, famines and hunger, space exploration, disease control, and other important things? Do I write letters expressing my opinions? Give time or money to things I believe in?

Friendships

What kind of friend am I? Do I have a clear idea of what the duties are of a friend? Or am I all take and no give? Or am I all give and no take? Do I allow my friends to give to me, knowing that giving is a joyful experience? Do I accept my friends as they are, or am I always trying to change them? Am I lonely? Am I willing to make new friends? Am I too dependent on my friends for my own happiness? Do I keep in contact with my friends who live far away from me by sending them notes, giving them a phone call, or sending them holiday greetings? Am I smothering as a friend, or do I allow maximum freedom for my friends? Am I jealous of my friends' friends? Do I gossip about my friends behind their back?

Do I genuinely wish the best for my friends, or do I secretly wish they'd fail so they would be more dependent on me? Am I willing to help my friends through thick and thin, or am I a fair-weather friend?

Work/School

Am I in the career I want? Am I willing to prepare for career advancement? Have I deliberately chosen a low-paying field and then complain constantly because others make more than I do? Do I do an honest day's work for an honest day's pay? Do I cheat the company by wasting time on the job or by stealing? Am I willing to change jobs or careers if my present one seems to be harming my happiness? Am I living up to my dreams, or have I lost track of them somewhere along the way and lowered my career sight? How do I strive to be better and better in my career? Do I keep up-to-date in my field? Am I friendly to others in my work setting, or am I unfriendly to them? Do I gossip about people I work with, or do I try to always say something nice about everyone? Do I gripe about my job a lot? Do I say unkind things about the place which gives me a job and thus feeds me? If I'm retired, do I keep myself busy and productive? If I'm a student, do I put studying before playing? Do I procrastinate because I fear failure when I have to write papers? Do I keep up-to-date in my readings and note-taking? Do I actively participate in my classes, or am I simply a passive observer? Do I compliment the instructor on particularly interesting lectures? Do I do the absolute minimum to get through my courses, or do I strive to do a bit of extra reading or preparation?

Mental Health

How is my mental health in general? Have I learned how to be gentle with myself? Am I open and honest with others? Do I share my problems and fears, or do I keep them hidden deep inside? Have I forgiven myself for past mistakes, or am I wallowing in guilt? How is my self-esteem? What kinds of things do I do each day to affirm that I'm a good person worthy of love? Am I functioning in my adult social roles? Am I relatively happy with life? If not, what am I doing to experience joy? Am I harboring resentments and angers? What efforts am I making to rid myself of them?

General Spirituality

How is my spiritual life in general? How do I show my kindness to people, animal, pets? Do I get away from the hectic demands of modern life to seek solitude to renew my spirit? Am I gentle with myself? Do I have a clear set of values to believe in? How does my behavior match–or not match–my value system? Am I able to forgive myself for past errors? Do I forgive others, or do I carry around grudges? Am I willing to make amends to persons I've harmed, especially to myself? Am I striving to be all I can be? Am I following my star, or have I lost the way and lowered my goals? If I have a religion, how am I practicing it? How about my prayer life? Do I meditate on a regular basis? Do I support things I believe in with my time and/or money? How do I express my gratitude for the blessings I have?

Applied Spirituality or Helping Others

How willing am I to help others? What do I give for those in need? Time? Money? Prayer? Am I more willing to understand than to be understood? More willing to listen than to talk? Do I counsel those in need when asked, or do I claim I'm too busy? Am I willing to allow myself to be helped, realizing that this will help the other person experience the joy of giving? How do I put my spirituality into practice? Give drink to the thirsty, food to the hungry, clothes for the needy, shelter for the homeless? Do I visit the imprisoned, the lonely, the sick? Do I give solace to those suffering, especially those who suffer because of their own human frailty? If I believe in prayer, do I pray for others, especially for those who I don't like too much? Do I perform my good works in secret, or do I do them in public so I can be praised for them?

Sexuality

How do I see my sexual health? Do I see sex as something basically good or basically evil? Do I see sex as a gift to be treasured, or as a curse to be tolerated? Am I thankful for my sexuality? Do I keep a sense of humor about my sexuality? Do I use my sexuality to celebrate life, or do I engage in it merely as a chore? Do I see sex as something which can serve many functions, or do I have a very narrow and confining view of it? How is my sex performance? Do I try to add new and fresh techniques to my performance? When I have sexual difficulties, do I try to work on correcting them? If I'm gay or lesbian, do I accept my sexual orientation as a positive thing? Am I sexually responsible about birth control and preventing sexually-transmitted diseases? How about foreplay? Is it exciting and always fresh, or am I in a boring rut? How about my body? Am I comfortable nude? How's my body image? Can I couple tenderness, touch, and the like with sexual activity? Do I use sex as a weapon or as manipulation to get what I want? Am I teaching children and others to see sex as a good thing? If I've promised to live a chaste life for religious reasons, how am I doing living up to my vows? Am I getting my intimacy needs met in a non-sexual way?

Family Relations

How is my relationship with my biological or non-traditional family? How is my relationship with my lover or spouse if I have one? How am I striving to be a better spouse or lover? What am I doing to add zest and excitement to the relationship? If I have children, do I realize that time and laughter are more precious in building treasured memories than are material things? Am I showing my child, by my example, how to love? How is my relationship with my parents? Am I meeting my obligations as a child? How is my relationship with other biological or adopted relatives? Can I be counted on to be there through bad times as well as in good times? Do I keep in contact with distant relatives? How do I show my love for those in the family who are experiencing "black sheep" behavior? Do I give them an extra dose of love? Am I living the kind of life which makes my family proud to call me their kin?

STEP TEN: CONTINUING SELF-EVALUATION

Step Ten is the first of the so-called "maintenance" steps, the others being Steps 11 and 12. Having "cleaned house" in the "working" steps, Steps 4 through 9, individuals are now faced with keeping their house clean.

Step 10 says: "Continued to take personal inventory and when we were wrong promptly admitted it" (Alcoholics Anonymous, 1981, p. 8). Like Step 4, this Step asks individuals to take personal inventory but more as an ongoing part of life. Further, it asks the individuals to weed their garden as soon as they spot a weed, knowing that left unattended, weeds grow larger and choke out the flowers.

Many persons take this Step every evening before retiring. They look over their daily events to see what they did right, what they did wrong, and how they could improve in the future. They might decide they need to admit their wrongs to someone and resolve to do so as soon as possible.

Others do this Step on a continuing basis in everyday life. Such persons are always in self-examination. They are consciously aware of their quest for improvement. They analyze their actions, but are not compulsive about it. When wrong, they feel bad about it. The hurt they experience is the result of a healthy conscience, and this hurt will not go away until they make amends for the wrong they have done. They are like the couple whose motto is, "Never let the sun set upon an angry heart."

As individuals grow in spirituality, the more on-going self-examination will become second nature to them.

Just as we saw that there are guides for making a Fourth Step, there are similar pamphlets, worksheets, and videos available for working the Tenth Step.

CLINICAL IMPLICATIONS

First, clinicians should believe that self-examination is critical for anyone wishing to develop a more spiritual way of living.

Second, we need to keep in mind that Step 4, in particular, is quite often overwhelming for the client. Procrastination, feelings of being overwhelmed, perfectionism, and the like are all problems which clients may encounter when approaching this Step.

Third, be aware of what kinds of guides or helps are available for doing Steps 4 and 10. Have some examples in your office for clients to peruse.

Fourth, practice these Steps yourself so you can identify more closely with the client.

Finally, reassure the client that self-examination is a life-long process, not an event. Thus, it never has to be perfect, simply sincere and honest.

To obtain a copy of *The WinterStar Life Assessment Guide,* send $5.00 in cash or money order to: WinterStar Press, 2421 Meadowbrook Dr. S.E., Cedar Rapids, IA 54403-2925.

REFERENCES

Alcoholics Anonymous. (1976). *Alcoholics Anonymous* (3rd edition). New York: Alcoholics Anonymous World Services, Inc.

Alcoholics Anonymous. (1981). *Twelve steps and twelve traditions.* New York: Alcoholics Anonymous World Services, Inc.

Kus, R.J. (1990). *The WinterStar Life Assessment Guide.* North Liberty, IA: WinterStar Press.

Wiederkehr, M. (1991). A prayer to own your beauty. In M. Wiederkehr's *Seasons of your heart: Prayers and reflections* (p. 71). San Francisco: Harper San Francisco.

The Clergyperson and the Fifth Step

Rev. Mark A. Latcovich, MDiv, PhD

SUMMARY. Individuals making their Fifth Step will often turn to members of the clergy to listen to their stories. In this article, the Rev. Mark A. Latcovich discusses the dynamics of the Fifth Step in the 12-Step way of life, how individuals can choose a clergyperson wisely, the role of the clergyperson in the Fifth Step process, and the hoped-for effects of a good Fifth Step. *[Single or multiple copies of this article are available from The Haworth Document Delivery Service: 1-800-342-9678, 9:00 a.m. - 5:00 p.m. (EST).]*

Step 5: "Admitted to God, to ourselves, and to another human being the exact nature of our wrongs" (Alcoholics Anonymous, 1981 p. 55)

One afternoon, when I was locking up the doors of the church after Sunday liturgy, a well-dressed man approached me in the church vestibule. He introduced himself and seemed rather anxious

---

Rev. Mark A. Latcovich is a priest for the Diocese of Cleveland and teaches both pastoral and systematic theology at St. Mary Seminary, Cleveland, OH. He currently is completing his doctorate in Sociology at Case Western Reserve University, Cleveland. Fr. Latcovich has served as a parochial vicar for nine years in various parishes in the Cleveland area. He has been a "soulfriend" to many in the Fifth Step process.

Address correspondence to Rev. Mark A. Latcovich, 28700 Euclid Avenue, Wickliffe, OH 44092-2527 USA.

[Haworth co-indexing entry note]: "The Clergyperson and the Fifth Step." Latcovich, Rev. Mark A. Co-published simultaneously in *Journal of Chemical Dependency Treatment* (The Haworth Press, Inc.) Vol. 5, No. 2, 1995, pp. 79-89; and: *Spirituality and Chemical Dependency* (ed: Robert J. Kus) The Haworth Press, Inc., 1995, pp. 79-89; and: *Spirituality and Chemical Dependency* (ed: Robert J. Kus) Harrington Park Press, an imprint of The Haworth Press, Inc., 1995, pp. 79-89. Single or multiple copies of this article are available from The Haworth Document Delivery Service [1-800-342-9678, 9:00 a.m. - 5:00 p.m. (EST)].

© 1995 by The Haworth Press, Inc. All rights reserved.   *79*

to talk with me. I invited him into my office. Once seated, he asked me if I was familiar with the Fifth Step of the Twelve Step Program in Alcoholics Anonymous (A. A.). "Not exactly," I replied. While I was familiar with the Twelve Steps of A. A., I really was not familiar with the specificity of the individual steps. Despite my unfamiliarity, however, he was ready to share those events in his life that weighed heavy on him. With firm conviction he persisted; "Reverend, could you give me the time that I need to tell my story? Help me make the Fifth Step? I want to confess a few things about my life that I am not too proud of!"

This scenario depicts my introduction to A. A.'s Fifth Step. As a clergyperson, this experience introduced me to another dimension of ministry that demonstrates the workings of nature and grace in a process that has liberated thousands of men and women. The purpose of this chapter is to offer some reflections on the nature and purpose of the Fifth Step within the A. A. program. Special consideration will be given to the pastoral and therapeutic role the clergyperson may play in assisting an individual in recovery through this process. While the Fifth Step does not necessarily require the presence of an ordained minister, it does require an individual who plays the particular role of *soulfriend*. A soulfriend serves as a spiritual teacher, mentor and guide, who elicits and invites a response to openness, support, and direction when individuals genuinely desire to discern and acknowledge their change of heart (Sellner, 1990).

THE DYNAMICS, POSITION AND FUNCTION OF THE FIFTH STEP IN THE A.A. PROCESS

In December of 1938, when Bill Wilson developed A.A.'s Twelve Steps, he developed a process of personal growth and recovery that was influenced in part by many Christian women and men who connected the dynamics of the small sharing groups with some of the principles inherent in Christian spirituality (Blumberg, 1977). Wilson's principles suggested that people could change their lives even when they found themselves at rock bottom. Reflecting on his own experience as an alcoholic, Wilson attributed his recovery process to the dynamic interaction of several components, namely, group support, personal introspection, and the interpersonal sharing of one's life story with others. Wilson synthesized this process into various steps that could in fact change an individual's direction and life course. His experience with The Oxford Group gave him the social support, affirmation and motivation he needed to overcome his destructive life path. However, the internal process of admitting that the pursuit of alcohol had dominated his life and had affected his relationships with others and with himself, required a change of heart. This internal reorientation, self-forgiveness and self-responsibility seemed to require the use of a special faculty within the person. In theological language this faculty is defined simply as the dynamics of conversion. This introspective process identifies the process of internal reorientation in three interrelated steps: *repentance* (the need to surrender one's sins and failings to God); *confession* (the need to admit one's faults and failings to the community and seek guidance); and *reconciliation* (making restitution for wrongs and accepting the forgiveness of God and others) as the process that leads to a fresh start and new life. The Fourth and Fifth Steps are important aspects of the alcoholic's recovery through the Twelve Step Process. These two Steps enable people to go through a process and experience that will enable them to take an honest look at who they are and then admit the truth of their inventory to self, God, and another human being (Keller, 1966: p. 121). The interconnectedness of Steps Four and Five reflect these dynamics of conversion taking the individual through this three-fold process.

Step Four is described in Alcoholics Anonymous' *Twelve Steps and Twelve Traditions* (1981) as a "vigorous and painstaking effort" (p. 42) to engage in a personal self-inventory. This inventory explores past actions, motives and conduct of the alcoholic. Usually, the A. A. sponsor assists the individual in this particular step by sharing his or her own story of past justifications and excuses for drinking.

> For most of us, self-justification was the maker of excuses; excuses, of course, for drinking, and for all kinds of crazy and damaging conduct. . . . We had to drink because times were hard and times were good. We had to drink because at home

we were smothered with love or got none at all. We had to drink because at work we were great successes or dismal failures. . . . But in A. A. we slowly learned that something had to be done about our vengeful resentments, self-pity and unwarranted pride. We had to see that every time we played the big shot, we turned people against us . . . . We had to see that when we were harboring grudges and planned revenge for such defeats, we were really beating ourselves with the club of anger we had intended to use on others. (pp. 46-47)

The self-inventory required in the Fourth Step helps persons identify negative and destructive behaviors and take responsibility for the effects they had on themselves and others. The honesty and accountability of this self-inventory is a process of personal repentance before oneself and God as we understand Him. The Fourth Step prepares the individual for the Fifth Step's confessional dimension: *sharing their life story with another.*

The Fifth Step is the telling of one's life story, a self-confession, and an opportunity for casting out one's mistakes, failures, and anxieties by telling another person. In this way those feelings and past deeds can lose their control over the person (Sellner, 1981). This step completes the inventory of the Fourth Step and allows the individual to connect with a spiritual mentor who can positively influence the person's own life story. The difficult side of this step is that it is "an ego deflator." Consequently, many A. A. members experience an intense fear and reluctance to do this step (A.A. 1981). On the other hand, the positive side is that this step allows alcoholics to understand God's grace and the spiritual dynamics in their lives on an emotional and spiritual level. The weight of the past can be lifted as the naming of past events releases emotional and psychological pain. When persons must deal with painful moments of self-knowledge and great remorse over past failures, they often feel an overpowering desire for clear discernment of what God may be calling them to do with their lives (Sellner, 1990). This is where the role of the clergy person provides an essential service in helping individuals feel the grace of reconciliation and experience insight into new and fresh directives for their lives.

MAKING A REFERRAL–
CHOOSING A CLERGYPERSON

Most individuals who choose to make the Fifth Step with a clergy person will usually check out on their own which clergyperson they will ask to facilitate this step. There are, however, times when they will ask a clinician or counselor for a clergy referral. First of all, clinicians need to consider the individual's religious preference. They may want to call around a general area to determine which clergy have knowledge of A. A.'s Fifth Step or a reputation for assisting in Fifth Step work. There often are professional and clergy A. A. groups that may provide clergy who can relate first-hand experience with this process, although clergy need not be members of A. A. in order to facilitate the Fifth Step process. Qualities that clergy should have are an openness to the process and comfort with persons recovering from substance abuse. If they were ordained from an accredited seminary or institution, they would have received some clinical and pastoral training in such matters. Most clergy are able to deal with people from every background and way of life. However, like any other professional group, some clergy persons may not be comfortable or knowledgeable about A. A. Therefore, before a referral is suggested or made, it might be important to consider the disposition and needs of the person being referred. Sex, age, background, sexual orientation, and religious tradition are important variables that need to be weighed in making a Fifth Step referral. For example, a person who drank because of an abusive relationship with a father or husband, may benefit more from a woman minister than a man. Likewise, an older individual may not feel comfortable making the Fifth Step with a minister who may be the same age as his/her son or daughter. Gay or lesbian persons may find homophobic clergypersons can provide neither the acceptance nor the environment necessary for a successful Fifth Step. A morally rigid pastor without any experience with A. A. may do more harm than good if he or she reacts with fire and brimstone assertions and sermons on the evils of drinking and drunkenness. Most individuals ready to make the Fifth Step need a clergyperson who can mediate for them a helpful image of God and society that are ready to welcome their change of heart and growth in sobriety.

THE ROLE OF THE CLERGYPERSON
IN THE FIFTH STEP

The role of the clergyperson in the Fifth Step process is to facilitate the individual's self-reporting. This term is preferable to self-confession because of the negative connotations the term confession might have for the individual such as admitting to a crime or sin. A self-report is a term that is neutral in meaning: it implies a sharing of experiences in a value-free context. The sense of remorse, guilt and even feelings of sin are often a part of their story. Telling one's story to God, oneself and another person is done in the context of a self-report. Often individuals will see the clergyperson as a representative of God and view their verbalization of their self-report to the minister as a way of talking to God (or their Higher Power) and to another person at the same time. Obviously, the articulation of their "story" is primarily a self-report that they need to hear above all else. It is a way of taking control again of their life by admitting it aloud, sharing it with another, as a means of self-disclosure. This self-disclosure is a subjective account and a report of those issues and insights gained from their personal inventory (Step Four). Therefore, the self-report is a process that initiates a dynamic for reconciliation and healing. Persons making a self-report are often nervous and afraid because they are exposing their state of mind which may include low self-esteem, feelings of estrangement, and feelings that the listener will view them as the worst person in the world.

Creating a Safe Environment for the Self-Report

The clergyperson's role during the self-report is to give the individual assurance by his or her non-verbal and verbal language. Nods indicating that the listener hears what people are sharing are appropriate and needed responses. They need to feel that the listener believes in them. People making the Fifth Step may be sharing a difficult or embarrassing situation about which they are ashamed. The clergyperson does well to remind them that "all of us are human" and cannot be perfect.

The Nature of Self-Reporting–Sharing a Story

Self-reporting has been defined as a process of self-censoring which is selective, discriminating, judgmental, and subjected to internal and external influences (Rambo and Reh, 1992). This self-reporting process reflects subjects' own experiences and their reaction to these experiences, with all of their self-judgments, fears, and mistakes. The clergyperson must allow the person to report these events from the frame of the person's own state of mind. Persons must be encouraged to tell their stories without any comments or judgments from the listener. Appropriate responses by the clergyperson will encourage self-reporters to continue in a positive manner and will allow them the opportunity to talk freely and frankly without fear of judgment. The process of self-reporting is quite emotional and may require moments of silence on the part of the person making the Fifth Step. The clergyperson must allow the individual to use that silence. He or she should not encourage the client to hurry through this process. If the minister reflects his or her "comfortableness" with silent periods, then the Fifth Steppers will be more apt to use those times productively to reflect, refocus or react emotionally to the part of the story they are trying to articulate. Self-reporting allows people to tell their story within a framework that encourages them to name in a reflective way the internal and external influences of their lives that have led them to hit rock bottom and have brought them back to life. The listener's role needs to encourage the individual with positive strokes. During painful moments or following a period of silence, the listener may want to summarize the person's thoughts prior to that silence. A verbal response accentuating the person's positive points and strengths will be helpful. Oftentimes people will focus on the negative aspects of their life stories, highlighting their weaknesses. The clergyperson needs to remind them about the positive choices they have made while remaining sober, especially the choice they are making at this moment to do this particular step.

Personal Guilt and Self-Judgment

At times when individuals make their self-reports, they may color their narratives with self-judgments, personal condemnations, or feelings of guilt. Usually people are critical of their past behavior. Derogatory language and self-effacing remarks indicate that they are highly judgmental of their past actions. The clergyperson may need to intervene during these comments and remind people that they are being too hard on themselves. The helper must remind people that their behavior and feelings about "who they are" may be based on their previous use of alcohol or drugs or on past negative experiences, but that no matter what they may have done in the past, the present can be used for changes and new growth. The presence of God and their honesty with themselves in relating their personal stories grants a provisional grace and new opportunity for their growth. The listener may need to interrupt and remind people that they are being "too critical of themselves." Usually, people appreciate the observation and continue with a lighter spirit. If storytellers can see the humor of their situation in retrospect, they may realize that they are "moving along" through the process.

The individual taking the Fifth Step may need to be reminded that these Twelve Steps are meant to be a positive process. The process reflected in the Fifth Step is merely an honest sharing of a life's story. While a person may not currently like himself or herself while accounting the story, the person needs to recognize that this image of self can and will change as the journey through the Twelve Steps continues. Being gentle with one's self during the Fifth Step process is an important and positive quality the clergyperson will want to continually remind people of, especially when they seem to feel guilty and ashamed of past actions. When the listener senses that someone may be feeling embarrassed or ashamed of a particular part of the story, a simple touch assuring the person to move forward in spite of negative feelings, is an appropriate gesture. A touch tells the person that the listener hears what is being said and can identify with the pain the person is experiencing in this process. A touch comforts and tells the person, "It's O.K. to feel that way."

Negative Self-Images

Individuals may begin to condemn themselves and divert from their story. This is usually the case when a person's self-image is poor or even shattered. People may lack self-worth and self-confidence. Thus, they may be bogged down in the negative feelings that they experience during their self-report. The clergyperson may need to verbally reassure them that their participation in this process, however difficult it may be, suggests that they believe they can change. They need to be reminded that their goodness and worth can be revitalized in time. Their progression through the steps and recovery will help them discover that their self-esteem and "at easeness" with who they are will come only as they move through the Twelve Step process (Royce, 1987). The process is taking each step, one day at a time.

While all of us must be accountable for our behavior, one's failings and personal mistakes do not make one less of a person. People's personal dignity remains intact even though they subjectively doubt their dignity. The clergyperson must help people to make their self-report within a positive perspective. It is the minister's role to continually remind people that they are good and capable of change, growth and self-forgiveness. The clergyperson's genuine belief in them just as they are will be their greatest source of help during this process. People need to feel that the clergyperson understands just how bad their situation may have been for them. Negative feelings need to be shared and accepted before positive ones can fill their place (Royce, 1985).

New Images of God

Since the Fifth Step includes an "admittance to God," it may be important for the clergyperson to ask about the self-reporter's image of God. A condemning, punishing, harsh, uncompromising, rigid and strict God who "is making a list and checking it twice" will make the Fifth Step all the more difficult for the person. When an individual is angry at God or senses God as "unapproachable or unforgiving," the process of reconciliation will be somewhat stifled. The clergyperson may need to re-present who God is. The use of the Hebrew or Christian Scriptures may provide a reference of God's mercy, compassion, forgiveness and power to save. The clergyperson's own belief and relationship with God will genuinely help the individual feel at home in God's presence. Re-imaging God for the person making the Fifth Step will enable the individual to also be less judgmental and condemning of him/herself. One practical way of accomplishing this shift in images of God is to offer to pray with the person. The clergyperson may pray with the person or ask the individual to pray in his or her own words, using everyday language. It may be appropriate for the minister to join in the person's prayer, thereby reminding the person of God's mercy and forgiveness.

Hoped-for Effects of a Good Fifth Step

At the completion of people's self-reports, they may be exhausted physically. They may be drained emotionally. A comment often made by many who have completed the Fifth Step is, "I feel like a great weight has been lifted from me." People feel cleansed. The telling of their story before God, self and others renews their hope in themselves that their life of sobriety can be a true way of life. The Fifth Step often allows them to chalk up a positive mark in their growth chart. People's honesty, dissatisfaction with their previous behavior, and ability to report both the negative and positive elements of their life with its influences (internal and external), failures and successes provide the dynamic that enables the Fifth Step to complete its specific task–reconciliation with self and others, renewed hope, and dedication to personal change and growth. The minister must now allow people to dedicate themselves to this new process of personal growth. Issues that may have been raised in the Fifth Step process may now need to be considered in some detail. The clergyperson may invite the person to rejoin his or her church in order to become a part of a faith community. In cases where the denomination of the person making the Fifth Step is Roman Catholic, Anglican, or Orthodox, sacramental absolution may be the appropriate ritual the clergyperson uses to conclude the session. However, it must be noted that the Fifth Step should not be seen as a sacramental confession. The Fifth Step stands on its own merits and must be seen as a subjective story that belongs to the individual. If the person asks to receive sacramental absolution and penance, the clergyperson needs to distinguish between the brief celebration of the rite with scripture, the laying on of hands, and the words of forgiveness and the conclusion of the Fifth Step. The person's need for forgiveness and healing is an ongoing process that many churches celebrate frequently within a person's life of faith. The Fifth Step is one important step that enables the individual to move through a process of recovery that continues to be a source of support for continued sobriety and growth.

CONCLUSION

I remember when the well-dressed man left my office some two hours later. He had literally changed before my eyes. His stress lines, and rigid muscular configurations had literally changed. His tears had cleaned him in a way no other medicine can. As he left my office, I remember embracing him and congratulating him on his new beginning. I guess, in retrospect, those were appropriate words. His smile and firm grip indicated to me that they were accepted. He thanked me with his eyes filled with a new glimmer of hope. The quickness and spiritedness in his walk back to his car indicated to me that the person who drove into the parking lot was not the same person who was now leaving to go home.

REFERENCES

Alcoholics Anonymous. (1981). *Twelve steps and twelve traditions*. New York: Alcoholics Anonymous World Services, Inc.

Blumberg, L. (1977). The ideology of a therapeutic social movement: Alcoholics Anonymous. *Journal of Studies on Alcohol. 38* (11), 11: 2134-39.

Keller, J. E. (1966). *Ministering to alcoholics*. Minneapolis: Augsburg Publishing House.

Rambo, L. R., & Reh, L.A. (1992). The phenomenology of conversion. In H. Newton Maloney and Samuel Southard (Eds.), *Handbook of religious conversion*. Birmington, Alabama; Religious Education Press: 229-258.

Royce, J. E. (1985). Alcohol and other drug dependencies. In *Clinical handbook of pastoral counseling*. In R.J. Wicks, R.D. Parsons, and D.E. Capps (Eds.). New York: Integration Books (Paulist Press): 502-519.

Royce, J. E. (1987). *The spiritual progression chart*. Center City, MN: Hazelden.

Sellner, E. C. (1981). *Step Five: A guide to reconciliation*. Center City, MN: Hazelden.

Sellner, E. C. (1990). What Alcoholics Anonymous can teach us about reconciliation. *Worship, 64*(4), 331-48.

Steps Eight and Nine of Alcoholics Anonymous

Sr. Mary Gene Kinney BVM, NCAC II
Sr. Letitia Marie Close BVM, NCAC II

SUMMARY. The alcoholic cannot stay sober living in the past or living in the future. Regrets about past behaviors and projections about future ones are old ways of thinking that the alcoholic's spiritual recovery process needs to continue to change by means of working the Eighth and Ninth Steps of Alcoholics Anonymous' Twelve *suggested* Steps. Step Eight encourages recovering persons to make a list of persons they have harmed and to become willing to make amends to them all. Step Nine says to make direct amends to such people whenever possible, unless to do so would injure them or others.

The purpose of this article is to explore why these two Steps are important for recovery from addiction; to mention ways these Steps may be worked; to list a few of the common difficulties or attitudinal barriers people often have toward attempting these Steps; and to suggest some beneficial outcomes of working these two Steps. Finally, clinical implications are given to help clients work Steps Eight and Nine. *[Single or multiple copies of this article are available from The Haworth Document Delivery Service: 1-800-342-9678, 9:00 a.m. - 5:00 p.m. (EST).]*

Sr. Mary Gene Kinney, BVM, NCAC II and Sr. Letitia Marie Close, BVM, NCAC II are Sisters of the Blessed Virgin Mary and certified addictions counselors in the Chicago area. The two sisters established the Intercongregational Alcoholism Program (ICAP) in Chicago in 1979 which is operated exclusively for nuns on a national level.

Address correspondence to: Srs. Kinney and Close at 1515 N. Harlem Avenue, #311, Oak Park, IL 60302, USA.

[Haworth co-indexing entry note]: "Steps Eight and Nine of Alcoholics Anonymous." Kinney, Sr. Mary Gene, and Sr. Letitia Marie Close. Co-published simultaneously in *Journal of Chemical Dependency Treatment* (The Haworth Press, Inc.) Vol. 5, No. 2, 1995, pp. 91-99; and: *Spirituality and Chemical Dependency* (ed: Robert J. Kus) The Haworth Press, Inc., 1995, pp. 91-99; and: *Spirituality and Chemical Dependency* (ed: Robert J. Kus) Harrington Park Press, an imprint of The Haworth Press, Inc., 1995, pp. 91-99. Single or multiple copies of this article are available from The Haworth Document Delivery Service [1-800-342-9678, 9:00 a.m. - 5:00 p.m. (EST)].

© 1995 by The Haworth Press, Inc. All rights reserved.

Many alcoholics enter the recovery process full of anger and rage at all of the harm done to them by others. Some truly believe that their addiction is the direct result of life events over which they have had no control. The thought that they have harmed anyone is extremely far removed from their construction of reality. Yet, the Eighth Step of Alcoholics Anonymous (A.A.), "Made a list of all persons we had harmed, and became willing to make amends to them all" addresses this phenomenon (1976). When they first encounter the Eighth step, many alcoholics react negatively to it. This reaction is also common enough among people who are in early stages of attending Al-Anon meetings. However, after some time of continued attendance at the Twelve Step program meetings, as well as continued contact with members of these mutual help programs, newly recovering persons work through Steps One through Seven and gradually understand that their "under the influence behavior" has had a negative impact upon others. This understanding often precedes the recovering persons' recognition of the need to take responsibility for making significant changes in attitudes and behaviors. So, it has been the careful working of Steps One through Seven of A.A. that brings about the degree of self-knowledge necessary for them to begin to address the damage that they have caused to others.

PRACTICAL TOOLS FOR REPAIRING DAMAGED RELATIONSHIPS

Steps Eight and Nine of A.A. are very important to the recovery process because they give recovering persons a practical way to deal with relationships that have been severely damaged or destroyed throughout the progression of addiction. Shortly after beginning the recovery process, alcoholics may become acutely aware of the havoc their own behavior has been causing in the lives of people about whom they do care. So, they begin to make the obvious amends to loved ones by stopping the use of chemicals, openly admitting that their use of chemicals has been a problem, and providing some descriptions of what they are doing about their problem. Some recovering addicts are aware that this is only "the tip of the iceberg" with respect to handling their relationship responsibilities, while others will think that this is sufficient to take care of the damage they've been a party to in their relationships.

Steps Eight and Nine are helpful because they address ways to deal with relationships with people. They help people set about amending relationships by means of admission, apology, restitution, etc. They assist people in examining their part in these relationships by means of:

- inquiry into some of the details of their past "drinking" behavior;
- evaluation discussion with other members of the Twelve Step program; and
- reading or "bibliotherapy" with respect to how the Steps are worked by others and how they may apply to themselves.

Furthermore, the actual action of working these two Steps indicates people's willingness to move outside of self, to repair the damages they have done in the past to others and to self, and to move into the future aiming for positive or healthy relationships.

The purpose of Step Eight is for alcoholics to *focus on the specific people they have harmed over the years* and to *become ready to do what is necessary to repair the damages* of the past. How can alcoholics see that others have experienced harm from their drinking episodes and behaviors? What comes to their minds as their part in the harm? Recovering addicts need to know these things because they need to change and to take responsibility for all of their behaviors, past as well as present. These changes help alcoholics move from self-loathing to self-approval, a movement that is essential for continued sobriety because in the past their only method for dealing with feelings about their relationships was to escape into drug-induced changes.

RECOVERY: A PROCESS OF ESTABLISHING A SPIRITUAL BASIS FOR LIVING

Recovery, or the establishment of a spiritual basis for living, is a gradual development, a process for alcoholics who have stopped drinking and drugging. At the beginning of this process, addicts learn some things about what can be changed in their lives and where they can get help in making these changes. For example, admitting that a dependence upon alcohol (perhaps already to the point of physical addiction) is a fact in their physiology is a change in their thinking, i.e., that they can control the effects of alcohol on them. In addition, they can learn to abstain from alcohol and other drugs trying some or all of the things other sober addicts have suggested. Feeling better physically and emotionally in the early recovery period is also important. Indeed, amazing things are happening in this recovery stage, and the alcoholic frequently has a growing desire to stay better.

SELF-KNOWLEDGE FROM STEPS ONE THROUGH SEVEN PREPARES WAY TO STEPS EIGHT AND NINE

Insight about oneself progresses through the effort to work the program from Steps One through Seven. When recovering alcoholics begin to see that their past drinking behaviors have actually hurt other people, they are ready to work Steps Eight and Nine. Also, when they speak of having positive, healthy relationships to others, they also are indicating their willingness to approach and to work on Steps Eight and Nine.

Step Eight has two parts: (1) "Made a list of all persons we had harmed," and (2) "became willing to make amends to them all" (Alcoholics Anonymous, 1981). Usually, the persons who belong on the "list" will already have been identified in Steps Four and Five. The flaws or faults that have been noted in the Fourth Step inventory will be connected with situations involving other people. It is these people who are placed on the Step Eight "list," as well as anyone else who comes to mind with whom there has been a strained relationship.

COMMON DIFFICULTIES IN WORKING STEPS EIGHT AND NINE

Confronting the terse orders of these Steps, however, may be even more uncomfortable than the experience of the Fourth and

Fifth Steps: "make a list of the persons . . . harmed; become willing to make amends . . . make direct amends . . . " (Alcoholics Anonymous, 1981). The "good news" is that the recovery process has progressed to a point where the alcoholics are interested in their part in the maintenance of better relationships. The "bad news" is that the Twelve Steps won't buy into their "let bygones be bygones" attitude. It's saying that they've got to *list all* persons they've harmed; they've got to *think specifically of their part* (harm-giving) in those relationships. They can't have the funeral until they've gone through the "wake"–the laying out, the recall, the loss, the damage, the deadliness. Indeed, "what an order," they'd rather not go through with it!

So, the clinician may be helpful here by breaking up the work on Step Eight into manageable proportions. For example, the clinicians can take clients through their fears, one at a time and can help them name each fear and say, "Yes, I have that fear." Some specific fears to be considered might include:

* fear of re-opening old wounds;
* fear of going back over the past and jeopardizing one's new-found peace of mind;
* fear of the reaction of the other person(s) involved;
* fear of rejection;
* fear of drinking or using other drugs again.

These fears often come out of pride (not wanting to look bad and thinking about how a particular individual might respond to the amends). Alcoholics Anonymous members will remind newcomers to simply make a list and not to think about actually making the amends at this time. Therefore, to "work" Step Eight is to simply make the list; focus on the relationship *as one has been responsible for it in the past*; let feelings of readiness to change come about. Learn your part, let go of the other persons' parts; think about what you can do to repair your damage; own up to that; think of possible restitution; change your present and future behaviors. Step Eight equals making the list and thinking about it.

PEOPLE COMMONLY ON THE AMENDS LIST

People who are most often on an alcoholic's amends list are spouse/lover; children; other family members; friends; co-workers; employers; clients; patients; students; employees. Since their own self has been seriously harmed by the addiction, some A.A. members put themselves on their amends list. Sometimes there have been extremely serious problems with another person. Perhaps it is true that the other person has also caused harm to the alcoholic. It is important at this part of the recovery process to put that person on the list also, so that the relationship can be looked at and the recovering person can determine what part of the problem she/he was responsible for.

WHY STEPS EIGHT AND NINE ARE IMPORTANT

It is important to encourage recovering people to advance in their process through Steps Eight and Nine. They have made progress spiritually, or else they would not be in the place of readiness for these Steps. Encourage them to *trust* their program of recovery, to keep proportion about the enormity of the problems of their past, to *listen to and to heed* experiences of recovered persons.

"Becoming willing to make amends to them all" means a willingness to accept responsibility for past behavior. There may be people on the list for whom it will take a long time to become willing to make amends. To be able to work the Eighth and Ninth Steps of A.A., one needs to have developed enough self-honesty, enough trust in the effectiveness of the Steps, and enough desire for healing personal relationships. These two Steps teach about true forgiveness and promote the healing of our relationships.

When approaching Steps Eight and Nine, it is not uncommon for the alcoholic to insist, "My drinking has never hurt anyone except myself! I drank by myself. I did not neglect my family. I never abused anyone. I always went to work. I paid my bills." It may be someone like Mary, a nun who did most of her drinking in secret, who recalls only four or five instances of being intoxicated in public, and who felt that she was the only one hurt by her drinking. When she said she could not make a list, her sponsor asked her if there was anyone she would go out of her way to avoid. Mary quickly said, "Oh yes!," and her sponsor told her to start her list with that person.

Working these Steps, therefore, requires significant attitudinal and behavioral changes by the recovering persons. They need to look at their part in past relationships, take action to repair the damage, and with greater self-knowledge move forward to have and to maintain healthy relationships. Step Eight is the Step by which chemically dependent persons move out from self towards healthy relationships with other people, with "God," and of course with self. The faithful working of Steps One through Seven have given the necessary self-knowledge to begin to address the damage addiction has caused to others. Steps Eight and Nine enable addicts to take responsibility for their past actions towards other people and to make restitution wherever possible.

Steps Eight and Nine are very important to complete recovery from addiction because these are the Steps that help and thereby enable the addicts to begin dealing honestly, soberly, and humbly with all their relationships. Isolation and self-centeredness are core psychological attributes of addicts and, as such, prevent them from developing the psychological growth necessary for achieving mature relationships. If they do not advance positively in relationships, they will let fear and false pride control. They are likely to begin distrusting themselves, their program, and they may drift away discouraged. These attitudes enable them to find reasons to drink and use drugs again.

However, healing their past sufficiently will require deepening their self-honesty and increasing their trust in the effectiveness of the Steps. Steps Six and Seven are operative in the addicts' working Steps Eight and Nine because they prepare addicts for future healthy relationships. The practice of being responsible for ourselves in relationships means being clear on what are our feelings and what are our limits. Step Eight is a practice by which the chemically dependent person moves out from self towards healthy relationships with people, "God," and self. The self-knowledge gained through working Steps One through Seven is used in "working" Steps Eight and Nine to start the addict taking responsibility for past behaviors toward others and to make the possible restitutions.

MAKING AMENDS GOES BEYOND "I'M SORRY"

A.A.'s Ninth Step is, "Made direct amends to such people wherever possible, except when to do so would injure them or others." This Step of the recovery process requires "direct amends" to people the addict admits harming. An amends is more than an apology, which means it must go beyond an "I'm sorry" statement. Rather, it should include the addict's plan for changing and for avoiding the old behavior. Furthermore, amends are not to be made for the purpose of achieving forgiveness or acceptance. Those may be the by-products of making amends, but they are not proof of an amend or the reason recovery requires amends.

Amends occur when alcoholics honestly identify what they have done, admit it to the other persons, and make a commitment to change their behaviors because it is right for them to do so. "Made direct amends . . . " means to take each person on the list, go to that person directly and acknowledge how the addict has harmed that person and how he/she plans to make it right. Sometimes money must be repaid or other types of restitution made. At other times, in cases of emotional damage, the alcoholic acknowledges what he/she has done and assures the other that the behavior will not happen again. An amends carries with it a change of behavior. It involves ownership of the problematic behavior.

Sometimes it may not be possible to make a direct amends because the person may have died or making a direct amends might cause further harm to the person. In such cases a letter may be written to the deceased person. Again, the purpose is for the person making amends to take responsibility for his/her own actions.

LESSONS TO BE LEARNED
FROM STEPS EIGHT AND NINE

Trust. While making the list in Step Eight, addicts learn to trust that good will come from being honest. Trust in their own ability to take responsibility for their actions grows.

Forgiveness. After the drinking and drugging has stopped, newly recovering persons discover the problems they have caused others and feel significant guilt and sometimes shame about the harm to others. Through these Steps alcoholics learn to forgive.

Working the Eighth and Ninth Steps as carefully and as well as they are able completes the process of bringing recovering persons up to date in their relational lives. That in itself is an essential foundation stone of a lasting sobriety and of spiritually-based principles for living. Once this foundation is in place, alcoholics have but to live in the present using Steps Ten, Eleven, and Twelve as the on-going spiritual principles by which their relationships (to self, "God," and others) are governed. The insecurity of living with past unresolved relationships is too much for alcoholics because this erodes peace of mind, self-respect, and trust, and will lead to loss of sobriety. Alcoholics cannot survive living in the past nor living in the future. They can and will survive and spiritually thrive living in the present day with their recovery program principles up to date.

Prayer and Meditation in Addiction Recovery

Robert J. Kus, RN, PhD

SUMMARY. In the Twelve Step way of life, three of the Steps call for prayer and one calls for meditation. After defining prayer, the author discusses various types of prayer, lists common formal prayers used in Twelve Step meetings, and discusses how God gets back to the individual who prays. He then discusses the two major types of meditation, reflection and centering, and provides clinical implications. *[Single or multiple copies of this article are available from The Haworth Document Delivery Service: 1-800-342-9678, 9:00 a.m. - 5:00 p.m. (EST).]*

More things are wrought by prayer than this world dreams of.

Alfred, Lord Tennyson

In the Twelve-Step way of life, three of the Steps call for prayer and one calls for meditation (AA, 1981, p. 6-9). The three that call for

Robert J. Kus is a nurse-sociologist who specializes in gay men's studies and alcohol studies. A former University of Iowa professor, he is currently studying to become a Roman Catholic priest.

Address correspondence to: Dr. Robert J. Kus, St. Mary Seminary, 28700 Euclid Avenue, Wickliffe, OH 44092-2527 USA.

[Haworth co-indexing entry note]: "Prayer and Meditation in Addiction Recovery." Kus, Robert J. Co-published simultaneously in *Journal of Chemical Dependency Treatment* (The Haworth Press, Inc.) Vol. 5, No. 2, 1995, pp. 101-115; and: *Spirituality and Chemical Dependency* (ed: Robert J. Kus) The Haworth Press, Inc., 1995, pp. 101-115; and: *Spirituality and Chemical Dependency* (ed: Robert J. Kus) Harrington Park Press, an imprint of The Haworth Press, Inc., 1995, pp. 101-115. Single or multiple copies of this article are available from The Haworth Document Delivery Service [1-800-342-9678, 9:00 a.m. - 5:00 p.m. (EST)].

© 1995 by The Haworth Press, Inc. All rights reserved.

prayer, or human-to-God communication, are Step 5 ("Admitted to God, to ourselves, and to another human being the exact nature of our wrongs"); Step 7 ("Humbly asked Him to remove our shortcomings"); and Step 11 ("Sought through prayer and meditation to improve our conscious contact with God *as we understood Him*, praying only for knowledge of His will for us and the power to carry that out"). Step 11 is the one Step which calls for meditation.

Many persons coming to the Twelve-Step way of life have a difficult time with prayer and meditation. Although they may be adults, their prayer-life and meditation skills may be on a child's level. Many see prayer and meditation as something "other-worldly" or too mysterious for the likes of them. Others simply have stopped praying as their disease progressed, as seen in Royce's *Spiritual Progression Chart* [See "The Effects of Alcoholism and Recovery on Spirituality" in this collection.]

Because one-fourth of the 12 Steps specifically recommend human-to-God interaction (prayer), it would appear that knowing how to pray is an important skill in the Twelve-Step way of life.

PURPOSE

The purpose of this article is to discuss the role of prayer and meditation in the Twelve-Step way of life. To do this, I will define prayer; discuss the various types of prayer; present common formal prayers which are often used in the Twelve-Step way of life; discuss how sobriety affects the types of prayer one says; discuss two types of meditation; discuss how God gets back to the one praying; and offer some clinical implications.

Before doing this, however, there are certain assumptions which this article makes which need to be pointed out.

ASSUMPTIONS

Step Two of AA states, "Came to believe that a Power greater than ourselves could restore us to sanity" (AA, 1981, p. 5). For many Twelve-Steppers, the "power greater than ourselves" is an AA group, a set of ideals, nature, or whatever. For most Twelve-

Steppers, however, this power is God or some supreme, supernatural Being.

Four of the Twelve Steps use the term "God" (3,5,6, and 11), and one, Step 7, simply refers to God as "Him." Contrary to popular misconception, the term "Higher Power" does not appear in any of the Twelve Steps (Alcoholics Anonymous, 1981).

For this paper, I am assuming that the individual is communicating with a supreme Being, no matter how this Being is envisioned. Although one can communicate with an AA group, we usually do not call this "prayer." Meditation, however, can be engaged in regardless of an individual's belief or non-belief in a supreme being.

A DEFINITION OF PRAYER

Simply put, prayer is human-to-God communication. As we'll see later, God gets back to our communication in a number of ways, but God's communication to us is seen as answering our prayers, not praying to us.

TAXONOMIES OR CLASSIFICATIONS OF PRAYERS

There are many ways to classify prayers. For simplicity's sake, this article is concerned with only two types of classification systems. These two ways of classifying prayers are according to their purpose or according to their formality or spontaneity.

Classification of Prayers on the Basis of Their Purpose

In this system, we classify prayers on the basis of their purpose. Are we asking God for something? Praising God? Thanking God?

Traditionally, this system identifies four basic types of prayer based on their purpose. These are prayers of adoration, contrition, thanksgiving, and supplication. These can be remembered by the mnemonic ACTS, the first letters of each of the types of prayers. A fifth category could be called "mixed," where the prayer contains more than one purpose, as in the Lord's Prayer.

A sixth category has been identified, however, and these are called "cursing" prayers. More will be said about this type of communication later.

Prayers of Adoration

Prayers of adoration are designed to worship God. Many of the Psalms, for example, are of this type. Psalm 149, for instance, entreats all of creation to praise the Lord–the sun and moon and shining stars and waters and sea monsters and storm winds and wild beasts and tame animals and young men and maidens and old men and boys. It ends with, "Praise the name of the Lord, for his name alone is exalted, and he has lifted up the horn of his people" (Ps 149, v. 13).

Prayers of Contrition

Prayers of contrition are those which ask God for forgiveness. Steps 4 through 7 are designed to help us make this kind of prayer. In Step 4, we are asked to make a "searching and fearless moral inventory of ourselves," while in Step 5 we admit "the exact nature of our wrongs to God, to ourselves, and to another human being." In Step 6 we become "entirely ready to have God remove all these defects of character," and in Step 7 we finally make the prayer of contrition: "Humbly asked Him to remove our shortcomings." Note the simplicity of the prayer: "God, please remove my short-comings."

Note that it is often much easier for many recovering persons to ask God or another human being to forgive them than to forgive themselves.

Prayers of Thanksgiving

Prayers of thanksgiving are designed to thank God for one's blessings. As individuals mature in sobriety, they are more likely to engage in thanksgiving prayers. They have more to be thankful for, and they are more aware of the many blessings they do have. Probably the earliest thank you prayer children learn is that before meals.

Prayers of Supplication

Prayers of supplication are prayers designed to ask God for something other than forgiveness. This type of prayer is perhaps the commonest one used by children, and it tends to be very popular in early sobriety. As one matures in sobriety, however, prayers of supplication tend to get overshadowed by prayers of thanksgiving. In Step 11, individuals are encouraged to ask for "knowledge of [God's] will for us and the power to carry that out."

Mixed Type Prayers

Mixed prayers are those containing more than one purpose. An excellent example of this type of prayer is the Lord's Prayer which Jesus taught his followers. "Our Father, who art in heaven, hallowed be thy name" is a prayer of adoration, while " . . . forgive us our trespasses, as we forgive those who trespass against us" is a prayer of contrition, and "Give us this day our daily bread" is a prayer of supplication.

Cursing Prayers

It is very unusual to consider cursing God to be a form of prayer, but if we define prayer as human-to-God communication, this has to be considered one form of prayer. In a research project exploring how gay men achieve and maintain sobriety in the AA context, I learned that before sobriety, and early in sobriety, many of the men cursed God for having been created gay (Kus, 1992). They saw this as a curse rather than a blessing. As they grew in sobriety, however, they came to accept their gay orientation as a divine gift. The cursing was abandoned, and thanksgiving was substituted. The "bad news" became "good news." In fact, abandoning their internalized homophobia (hatred of being gay) is one indication of how gay alcoholic men are growing in sobriety.

Alcoholics and other addicts are not immune to this type of prayer, especially in the final days of pre-recovery and in early recovery. One might curse God for the loss of a loved one or for having been given a disease such as alcoholism, cancer, or AIDS.

Having looked at how prayers may be classified on the basis of their purpose, let us look at how they may be classified on the basis of their spontaneity or formality.

Formal vs. Spontaneous Prayers

Formal prayers are those prayers which are written down and often memorized, while *spontaneous prayers* are those which are not written down and which arise from the individual talking to God in his or her own words.

Generally, we learn formal prayers as children before we are comfortable with saying spontaneous prayers. Many newcomers in the Twelve-Step way of life may initially find formal prayers easier as they require no creativity.

Three of the most common formal prayers in the Twelve-Step way of life are the Lord's Prayer, the first part of the Serenity Prayer, and the Prayer of St. Francis of Assisi.

The Lord's Prayer

Although this prayer is said in Christian churches on a regular basis, there is nothing specifically "Christian" about it. It was formulated, some biblical scholars believe, by Jesus–a Jewish rabbi–and it can be easily used by anyone believing in the concept of one God.

> Our Father, Who art in heaven, hallowed be Thy Name. Thy kingdom come. Thy will be done, on earth as it is in heaven. Give us this day our daily bread. And forgive us our trespasses, as we forgive those who trespass against us. And lead us not into temptation, but deliver us from evil. For Thine is the kingdom and the power and the glory, forever and ever. (Pittman, 1990, 1-2)

The Serenity Prayer

The Serenity Prayer is attributed to American theologian Reinhold Niebuhr. The first part of the prayer has become so popular in Alcoholics Anonymous and other 12-Step groups that many refer to it as the "AA Prayer." The whole prayer follows; above the dotted line is what is traditionally said in 12-Step meetings, while the part below the line is usually deleted. In fact, many AA members are astonished to learn that what they believe to be "The" Serenity Prayer is actually only the first part of the Prayer!

God, grant me the serenity
To accept the things I cannot change;
The courage to change the things I can;
And wisdom to know the difference.

- -

Living one day at a time;
Enjoying one moment at a time;
Accepting hardship as the pathway to peace;
Taking, as He did, this sinful world as it is,
not as I would have it;
Trusting that He will make all things right
if I surrender to His Will;
That I may be reasonably happy in this life,
and supremely happy with Him forever in the next. (Pittman,
1990, p. 1)

The Prayer of St. Francis

Finally, there is the Prayer of St. Francis of Assisi which was one
of AA co-founder Bill Wilson's favorites and which he included in
Twelve Steps and Twelve Traditions (AA, 1981 p. 99).

Lord, make me an instrument of Your peace!
Where there is hatred, let me sow love.
Where there is injury, pardon.
Where there is doubt, faith.
Where there is despair, hope.
Where there is darkness, light.
Where there is sadness, joy.
O Divine Master, grant that I may not so much seek
To be consoled as to console.
To be understood as to understand.
To be loved as to love.
For it is in giving that we receive.
It is in pardoning that we are pardoned.
It is in dying that we are born to eternal life. (Pittman, 1990, p. 2)

Although there are other formal prayers woven in various parts
of AA literature, these three are perhaps the most well-known and
used of the formal prayers.

There are many prayer books on the market today for every taste. One of the richest collections, from a 12-Step point of view, is one compiled by Bill Pittman titled, *The 12 Step Prayer Book* (Seattle: Glen Abbey Books, 1990).

Spontaneous prayers may be very simple such as "Help!" or "Thanks!" Or they may be more complex.

Often individuals make up prayers at the beginning of the day. An example of such a spontaneous prayer might be:

> God, thanks for another day. Please help me through this day. Help me to know your will and give me the power to carry it out. Please help me in my work and in my leisure. And if I forget to say thanks for the many blessings you send me during the day, let me say "Thanks!" now. Amen.

Likewise, many persons say spontaneous bedtime prayers. An example of this might be:

> Great Spirit, thank you for walking with me on my life journey today. We made it safe and sound and sober! Thanks for all the blessings I have—my friends and family and food and other earthly goods. Thanks in particular for my sobriety and for the continual growth you are granting me. Overlook my shortcomings and help me improve even more tomorrow. Amen.

Because they are spontaneous, such prayers are unlimited. They may be used for specific requests, for thanksgiving, for praise, or for forgiveness.

TOWARDS A DEFINITION OF MEDITATION

In general, people in Eastern cultures tend to be more comfortable with meditation rather than prayer, while persons in Western societies tend to be more familiar with prayer rather than meditation. Many Americans have a very fuzzy notion of "meditation" at best. Some see it as a form of prayer, while others confuse it with contemplation. However, thanks in large measure to the Maharishi

Mahesh Yogi and his Transcendental Meditation movement, millions of Americans have learned basic meditation techniques and are deriving many benefits from meditating.

Many AA members, based on my own research, see prayer as "me talking to God," and meditation as "me being quiet long enough to hear what God is saying to me." For purposes of this paper, meditation will be defined in two ways. First, it is a form of reflecting on a sacred truth, slogan, virtue, or whatever for spiritual purposes. Second, it is a form of centering in which the individual tries to clear his or her mind to allow God to enter.

MEDITATION AS REFLECTION

Meditation as reflection is very common in the Twelve-Step way of life. In fact, there are a number of daily meditation books available which invite the reader to reflect on a particular concept or virtue or defect and see how it applies to his or her life. The typical format for such daily meditation guides are: a brief saying from a famous person; a reflection on the theme; a resolution for action. For example, in *Touchstones: A book of daily meditations for men,* we see that the theme for March 23rd is the sacredness of the human body. The March 23rd page begins with a quote from nurse-poet, Walt Whitman: "If anything is sacred, the human body is sacred" (Hazelden, 1986). There follows a discussion of the role of sex, the human body, and spirituality. At the end, there is a resolution based on the discussion: "May I find ways to include sexuality in my spiritual awakening."

The "granddaddy" of all such meditation guides, first published in 1954, is *Twenty-four hours a day* (1975), a meditation guide for AA members written anonymously by one of the early AA writers. Some of the other popular daily meditation guides, most written anonymously and published by Hazelden, are:

- *Answers in the heart: Daily meditations for men and women recovering from sex addiction* (1989)
- Beattie's *The language of letting go: Daily meditations on codependency* (1990)
- Brady's *Daybreak: Meditations for women survivors of sexual abuse* (1991)

- Casey's *Worthy of love: Meditations on loving ourself and others* (1990)
- Casey's *If only I could quit: Recovery from nicotine addiction* (1989)
- Cordes' *The reflecting pond: Meditations for self-discovery* (1988)
- *Day by day: Daily meditations for recovering addicts* (1974)
- Dean's *Night light: A book of nighttime meditations* (1986)
- *Each day a new beginning: Daily meditations for women* (1984)
- Fossum and Fossum's *The more we find in each other: Meditations for couples* (1992)
- *In God's care: Daily meditations on spirituality in recovery* (1991)
- *Keep it simple: Daily meditations for Twelve-Step beginnings and renewal* (1989)
- L.'s *Inner harvest: Daily meditations for recovery from eating disorders* (1990)
- L.'s *Food for thought: Daily meditations for overeaters* (1980)
- Larsen and Hegarty's *Days of healing, days of joy: Daily meditations for adult children* (1989)
- Limon's *Beginning again: Beyond the end of love* (1991)
- Pitzele's *One more day: Daily meditations for the chronically ill* (1988)
- Roeck's *Look to this day: Twenty-four hours a day for everyone* (1978)
- Tillevas' *The color of light: Daily meditations for all of us living with AIDS* (1988)
- *Today's gift: Daily meditations for families* (1984)
- *Touchstones: A book of daily meditations for men* (1986)

Two other daily meditation guides are *Daily reflections: A book of reflections by A.A. members for A.A. members* (AA, 1990) and Hifler's *A Cherokee feast of days: Daily meditations* (Council Oak Books, 1992).

MEDITATION AS CENTERING

The second type of meditation is non-reflective. This type of meditation, which has various subtypes, has three basic features: assuming a comfortable body position, maintaining physical immobility, and continuously focusing attention on some object, sound, or bodily process (Woolfolk and Richardson, 1978, p. 142). As Woolfolk and Richardson note, if you do these things, you are by definition meditating.

A recommended approach for getting started with non-reflective or centering meditation might be as follows. First, find a quiet place to meditate. Second, try meditating at approximately the same times each day, times which seem most conducive to meditation. Third, when meditating, get into a comfortable position wearing comfortable clothes if possible. Beginners often feel a need to have their back supported. Fourth, clear the mind of all thoughts as much as possible. Allow stray thoughts to float through your mind. To help with this process, engage in focusing on an object, a bodily process, or sound.

If the eyes are closed, one might concentrate on one's breathing, saying "in" on inhaling and "out" on exhaling. Or one might use a mantra, a sound or word such as "om" or "Jesus" which one repeats rhythmically with one's breathing. This helps to clear the mind of all thoughts, allowing one to be open to insights or communication from God. One might focus on a sound such as the tinkling noises of windchimes or "waterfall" sounds from white-noise machines used to enhance sleep. If one chooses to have his or her eyes open, one might focus on a flower or flame from a candle.

Many writers in this area recommend that the novice practice meditation for 15-20 minute periods twice a day. Like anything else, the more one practices, the greater the facility one will achieve.

It is important, also, that the meditator should not focus on whether the meditation is good or bad. As Woolfolk and Richardson say:

> A third problem that people have in learning to meditate is self-evaluation. We all like to feel that whatever we do we do well. Many people will not even attempt activities at which they feel they cannot excel. However, the lexicon of success

and failure does not apply to meditation. One does not meditate "well" or "poorly." If one is attending to the object of meditation, one is meditating. If one's attention is not focused upon the object of meditation, then one is not meditating. Meditation is, by definition, value-free. One simply is either meditating or not meditating. It is, therefore, self-defeating to try to do well while meditating. The chances are that if someone is trying to meditate well, then she [sic] will be thinking about how well she [sic] is doing rather than maintaining her [sic] focus on the object of meditation. Trying to meditate well will therefore keep one from meditating at all. (1978, pp. 143-144)

The benefits of meditation are numerous and include such things as a "calmer, more spiritual outlook, a sense of physical and spiritual well-being, a sense of harmony with the Lord and his creation, and a more positive attitude toward others" (Antonsen, 1979, p. 529).

HOW GOD COMMUNICATES WITH HUMANS

So far, we have focused on human-to-God communication. But how about God-to-human communication? How does God communicate to us? Unfortunately, God does not communicate to us in telegrams. Therefore, many people find it difficult to imagine God communicating with them at all. But, the more people grow in sobriety and the spiritual life, the more they are able to recognize God communicating with them in a number of ways.

One, God speaks through individuals. These individuals may be AA members sharing themselves in AA meetings or in pre- or post-meeting gatherings, sponsors, bosses, friends, spouses or lovers, and others. When we realize God speaks through other humans, the more likely we are to listen attentively and reflectively. Two, God speaks through writers of inspirational books, biographies and autobiographies, meditation books, and the like. Three, God communicates with us by sending us life experiences, both pleasant and unpleasant. Our challenge is, of course, to figure out what messages we should be gleaning from our various experiences.

Four, God speaks through "coincidences," which many 12-Steppers refer to as "when God chooses to remain anonymous." Five,

God speaks through nature. The wonderment of the cosmos, the soothing nature of a stream or lake, the calming effects of the woods, the beauty of flowers, the simplicity and innocence and earthiness of our pets, and the like are all reflections of God in our universe. Six, many feel God speaks through dreams. Seven, God may speak to us via flashes of insight into our lives.

Eight, God communicates to us by granting us favors which we ask for, by denying us what we want, or by delaying what we want. Nine, God may speak to us via movies or television. Many persons have found answers to life problems from films, and many have been stimulated by the inspirational stories of others to change the directions of their own lives for the better. Finally, God communicates to us by sending us serenity, one of the signs that we are doing God's will for us.

In short, God's presence is everywhere around us. One sees when one believes. In AA, the traditional notion of "I'll believe it when I see it" is transformed more accurately into "I'll see it when I believe it!"

CLINICAL IMPLICATIONS

From the above discussion, the following recommendations may be made for clinicians faced with helping recovering clients deal with prayer and meditation.

First, analyze your own prayer life. How do you pray? What are some of the obstacles you have found in your own life to praying? What did you do to overcome them? Second, clinicians should be aware of the different types of prayer. Third, become familiar with prayer books which you can point out to clients. As noted above, an excellent source for 12-Steppers is Pittman's *The 12 Step Prayer Book* (Seattle: Glen Abbey Books, 1990). Fourth, assist your clients with the spontaneous type of praying. Many persons do not know how to pray spontaneously.

Fifth, encourage consistency in praying. Like any other human activity, the more one prays, the easier and better it becomes. Sixth, be familiar with the basics of meditation and where you can get further information. As noted in this article, meditation is not as mysterious as many believe. Seventh, be familiar with a rich variety of reflection-type meditation books on the market today. Call Hazelden, for example, to get a copy of their catalog of such books (800)-328-9000. Eighth, encourage daily meditation at set intervals. Many 12-Steppers find it useful to read from a meditation book every morning upon awakening and each night before retiring. Those who do centering-type meditation also find it helpful to get into a routine.

Ninth, talk with others about their prayer and meditation experiences. Others' experiences may be helpful to your own clients. Tenth, help your clients learn to recognize how God interacts with them through others' talk, through books, through movies, through nature, and the like. Finally, give your clients positive strokes for their efforts at improving their prayer and meditation life.

REFERENCES

Alcoholics Anonymous. (1981). *Twelve steps and twelve traditions.* New York: A.A. World Services, Inc.

Alcoholics Anonymous. (1990). *Daily reflections: A book of reflections by A.A. members for A.A. members.* New York: A.A. World Services, Inc.

Antonsen, C. (1979). Prayer. In *New Catholic Encyclopedia* (Vol. XVII Supplement: Change in the Church) (pp. 528-529). New York: Publishers Guild.

Beattie, M. (1990). *The language of letting go: Daily meditations on codependency.* Center City, MN: Hazelden.

Brady, M. (1991). *Daybreak: Meditations for women survivors of sexual abuse.* Center City, MN: Hazelden.

Casey, K. (1990). *Worthy of love: Meditations on loving ourself and others.* Center City, MN: Hazelden.

Casey, K. (1989). *If only I could quit: Recovery from nicotine addiction.* Center City, MN: Hazelden.

Cordes, L. (1988). *The reflecting pond: Meditations for self-discovery.* Center City, MN: Hazelden.

Dean, A.E. (1986). *Night light: A book of nighttime meditations.* Center City, MN: Hazelden.

Fossum, M. and Fossum, M. (1992). *The more we find in each other: Meditations for couples.* Center City, MN: Hazelden.

Hazelden. (1989). *Answers in the heart: Daily meditations for men and women recovering from addiction.* Center City, MN: Hazelden.

Hazelden. (1974). *Day by day: Daily meditations for recovering addicts.* Center City, MN: Hazelden.

Hazelden. (1984). *Each day a new beginning: Daily meditations for women.* Center City, MN: Hazelden.

Hazelden. (1991). *In God's care: Daily meditations on spirituality in recovery.* Center City, MN: Hazelden.

Hazelden. (1989). *Keep it simple: Daily meditations for Twelve-Step beginnings and renewals.* Center City, MN: Hazelden.

Hazelden. (1984). *Today's gift: Daily meditations for families.* Center City, MN: Hazelden.

Hazelden. (1986). *Touchstones: A book of daily meditations for men.* Center City, MN: Hazelden.

Hazelden. (1975). *Twenty-four hours a day.* Center City, MN: Hazelden.

Hifler, J.S. (1992). *A Cherokee feast of days: Daily meditations.* Tulsa, OK: Council Oak Books.

Kus, R.J. (1992). Spirituality in everyday life: Experiences of gay men of Alcoholics Anonymous. *Journal of Chemical Dependency Treatment,* 5(1): 49-66.

L., E. (1980). *Food for thought: Daily meditations for overeaters.* Center City, MN: Hazelden.

L., E. (1990). *Inner harvest: Daily meditations for recovery from eating disorders.* Center City, MN: Hazelden.

Larsen, E. and Hegarty, C.L. (1989). *Days of healing, days of joy: Daily meditations for adult children.* Center City, MN: Hazelden.

Limon, W. (1991). *Beyond the end of love.* Center City, MN: Hazelden.

Pittman, B. (1990). *The 12 step prayer book: A collection of favorite 12 step prayers and inspirational writings.* Seattle: Glen Abbey Books.

Pitzele, S.K. (1988). *One more day: Daily meditations for the chronically ill.* Center City, MN: Hazelden.

Psalm 149. *New American Bible.* New York: Thomas Nelson.

Roeck, A.L. (1978). *Look to this day: Twenty-four hours a day for everyone.* Center City, MN: Hazelden.

Tilleras, P. (1988). *The color of light: Daily meditations for all of us living with AIDS.* Center City, MN: Hazelden.

Woolfolk, R.L. and Richardson, F.C. (1978). *Stress, sanity, and survival.* New York: New American Library.

Applied Spirituality:
Expressing Love and Service

Douglas J. King, MArch

SUMMARY. Applied spirituality, in Twelve-Step groups, usually refers to being of service to others. After looking at how some AA members engage in applied spirituality, the author discusses both short-term and long-term activities which individuals in recovery may experience. After identifying barriers and misunderstandings newcomers to recovery have regarding applied spirituality concepts, strategies for helping clients overcome these barriers are given. The importance of service work in recovery, stages of applied spirituality in recovery and potential pitfalls which persons in long-term recovery may experience are all explored. Finally the author gives practical suggestions to clinicians for helping their clients in the realm of applied spirituality. *[Single or multiple copies of this article are available from The Haworth Document Delivery Service: 1-800-342-9678, 9:00 a.m. - 5:00 p.m. (EST).]*

EXAMPLES OF SPIRITUALITY IN ACTION

The Twelve Step movement, one of the greatest spiritual movements in modern history, finds the concept of "applied spirituality"

Douglas J. King is currently an architect specializing in the design of large-scale, high-rise, health care facilities. Mr. King has been involved in various recovery programs since 1979. He has sponsored numerous people in recovery. He has founded many A.A. groups for gays and lesbians, and is the co-founder of the Lambda Service Group, an organization which conducts outreach and education regarding alcoholism in the gay and lesbian communities.

Address correspondence to: Mr. Douglas J. King, 1742 W. Byron, Chicago, IL 60613.

[Haworth co-indexing entry note]: "Applied Spirituality: Expressing Love and Service." King, Douglas J. Co-published simultaneously in *Journal of Chemical Dependency Treatment* (The Haworth Press, Inc.) Vol. 5, No. 2, 1995, pp. 117-134; and: *Spirituality and Chemical Dependency* (ed: Robert J. Kus) The Haworth Press, Inc., 1995, pp. 117-134; and: *Spirituality and Chemical Dependency* (ed: Robert J. Kus) Harrington Park Press, an imprint of The Haworth Press, Inc., 1995 pp. 117-134. Single or multiple copies of this article are available from The Haworth Document Delivery Service [1-800-342-9678, 9:00 a.m. - 5:00 p.m. (EST)].

© 1995 by The Haworth Press, Inc. All rights reserved.

117

critically important. Applied spirituality refers to helping or serving others. This aid can occur within the recovery community or in the myriad activities of everyday life. An example of the former would be giving a ride to a carless person to an NA (Narcotics Anonymous) meeting, and of the latter would be spending more quality time with one's children. It is important to recognize that in Twelve Step groups this concept has additional importance; the act of helping others results in the paradoxical side effect of helping the people who are providing service recover from their particular addiction.

I have witnessed this phenomenon repeatedly in my fifteen years of association with members of Alcoholics Anonymous and other recovery programs. Being of service to others is an important ingredient in developing a healthy spirituality, and a healthy spirituality leads to a lasting and meaningful recovery from addiction.

Included below are descriptions of a few AA members whom I have come to know. These persons, whose names I have changed to protect their anonymity, have achieved a high degree of spiritual awareness in their recovery from alcoholism. They exemplify how a person can grow spiritually within Twelve Step recovery programs and how serving others is a critical component of that spiritual growth and its resultant recovery from addictions.

Abraham

Abraham has been recovering from alcoholism and cocaine addiction for nine years. His family owns a large candy factory in a large midwestern town where he is employed. Early in his recovery he began to attend the gay Alano Club (an Alano Club is an organization that is formed to allow many Twelve Step meetings to take place in one location) in his town. He quickly became involved in helping to put on the parties which frequently occurred there, initially providing the refreshments. As time went on, he became a member of the club's Board of Directors and began to initiate such activities as Club involvement in the Annual Civic Gay Pride Parade and fundraising for the purchase of a new building. In the past few years, Abraham has been involved in soliciting gay and lesbian community support for his alderman, and he serves on the Board of

Directors of an organization which feeds homebound Persons With AIDS.

Charles

Charles, during his "using days," was a manager of an infamous gay hustler bar. Early in his recovery, he got involved in the activities of a large Alano Club in a large midwestern city. He also started a hairdressing business. Then he started a second hairdressing outlet and began managing a large gay bar. Having a great entrepreneurial spirit, Charles and several friends started the first Alano Club in the country devoted primarily to gay and lesbian recoverees. After about fifteen years of sobriety, Charles decided to change his life, and he applied to become the National Director of an AIDS outreach program for a major religious denomination, a position for which he was accepted. Interestingly, during the interview the Church said that the most impressive item on his resume was the work he had done in starting the gay Alano Club.

Alex

In his drugging and drinking days, Alex made his living as a drug runner. He would fly to Miami and pick up thousands of dollars worth of drugs which he would transport back to his home in Northern Michigan, thus supplying much of the area with cocaine. When he entered recovery, Alex was on probation and had lost his driver's license for several years. He "came out" as a gay man in early recovery. Because he was having trouble finding acceptance in the predominantly "redneck" AA meetings in his small semi-rural town, when he was about two weeks sober, he was encouraged by others to start a gay AA group in his hometown to increase his support network. With no car, no money, and not knowing other gay people in recovery, he set out on his task. Through the assistance of several local therapists, he was introduced to several prospective members for this gay AA group. Today this group thrives, and dozens of people have found sobriety as a result of it. Through this activity Alex found himself attracted to the helping professions. As a result, he went back to college in early sobriety. Eight years into recovery, he is now working as an MSW therapist in Northern Michigan specializing in the treatment of individuals with schizophrenia and other chronic mental disorders.

Alonzo

Alonzo was a jet-set type in his partying days. His lover was a popular and well-known novelist, and Alonzo would spend his days getting drunk with the social elite of the particular country in which they were residing at the time. Alonzo and his lover would move to a different European country every couple of years to establish the setting for his lover's next novel. After about ten years of this glamorous living, Alonzo finally "hit bottom" with his alcoholism and sought recovery in Italy. However, AA had not yet been started in Italy at that time (1968), so Alonzo, with the support of the AA New York Central Office, started AA in that country. Ironically, this adventure became the setting for his lover's next novel. In gratitude for this activity, and for the positive exposure the novel gave AA in Italy, Bill Wilson (co-founder of AA) wrote Alonzo and his lover a thank you letter. Over the next quarter century, Alonzo has been very active in "service work." He is well-known in his native Mexico AA, and he has been one of the official greeters for Mexico AA at various AA World Service Conferences for the past twenty years. Alonzo worked for years in the Central AA Office of Mexico. He was instrumental in starting the first gay AA Group in Mexico, and he recently started a Twelve Step group for persons with HIV-positive status in recovery in that country. He is also active in supporting the civil rights movement for gays and lesbians in Mexico, and he has opened up his residence to several PWA's (Persons with AIDS).

APPLIED SPIRITUALITY IN RECOVERY: A HISTORICAL PERSPECTIVE

Applied spirituality is rooted in the earliest history of Alcoholics Anonymous. Bill Wilson credits maintaining sobriety in his first six months of recovery from alcoholism (in early 1935) to his diligent interactions with other alcoholics. He noted, however, that none of the people he met at that time ever got sober because of his "preachy" efforts. When he shared his story with AA co-founder Dr. Bob Smith in June of 1935, Dr. Bob's advice was to simply tell his own story of what it was like, what happened, and what it was like to be in recovery. What alcoholics do need is evidence that someone just like him or her is no longer drinking and is now living a decent life. It was at this initial meeting that Bill Wilson also realized that he needed to talk to help Bob Smith to help himself.

This humble awareness that an alcoholic can stay sober by helping another alcoholic is one of the primary principles of Alcoholics Anonymous. This basic idea also set AA apart from any similar movement which previously existed. For the first time in history, the afflicted were taking a major role in their own recovery.

By AA's fifteenth anniversary, in 1950, the Twelfth Step had been written. It states, "Having had a spiritual awakening as a result of these steps, we tried to carry this message to alcoholics, and to practice these principles in all of our affairs" (AA, 1952, 1953, 1981, p. 8). At the first National Alcoholics Anonymous Conference which celebrated the anniversary of AA, a very ill Dr. Bob Smith gave his last talk. In it Dr. Bob (*Grapevine*, 1951) said:

> Our 12 Steps, when simmered down to the last, resolve themselves into two words: *love* and *service*. We understand what love is and we understand what service is. So let's bear those two things in mind. . . . (p. 49)

Dr. Bob also reminded the AA members in attendance that none of them would be sitting in the convention sober if others before them hadn't taken the time to explain little things to them, to pat them on the back, to take them to meetings, and to do all the other little things AA members do for each other. He cautioned his fellow AA members to never forget to help those who are less fortunate (*Grapevine*, 1951).

On a more contemporary note: M. Scott Peck, in his classic work *The Road Less Traveled* (1978), defines love as "the will to extend one's self for the purpose of nurturing one's own or another's spiritual growth" (p. 81). This passage sums up the interrelationship between love, service and spirituality. When we are talking about "applied spirituality" we are discussing "unconditional love in action." To practice "applied spirituality," we are embracing acts that contain elements of both "service" and "unconditional love" and benefit both server and those served. As the concepts of applied spirituality are discussed in this article, Dr. Peck's definition of "love" will come to life as we see newcomers to recovery become increasingly more loving in their actions as they progress in recovery.

RECOVERY ACTIVITIES WHICH MANIFEST "APPLIED SPIRITUALITY"

Examples of recovery-related activities which comprise acts of applied spirituality fall into two broad categories: (1) day-to-day activities which appear menial, but are a part of every Twelve Step meeting, and (2) more involved activities which require more of a commitment to fulfill.

Day to Day Activities

The activities which occur at virtually every 12 Step meeting in the world include such things as:

- Setting up and taking down tables and chairs;
- Greeting newcomers and visitors (and providing information for them);
- Preparing and distributing refreshments;
- Cleaning up the meeting room after the meeting;
- Volunteering at Alano clubs to clean up and answer the phone;
- Accompanying fellow recoverees on 12 step calls;
- Sharing oneself with others at meetings;
- Reading a passage from recovery literature at a meeting;
- Calling someone in the group on the telephone;
- Providing transportation for someone to and from a meeting;
- Being available on the calling list of contacts for newcomers.

These types of activities (and others) provide an opportunity for newcomers to recovery to begin to contribute and become part of the group and thus develop feelings of "fellowship." This experience of "fellowship" should not be underestimated in its ability to help newcomers feel welcome and motivated toward seeking recovery. The information shared at Twelve Step meetings is indeed helpful; but the camaraderie with other persons whom newcomers can identify with will go a long way towards promoting their desire to return to the meetings. Alcoholics or addicts who have spent the previous few years in the tortured solitude of addiction and in the gripping pain of resentment and fear will enjoy the healthy banter that occurs in many AA groups.

The second group of activities are events which newcomers to recovery gradually begin to take part in as their growth in recovery advances. In many groups this process of allowing newcomers to increasingly take on more responsibility at groups is a conscious, purposeful, act. Usually during their first year of sobriety, people are given the chance to begin to chair (be secretary at meetings) which entails a weekly commitment of between three and six months depending upon the group. Clearly, being the chair of a meeting or doing other similar tasks, are not ego-feeding propositions, but instead are integral parts of the growth process of recovery. Below are listed some activities which require a commitment and which might occur in the recoveree's program after around a year of involvement in a Twelve Step program.

Activities Involving Greater Commitment

- Chairing the meetings;
- Sponsoring newcomers;
- Doing Twelve Step work;
- Being involved in the management of an Alano Club;
- Taking on a leadership role in putting on AA conferences;
- Speaking at speaker meetings;
- Being involved in AA's service structure which extends beyond one's community and links the local AA groups with AA as a whole.

Some of these activities, especially sponsorship and leadership roles in administering AA conferences, could require several years of sobriety. However, depending on the individual's talents and personality, these ranges could vary.

Activities in Everyday Life

A special note should be made about two broad categories of service-related activities that occur in everyday life: those which occur in the community-at-large and those that occur in a person's life on a daily basis.

As newcomers progress in sobriety, opportunities may present themselves for involvement in community-wide activities such as groups which educate the community about AIDS, church groups, or professional or school-related organizations. Such commitment by persons relatively new in recovery should be monitored closely. If such an obligation is too demanding and thus preventing the development of a newcomer's recovery program, it should be discouraged. However, if new recoverees have the time available for both their recovery program and outside activities, they should be encouraged.

The other category of activities which newcomers can involve themselves in are those that occur within their everyday lives. Examples of "doing spirituality in everyday life" can include doing good works (corporal and spiritual works of mercy), maintaining sobriety, communicating with the Higher Power, sharing oneself with others, fulfilling adult social roles, living an "examined life," seeking forgiveness, performing rituals, developing discipline, and doing the little everyday tasks as best we can (Kus, 1990, pp. 55-63). These activities could be as humble as doing one's job well, paying one's bills on time, and engaging in good citizenship. The important idea to impart to newcomers is that acts of applied spirituality, or "service work," can occur in everyday life. Additionally, newcomers are probably engaging in many acts of applied spirituality already; these deeds may just be too unpretentious for the newcomer to see without the clinician's assistance.

BARRIERS AND MISUNDERSTANDINGS IN COMMUNICATING APPLIED SPIRITUALITY TO NEWCOMERS

The activities previously listed are the "bread and butter" events which form the core of involvement in virtually all recovery programs. The scope of involvement is quite broad. For example, if a man is an accountant by training, he may find himself gravitating to the treasurer position of his group, Alano Club, or conference. Or if persons have a bent for creativity, they may find they would like to decorate the clubs, meeting rooms or conference facilities. The range of involvement is limitless. The primary limiting factor is a negative attitude towards "service work." The following is a short list of excuses which clinicians might hear newcomers use to avoid becoming involved in activities which are helpful to others:

a. They are afraid of rejection if they reach out to others to become involved in the group activities.
b. They are too busy in their lives to be involved beyond going to meetings.
c. They see this "do-goodism" as smacking of religiosity or piousness.
d. They are not "good enough" at a task to start it.
e. They feel that this type of activity is beneath them: "Let others do that, I have more important things to do."
f. They don't feel comfortable doing things in groups.

To overcome these and other barriers, counselors need to understand the basis for these attitudes. Many people in recovery have perfectly natural reasons for having suspicion, if not outright defiance, about being involved in a benevolent way with others. Frequently, newcomers come from frightfully confrontational home environments where their model of group interaction was a deep-seated selfishness that permeated each person's interaction with the other family members. Unfortunately, much of our society reinforces this strong individuality and "looking out for number one" attitude. Asking for help is not considered the "American Way." Rarely does life offer such non-confrontational, non-competitive, mutually beneficial, warm, gentle, human interaction which is readily available in Twelve Step groups. So, when confronted with such a different environment, it is likely that newcomers may be deeply suspicious and reluctant to embrace the recovery environment. However, mistrust and reluctance melt quickly when newcomers see that many of these folks are "just like me" with the problems they share.

Frequently people who are early in recovery need help getting involved in the Twelve Step group activities. The clinician can provide assistance in ways that vary from the subtle to the downright confrontational. Some suggestions are as follows:

A. *"Start Small":* The clinician can help those in early recovery get started by having them do some of the "small tasks" which need to be done at each meeting. A Twelve Step meeting which meets in the clinician's base facility is a good place to start. Newcomers (those at their third or fourth meeting) can set up the meeting room chairs and tables, or make the coffee, or do a simple reading from the AA literature which is part of the group ritual, etc. By contributing in a small way, newcomers can become accustomed to the idea that everyone becomes involved in the welfare of the group.

B. *Don't couch the service work activities in spiritual/religious terms:* The clinician would be wise not to use heavily weighted spiritual/religious terms in helping newcomers get involved. In early recovery it is important to develop the simple habits of contributing to the group instead of unintentionally misleading newcomers into believing they are joining a cult or religious organization.

C. *Start newcomers in service-related activities as early as possible in their recovery:* People early in recovery may be weak emotionally and physically, and their spirits may be down, but the simple act of being kind to another person or group can be a catalyst for making recovery attractive. The positive self-esteem garnered by performing simple acts of kindness is truly infectious. Many sponsors ("mentors in recovery") try to have people they sponsor get involved in helping others right from the start of their recovery. For example, Alex, whom I described earlier, started an AA group when he was two weeks sober with the support of his sponsor. In AA's earliest days people with barely more than weeks of sobriety were setting up groups in major metropolitan areas. Early recovery is the time for the clinician to use newcomers' heightened fear of relapse as emotional leverage to urge them to become more involved in their recovery and ultimately improve their lives.

D. *Confront religious/spiritual prejudice:* Counselors need to explain to newcomers that recovery is truly non-denominational.

Addiction affects people of all races, religions and upbringings. The Twelve Step way of life is not a religion. What many Twelve Step groups are providing is reinforcement of simple basic principles for preventing relapse from their particular addiction. The bottom line of recovery for many members is "life or death." As newcomers progress they will understand that the Twelve Step program has less and less to do with an individual's particular affliction and more and more to do with rebuilding the person's life. The paradox of recovery is: by focusing on the fundamentals of abstinence from the addiction, the luxury of delving into the spiritual becomes a possibility; and this healthy spiritual condition will, in turn, insure long-term sobriety.

The depth of this personal resurrection of mind, body and spirit is bounded only by the newcomer's imagination. Few fellow recoverees are going to dictate how newcomers will choose to spend their lives in recovery. However, the older members will be, hopefully, observant enough to help newcomers alter their behavior if they are headed for relapse. This type of mutual support permeates recovery programs and is spiritual rather than religious in nature. At its essence, members of Twelve Step groups are helping each other to survive.

E. Challenge distancing techniques: Sometimes newcomers to recovery "distance" themselves from group activities. Common distancing techniques include non-attendance at meetings; arriving late and leaving early; refusing to talk to others; and looking unfriendly. Newcomers distance themselves for many reasons: fear of rejection; low self-esteem; poor communications skills; not knowing what kinds of things to say in group settings; previous rejection in groups; and feelings of uniqueness. Meetings and post-meeting get-togethers are excellent ways of helping such persons get over feelings of being "terminally unique." Being invited to participate in group work, such as sharing their story in a small group of folks after a meeting or going on 12 step calls with more experienced members, are good ways to help such persons open up.

F. Get them involved in the group process: Clinicians should get newcomers to engage in group-related activities as early in recovery as practical and encourage them to secure a sponsor for additional emotional support. An astute sponsor will include newcomers in group-related activities such as going out for coffee before or after the meeting, helping with the set up of meetings, or going to social events that are being hosted by members of the group.

This spirit of inclusion is vital to recovery and should be constantly reinforced. All Twelve Step programs have two major components, "The Program of Action" (which comprises the 12 steps, 12 traditions and 12 concepts of World Service) and "The Fellowship" component. Frequently "the program" part of the equation receives the most attention in early recovery, but it is "The Fellowship" that contributes to newcomers' wanting to return to the group and is the living, breathing evidence to newcomers that recovery is indeed "worth it" and attainable.

G. *Confront "Busyness"*: Occasionally newcomers who enter recovery have very busy lives. These individuals might have viable time demands which include jobs which require extraordinary time, families with wants, social and love lives. Frequently, in early recovery, these demands are particularly pronounced because of the prior neglect of these issues. For example, big job demands might be the result of a person's sloth while in the grips of addiction; the family needs may be from neglect; the social and love lives might have sprung up as a result of a new-found energy and zest for living newcomers frequently experience in early recovery.

These distractions are a virtual minefield of timetraps. They can detour even the most earnest recoveree. The foundation of early recovery–going to meetings, communicating with a sponsor and/or a therapist, being involved in Twelve Step groups beyond simple attendance at the meetings, and developing a spiritual life–involves a significant time commitment. This early recovery involvement later allows newcomers to become more invested in career, family, romance and the like as their recovery stabilizes. In short, newcomers need to focus on their priorities. Recovery comes first; the other issues will be of little consequence if the newcomer's recovery is not solid.

If newcomers use "I am too busy" as an excuse to not become involved in the "service" aspects of recovery, it helps to remind them of the amount of time they spent engaging in their addiction and to stress that issues outside of recovery can be better dealt with once a quality recovery program is developed.

APPLIED SPIRITUALITY AND THE PROGRAM

The clinician would be prudent to focus on the short-term activities (previously listed) in their clients' early recovery. This allows for low-risk involvement that minimizes the chance of failure. Clients can gradually gravitate to longer-term involvement once they become more comfortable with their particular Twelve Step group. Below is a description of how a person might progress in early recovery in terms of "service work" involvement.

First Ninety Days: Program Orientation

The newcomers' focus is on becoming comfortable within the group. Perhaps they will have been asked to read a simple reading like the "AA preamble," "How it works," or a page from a meditation guide. They have assisted in setup and cleanup of the group meeting space and have secured a sponsor. They will have begun to interact socially with the group outside the meeting, if this is a custom of that group.

Ninety Days to Six Months: Recovery Attitude/Activity Formation

Newcomers are now recognized as familiar faces within the group and are being included in more and more activities such as group-initiated social events and parties. They are hopefully engaged with their sponsors on working the spiritual aspects of Step Two (to come to believe that a power greater than themselves can restore them to sanity), and Step Three (turning one's life and will over to the care of God as they understand Him), and are beginning to experience the serenity the program speaks of. They are continuing with the activities they did in the first ninety days and may have even begun to assist other newcomers by accompanying a more experienced member on Twelve Step calls, or by talking with new people before or after the meeting, or by telephoning them at home outside of the meeting.

Six Months to a Year: Internalizing Recovery

The newcomers are developing their spiritual lives, i.e., learning to pray, meditate, and relax and learning to "let go" of fears and angers. Feelings of serenity have probably become more frequent: they are now an established member of the group and may even become a "secretary of a meeting" at around a year in recovery. They have probably transformed their social life to where almost every significant person in their life is a co-recoveree. They, and their sponsor, may have initiated working on the Fourth Step (taking a searching and fearless moral inventory) by now.

A Year to Two Years: Longer Term Goal Focus

The newcomers have perhaps been secretary of a group and are now giving "leads" or talks where they share their experience and story with the group in some detail. They have by now done their Fourth Step; Fifth Step (admitting to God, selves, and another human being the exact nature of their wrongs); Sixth Step (becoming entirely ready to have God remove these defects of character); Seventh Step (humbly asking God to remove their shortcomings); and Eighth Step (making a list of persons they had harmed and becoming willing to make amends to them). Further, they are probably involved in the amends-making process of Step Nine. They may have developed deep and lasting friendships with others within the recovery group and now find that their lives are packed with activities ranging from going to meetings, giving leads, social involvement and some Twelve Step work or other related service work (like involvement in their local Alano Club or AA Conference Committees). At around two years, newcomers are becoming stable enough to work on issues surrounding career, family, and romance. This coincides with the Ninth Step work they have done with their sponsors, which focuses primarily on repairing the past wreckage of their addiction. The important concept for the clinician to recognize is that preparation to work on these issues takes time. This time is not measured in weeks, nor months, but years.

After Two Years: Keeping Grounded in Recovery

A frequent occurrence for persons in later recovery is the gradual drifting from a focus on recovery into a focus on broader life issues like career, romance, family, etc. This shift can be subtle and may occur over many years. In fact, AA and other Twelve Step programs are populated with individuals who, unfortunately, had to learn the hard way that one is never cured from the disease; and relapses sometimes occur after many years of recovery. A recoveree should be reminded to never forget the fundamentals of recovery. It may be very easy when clean and sober ten or fifteen years to go weeks without meetings and to still feel quite serene and comfortable with life. But the old habits of resentments, fears, and nameless anxieties may slowly drift back into their lives. Therefore, consistent involvement in recovery helps maintain a long-term reprieve from the disease. A common joke in AA which summarizes this phenomenon is: the *"ism"* of alcoholism stands for *incredibly short memory.*

Conversely, some individuals will use "service work" activities to avoid working on life issues which are causing them problems. The recovery community often mistakenly encourages such "super service workers" as individuals who are deeply committed to recovery. One man, for example, was very active in various recovery-related activities: chairing meetings, writing and speaking on recovery, sponsoring numerous people, and being actively engaged in the local AA conference, all the while receiving accolades for his efforts. However, he was neglecting issues such as the renovation of his newly-bought house and was neglecting spending time with his lover, who was going through emotionally rough times himself. This person's avoidance of dealing with basic issues in his life was brought home to him when one night an older member dropped him off at his home and saw his front steps ready to fall apart. As the driver parked, the young man was being enthusiastic about some Twelve Step activity he had been involved with. The older man calmly turned to the younger man and said, "I think you need to Twelve Step your front steps."

Because living balanced lives in recovery is so important, clinicians should be watchful of individuals who "hide out" in recovery by becoming so involved that they avoid other life issues. Twelve Step program involvement can become as addictive as any substance, and the co-recoverees can be as enabling, in this addiction, as any friend or spouse of an addict.

I close this section with an example of a person whom I assisted in his early recovery. This individual focused primarily on developing a strong recovery program early in sobriety. He weathered calamity and now finds himself living a very useful and exciting life.

Matt

Matt was a mid-thirties family man with two children, a nice house, two cottages, and a great job with a good salary working for his father managing a large car dealership. Matt had gradually begun to drink and drug more and more in his late twenties and early thirties to where it was becoming a problem for him. He also was beginning to identify that he was gay. This awareness, coupled with his homophobic family and conservative living environment, resulted in his entertaining suicidal thoughts. Ultimately this led to several suicide attempts with subsequent hospitalization and treatment for chemical dependency. In his early recovery, he did not disclose his sexual orientation to anyone, but acted on it in clandestine anonymous sexual escapades. After his repeated drug and alcohol relapses, his wife filed for divorce. Matt began to attend gay AA groups in out-of-town cities and slowly became aware of others who had experiences similar to his. After about a year of sobriety, during which he focused on doing the Steps and developing his spiritual life, Matt quietly began to get involved in a gay parents group. He also started a gay AA group in his local town to increase his support network.

Shortly thereafter, while on a vacation far from home in San Francisco, Matt attended the annual Gay Pride Parade. Out of the several hundred thousand people at this event, he had the misfortune of running into his father's neighbor who promptly informed Matt's father what he saw. Matt was immediately fired from his well-paying job (which included losing his company car) and being denied contact with his children by his estranged wife.

To overcome this calamity, which occurred in his second year of recovery, Matt decided to return to school. He switched from his sales background to social work. He started both a student organization for gays and lesbians at his college, and a support group for gays and lesbians in his community which today helps hundreds of people with "coming out" (gay and lesbian self-acceptance) every year. Upon graduation from college, Matt secured a job with a nationally-based Gay/Lesbian political organization in Washington, D.C. and is today enjoying a very useful and productive life in recovery.

CLINICAL IMPLICATIONS

Applied spirituality is a very important part of the Twelve Step way of life. To assist their clients in appreciating and practicing applied spirituality, clinicians should consider doing the following things:

One, the clinician should encourage newcomers to engage in helpful "service-oriented" activities as early in recovery as is practical.

Two, the clinician can often utilize the quality and quantity of "service related" activities clients are engaged in as a sign of their commitment to recovery. Also, the clinician can leverage the heightened fear of relapse to motivate early recoverees towards involvement in the program.

Three, the clinician needs to be aware that many activities which may not be immediately linked to recovery are also useful and conducive to promoting a client's growth. Any activity which is done to benefit another person or the community is an act of spirituality.

Four, the clinician can teach newcomers that doing service-related activities is a path to self-esteem and developing self-worth.

Five, the clinician may want to have a list of activities that can be suggested to clients to do to benefit others, in the event clients don't believe they have any beneficial talents.

Six, the clinician may want to have a list of short-term activities to have their very early clients do, perhaps within an in-house Twelve Step meeting or therapy group. A separate list may be developed of activities which are more long-term in focus that more advanced newcomers can engage in. These longer term commitments may encompass the community-at-large and everyday life-related activities.

REFERENCES

Alcoholics Anonymous. (1969). *The AA service manual.* (1st ed.). New York: AA World Services, Inc.

Alcoholics Anonymous. (1976). *Alcoholics Anonymous.* (3rd ed.). New York: AA World Services, Inc.

Alcoholics Anonymous. (1962) *Twelve concepts for world service.* (1st ed.). New York: AA World Services, Inc.

Alcoholics Anonymous. (1952, 1953, 1981) *Twelve steps and twelve traditions.* New York: AA World Services, Inc.

A.A. Grapevine. (1951). This is the story of Dr. Bob. *AA Grapevine, 8*(1), 10-44.

Kus, R.J. (1992). Spirituality in everyday life: Experiences of gay men of Alcoholics Anonymous. *Journal of Chemical Dependency Treatment, 5*(1), 49-66.

Peck, M. Scott. (1978). *The road less traveled.* (1st ed.). New York: Simon and Shuster, Inc.

Robertson, N. (1989). *Getting better: Inside Alcoholics Anonymous.* (1st ed.). New York: Ballantine Books.

Spirituality, Art Therapy, and the Chemically Dependent Person

Mary Ann Miller, RN, CARN, BLS

SUMMARY. Art therapy is a fascinating and powerful tool found helpful in the treatment of alcoholism and other forms of chemical dependency. After defining what art therapy is, the author discusses the value of art therapy for the chemically dependent client. Finally, the author discusses how art therapy is used in the Chemical Dependency Center at The University of Iowa Hospitals and Clinics to help clients explore their spirituality. *[Single or multiple copies of this article are available from The Haworth Document Delivery Service: 1-800-342-9678, 9:00 a.m. - 5:00 p.m. (EST).]*

Addiction–when confronted, brings a person face-to-face with his or her own dark side–the capacity for the horrible and destructive. Creativity requires living in the tensions of the opposites, while addiction seduces us by promising to take the tensions away. Addiction is linear, a progressive, degenerative disease; but, creativity is regenerative and cyclical, a process of death and rebirth. (Leonard, 1989, p. 6)

Mary Ann Miller is currently the head nurse of the Chemical Dependency Center at The University of Iowa Hospitals and Clinics. In addition to being a Certified Addictions Registered Nurse, Ms. Miller has been conducting art therapy groups at the Chemical Dependency Center for the past ten years under the supervision of her teacher and mentor, Janie Rhyne, PhD, ATR.

Address correspondence to: Ms. Mary Ann Miller, RN, Chemical Dependency Center, The University of Iowa Hospitals and Clinics, Iowa City, IA 52242.

[Haworth co-indexing entry note]: "Spirituality, Art Therapy, and the Chemically Dependent Person." Miller, Mary Ann. Co-published simultaneously in *Journal of Chemical Dependency Treatment* (The Haworth Press, Inc.) Vol. 5, No. 2, 1995, pp. 135-144; and: *Spirituality and Chemical Dependency* (ed: Robert J. Kus) The Haworth Press, Inc., 1995, pp. 135-144; and: *Spirituality and Chemical Dependency* (ed: Robert J. Kus) Harrington Park Press, an imprint of The Haworth Press, Inc., 1995, pp. 135-144. Single or multiple copies of this article are available from The Haworth Document Delivery Service [1-800-342-9678, 9:00 a.m. - 5:00 p.m. (EST).

© 1995 by The Haworth Press, Inc. All rights reserved.

135

As Linda Leonard has so aptly stated in her book, *Witness to the Fire: Creativity and the Veil of Addiction* (1989), addicted persons have spent a great deal of time viewing life from their dark side, using any innate creative force in pursuing a chemical. Because it helps people work toward the light and shift the creative force toward a rebirth and a different way of seeing, art therapy is a useful tool in the area of spirituality.

A DEFINITION

Art therapy can be defined as "the creation of visual art work for the purpose of healing or personal growth by individuals and the visual and verbal sharing of the resultant art work in a group setting" (Kus and Miller, 1992, p. 393). Healing and personal growth are aided by an increase in spiritual awareness, and sharing in a group has numerous benefits.

ART THERAPY
AND THE CHEMICALLY DEPENDENT CLIENT

In her book *The Gestalt Art Experience*, art therapist Janie Rhyne states that the value of art therapy as a counseling tool includes the following:

1. A vehicle for non-verbal communication.
2. The facilitation of fantasy.
3. Sharpened visual perception.
4. Recognition of emotional states.
5. The development of alternative forms of expression.
6. Breaking rigid patterns.
7. Saying forbidden things.
8. An increase in self-understanding.
9. Recognition and resolution of routine anxieties.
10. Explorations of time, space and community.
11. Explorations with relationships.
12. Play. (1984, p. 10)

Specifically for the chemically dependent person, each of the above has a particular emphasis. As a vehicle for communication, art, in contrast to other group work including Alcoholics or Narcotics Anonymous, provides a way to explore oneself without having to speak. Although most patients show an increase in participation in group work as treatment progresses, initially most people are very frightened by exposure. Thus, even at the outset of treatment, art can be a safe way to communicate.

Art work is a way to explore one's fantasies. Often these expressions come from dreams and the unconscious, and they can provide a background for validation or be presented as a dichotomy to help the patient view the reality of the idea expressed.

Sharpened visual perception helps one to see. Art becomes an exercise in showing what is real. While people are chemically intoxicated, their vision becomes blurred; thus, a means of seeing clearly enhances a clearing of all the senses and helps the patient connect with reality. As art therapist Peggy Papp states:

> The major goal of therapy, as of art, is to change a basic perception so that one sees differently. Through the introduction of the novel or unexpected, a frame of reference is broken and the structure of reality is rearranged. (1984, p. 22)

Because of numbing-out through chemicals, the recognition of emotion is often overwhelming to patients. Feelings hit as explosions until a balance can be achieved through time and sobriety. Art seems to evoke emotions one may not be aware of or to have allowed oneself to be in touch with on a conscious level. Most addicted persons have coped through numbing-out for many years, so the recovering person's emotional life is no small area to explore. It is very useful for the therapist to validate the individual's feelings and assure the patient that feelings are neither right nor wrong. They are universal, human, and ancient.

> With the integration of the arts and therapy, psychotherapists are harking back to the most ancient and time-validated methods of healing. . . . Art allows for the expression of inner chaos and pain through a reassuring external order. The arts bring creative action to psychotherapy and break expressive bound-

> aries. The full physical catharsis of the body and the more varied and far-reaching communication of artworks penetrate previously inexpressible places in people and further total expression and total perception. (McNiff, 1981, p. 113)

If a patient has been out of control when feelings erupt, intoxicated or not, art can be one method of control. As an example, one can draw or knead clay as a mean of working through anger or anxiety. Many patients have other talents which art group evokes such as creative writing, playing a musical instrument and dance. These skills can be encouraged as a means of expression and control and as a way to feel better without reaching for a chemical. Art can, in this way, help to break patterns of rigidity and serve as an option or alternative activity.

> Thus, the expressive therapies of art, dance, drama, music, and poetry have an essential unity and complement each other in practice. In our work as psychotherapists, we find that people have different expressive styles with strengths and weaknesses. One person will be more visual, while another will emphasize the kinesthetic or verbal modalities. (McNiff, 1981, p. viii)

Denial as a part of the illness of chemical dependency can be very powerful. Besides the denial of addiction, there is often also a denial of feelings and guilt from acting against one's values as the illness progresses. Individuals often have secrets and shame to bear which if they do not confront, will keep them vulnerable to the power of hidden secrets and shame. Art work often uncovers these hidden feelings of shame and guilt and brings them into the present to be dealt with openly. Regarding self-expression, McNiff (1981) says:

> Expressive action with objects may allow for the venting of emotions that would either be too threatening or inappropriate to act out in a situation other than a therapeutic dramatization. One of the great advantages of the arts in therapy is that they allow for the cathartic expression of anger, fear, and painful memories through all of the senses, thus maximizing the

effects of expulsion. For the person who cannot directly communicate threatening feelings through language, the nonverbal arts provide an opportunity for their expression in a less intimidating form. (p. xiv)

As a means to explore time, space, sense of community and relationships, art provides a way to arrange symbols of these issues in ways that are meaningful to the individual. Time and space can be seen more clearly if events are drawn on paper to punctuate years of living. Past, present, and future can be studied through life events. Through working together with others in treatment, both the treatment and global communities can be looked at as well as the outside community of which the individual is a part.

Chemically dependent people often need to secure tools to help fill their time when they would otherwise have been involved with buying or using their chemicals. In treatment, patients are exposed to some alternatives through recreation, music, and art therapy. Art work in particular can be done simply for fun. Many patients are amused that they are using scissors, paste, and crayons for the first time since kindergarten. It helps them get into the child-like portion of themselves and enjoy. It is permission to be creative and to have fun. Most chemically dependent people have not enjoyed life in a sober way or without chemicals being the priority in a long while before coming to treatment. If they grew up in an alcoholic home or a home with other stresses, childhood was a myth that other children lived. Not having to be perfect to be validated and having permission to be messy also helps to decrease the rigidity, extremism, and compulsivity exhibited by most clients.

According to Kinney and Leaton (1982), *psychological needs* that must be satisfied before an addicted person can learn new coping skills include:

1. The need to share thoughts and feelings with other persons who are accepting and understanding.
2. The need to feel competent by gaining recognition from others.
3. The need to know one belongs and is united with others in some way.

4. The need for affection and assurance that someone really cares.
5. The need for pleasurable nourishment that comes through the senses.

It would appear that art work provides all of the above.

To create a safe environment and promote interest, the therapist needs to state certain *expectations*:

1. Anything is acceptable and one cannot be wrong. There should be an unstructured feel to the work.
2. The therapist is there to help, but will not be analyzing the work. The patient shares what the art means to him or her.
3. The work does not have to be perfect. The patient is taking some risks so this would not be a time for perfection and control.
4. The main focus is on the process, not the finished product. The therapist should state that the main goal is for each person to express in an individual way.
5. To alleviate the fear of exposure, emphasis should be made that the therapist considers everyone to be an artist, not just those people labeled as artists and whose work is displayed in museums. Ways in which people create can be discussed—cooking, sewing, carpentry, fixing machines, raising children, choosing clothing, surviving life. This discussion can help to demystify the arts as elitist and removed from daily living. Fear can also be decreased by sharing previous patients' work on the same project.

There is an increase in self-esteem due to completing a work of art of one's own creation. The idea of a success and completion rather than failure and quitting is realized. Displaying the work on the unit bulletin boards where clients have a constant reminder of their accomplishments validates their work. Upon discharge clients may take their work home with them and continue to learn from it.

THE UNIVERSITY OF IOWA PROGRAM

At the University of Iowa Hospitals and Clinics Chemical Dependency Center, art therapy group is held weekly in two sessions. The first session includes the establishment of rapport and the introduction of the assignment. This session lasts approximately one hour. Patients begin to work on the assignment which is due three days later. They are allowed to work in the privacy of their own room, outdoors, or wherever they feel comfortable. Three days later, the patients are divided into small groups, and each patient presents his or her project to the group.

Since clients on our inpatient unit stay approximately three weeks, there are three art projects completed as part of their plan of care: (1) A self-image/identity project, (2) A family/relationship project, and (3) A spirituality project. The three projects are quite different assignments, but do overlap at times. Although I view all three as spiritual, I will focus here on the specific spirituality project assigned.

Because our treatment program is based on the Alcoholics and Narcotics Anonymous philosophy and is holistic in nature, *spirituality* is a major area of focus from admission through discharge. During the initial assessment, patients are asked about their spiritual, ethnic, and cultural background and where they see themselves at this point in their lives. They are then given a one page spirituality questionnaire which they complete on their own. The questionnaire asks about their past and present spiritual background and practices. They are also asked if they feel any anger towards their spirituality and where they are in the process of self-forgiveness. This information is then used to help formulate their treatment plan and, if indicated, becomes part of their master problem list. Each client then participates in counseling groups regarding spirituality, has an opportunity to attend church and visit with clergy, completes spirituality art group, and attends four AA or NA meetings per week. To monitor for change during treatment, a second questionnaire is given near the end of treatment to obtain input and validate our program in this area. Ninety percent (90%) of patients state that art group increased their spiritual awareness.

The *goals* of spirituality art group are (1) To begin to become aware of one's own personal spirituality, and (2) To begin to define and relate to a Higher Power. To work in this area, patients are asked to create a project that portrays their personal spirituality.

Thomas Moore, in his book *Care of the Soul* (1992), says:

In our spirituality, we reach for consciousness, awareness, and the highest value; in our soulfulness, we endure the most pleasurable and the most exhausting of human experiences and emotions. These two dimensions make up the fundamental pulse of human life and to an extent, they have an attraction to each other. (p. 10)

He also says that spirituality is not religion and that the soul is always in process so it is "difficult to pin down with definition or a fixed meaning."

To help patients focus and to dispel the rather prevalent rationalization that if one doesn't believe in God one can't work the AA/NA program, my approach is to be as open and permission-giving as possible. A client cannot be wrong in this group because there is no one "correct" answer.

I give each client a handout of an article I found in LIFE magazine in December 1988, entitled, "The Meaning of Life." In it are short paragraphs of what forty people, some famous, some not, have to say on the subject. I ask them to read it for inspiration.

I explain briefly about a few *cultures and religions* of the world and their view of things spiritual. I offer them the opportunity to view the Joseph Campbell-Bill Moyer video on "The Power of Myth" and Bill Moyer's video "Amazing Grace."

I ask them to think about the *close calls* they have had in their lives. Since addicted persons are very often risk-takers, they are aware of this. I ask them to think about why they are still here after driving intoxicated, surviving accidents, over-dosing, living on the streets, and engaging in self-destructive behaviors. In general, I find most addicted persons in the group have "lived on the edge," but they often are very fearful of death and quite superstitious.

I ask them to think of *dreams* as a source of spiritual information. Some patients have had repetitious dreams over their lifetime, and some receive messages. Many patients speak of having a guardian angel, usually a grandmother who watches over them. A few relate out-of-body experiences when near death.

I ask them to think of the *rituals* they planned and observed while using, for example: certain music, certain places, certain times of day, special ways they laid out their "works." I suggest to them that their chemical use was their Higher Power; the ritualistic aspects of using were similar to the ritual used in religious ceremonies.

We speak about the loss, shame, and guilt addicts may feel because of not living their value systems due to using chemicals; we explore how important it is to work on forgiveness of self. As Royce (1987) has noted, chemical dependency affects one's values and behaviors in a very negative way. We speak of the loss and grieving of giving up their chemical itself and the void this creates. We also explore the idea that because their addictive past has presented them with the "dark side" of life, they can, in recovery, come to know the "light side" of life, to experience rebirth and serenity. In fact, we discuss that the joy and peace which recovering persons experience are often far richer and more intense than that experienced by those who have not known the destructive side of life.

I offer the patients many kinds of *art supplies*: papers, pencils, glue, scissors, paints, and magazines to make collages. I also offer opportunity to use "found objects" and to go outdoors to gather materials such as stones, leaves, flowers, and the like to build a project.

When the projects are completed and we *process in group*, I make a point of asking what type of religious background they may have had if they have had one. This is mainly a way to facilitate sharing and for the group to know each other better. If not evident from their project, I ask what Higher Power means for them when they attend AA or NA meetings. I document their answers in the medical record for reference. At the end of the group, I talk about the Serenity Prayer. I do this because over the ten years I have done the spirituality art group, I would estimate that only two patients a year refer to it in their art projects. I find this of interest since the prayer is in many recovery books, talked about at AA/NA meetings, read at the beginning of each treatment day, and posted about the unit. I have no answer to this puzzle.

Patients' projects over the years have been varied and beautiful. Atheists have done a variety of spirituality projects including drawing a monkey holding a Christian Bible, a large black void, and the like. Despite a non-belief in a God, atheist clients do believe in some type of concept of Higher Power, even if this power is an AA group, a set of values, or a sponsor. Also many self-defined atheists often come to believe in more traditional concepts of God as they experience recovery. The majority of our patients have a Christian background, but some patients have adopted the religion of Islam. We have a small percentage of Native Americans who tell us stories about the Great Spirit. Besides drawing, painting, and making collages out of magazines, patients have built churches out of cardboard, crosses out of tongue blades, mobiles out of coat hangers, and several have gathered objects from nature and put together beautiful living gardens.

In 1992, I gathered data on fifty spirituality art projects to see if there was any pattern or common definition of Higher Power. I evaluated each of the fifty projects and computed that 24% had chosen mountains as a symbol of their Higher Power. From this convenience-sample study, I concluded that "nature" is the most common choice to symbolize their Higher Power within our patient population, a population made up primarily of urban white men whose average age is twenty-seven years.

I often say, "A picture is worth a thousand words," so to write about art projects is a difficult task. Suffice it to say, it is often a spiritually uplifting experience to view addicted persons' view of the mystery. It gives me great satisfaction that ninety percent of our patients feel that art group increases their awareness of their personal spirituality. It certainly increases mine.

REFERENCES

Kinney, J., & Leaton, G. (1982). *Understanding alcohol*. St. Louis: C.V. Mosby Company

Kus, R.J., & Miller, M.A. (1992). Art therapy. In G.M. Bulechek & J.C. McCloskey (Eds.), *Nursing interventions: Essential nursing treatments* (2nd ed.) (pp. 392-402). Philadelphia: W.B. Saunders.

Leonard, L. (1989). *Witness to the Fire: Creativity and the veil of addiction.* Boston: Shambhala Publications, Inc.

McNiff, S. (1981). *The Arts and psychotherapy.* Springfield, IL: Charles C.Thomas.

Moore, T. (1992). *Care of the soul.* New York, NY: Harper Collins Publishers, Inc.

Papp, P. (1984, September-October). *The links between clinical and artistic creativity. Networker,* pp. 20-28.

Rhyne, J. (1984). *The Gestalt art experience.* Chicago, IL: Magnolia Street Publishers.

Royce, J. (1987). *The spiritual progression chart.* Center City, MN: Hazelden.

Music Therapy, Spirituality
and Chemically Dependent Clients

Joey Walker, MA, RMT-BC

SUMMARY. The purpose of this article is to discuss music therapy and how it can be used with the chemically dependent population. The article includes (a) a definition, examples, and an overview of music therapy, (b) rationale and benefits gained from using music as a therapeutic tool, (c) specific music therapy techniques such as songwriting, lyric analysis, music movement and relaxation, and creativity through music which can be used to help with spirituality issues, and (d) recommendations for clinicians who are not music therapists. *[Single or multiple copies of this article are available from The Haworth Document Delivery Service: 1-800-342-9678, 9:00 a.m. - 5:00 p.m. (EST).]*

DEFINITION OF MUSIC THERAPY

According to "Music Therapy as a Career" (1993), a brochure from the National Association for Music Therapy, Inc., music therapy is:

> an allied health profession in which music is used within a therapeutic relationship to address physical, psychological,

Joey Walker is a music therapist at The University of Iowa Hospitals and Clinics. In addition to working with chemically dependent clients, she also sees patients in the general hospital as well as in adult and child psychiatry.

Address correspondence to: Ms. Joey Walker, Activities Therapy, The University of Iowa Hospitals and Clinics, 2701 C-JPT, 200 Hawkins Drive, Iowa City, IA 52242 USA.

[Haworth co-indexing entry note]: "Music Therapy, Spirituality, and Chemically Dependent Clients." Walker, Joey. Co-published simultaneously in *Journal of Chemical Dependency Treatment* (The Haworth Press, Inc.) Vol. 5, No. 2, 1995, pp. 145-166; and: *Spirituality and Chemical Dependency* (ed: Robert J. Kus) The Haworth Press, Inc., 1995, pp. 145-166; and: *Spirituality and Chemical Dependency* (ed: Robert J. Kus) Harrington Park Press, an imprint of The Haworth Press, Inc., 1995 pp. 145-166. Single or multiple copies of this article are available from The Haworth Document Delivery Service [1-800-342-9678, 9:00 a.m. - 5:00 p.m. (EST)].

© 1995 by The Haworth Press, Inc. All rights reserved. *145* cognitive, and social needs of individuals. After assessing the strengths and needs of each client, the qualified music therapist provides the indicated treatment including creating, singing, moving to, and/or listening to music. Through musical involvement in the therapeutic context, clients' abilities are strengthened and transferred to other areas of their lives.

In simpler terms, music therapy is the practice of using music to work toward other nonmusical goals. The emphasis in music therapy is on the therapy, while the music is a tool to help an individual change nonmusical behaviors. To illustrate this point, some examples are presented here.

Examples of How Music Therapy Can Be Used Effectively

Music therapy can be used with groups or individuals of all ages. Music is an important part of our culture, and almost everyone relates to music in some manner. Music can be a non-threatening medium to use to work toward goals. For example:

1. Music can be used to teach academics or other skills. A developmentally disabled client may be unable to distinguish when it is appropriate to hug people and may go out in public and attempt to hug anyone. Learning and memorizing a song that goes "When we meet people we shake hands, shake hands, shake hands, etc." may assist the client to generalize his shaking hands behavior to public situations. Just as we learned our "ABC's" to music when we were children, it is often easier to remember concepts when they are put to melodies and/or rhythm.

2. Music can stimulate memories of past events and it is used with the elderly to assist in communicating about events which are happening now and in the past. People with dementia who may not be communicating or may have no idea where they are, may be able to sing or sit down and play the piano or dance with their spouse to familiar music of their young adulthood.

3. Music is often used for expression of feelings, to improve self-esteem and to elevate mood. Patients who are hospitalized for long periods, especially those in isolation, may be able to learn a new skill such as playing the guitar or keyboard. Although one goal may be learning to play the guitar, the music therapist probably has

additional goals in mind. The patient may have a change of appearance during hospitalization due to medication, illness or surgery and may have greater issues with self-esteem. Being able to learn a new skill, have an outlet for expression, and gain a new leisure activity may elevate mood and self-esteem.

4. Music is social in nature–people attend concerts, dances, play instruments together, or sing in choirs or groups. For some clients with psychiatric problems, isolation can be an issue. After sessions with a music therapist, a client may continue to attend musical gatherings in his or her community and gain a sense of belonging.

These are only a few examples of how music can work toward the best quality of life for each client. In addition to serving individuals with developmental, physical or emotional disabilities, music therapists also are employed in rehabilitation centers, hospice programs, correctional facilities, halfway houses, university settings, outpatient clinics, adult day care centers, schools, oncology treatment centers, pain/stress management clinics and in private practice.

OVERVIEW OF MUSIC THERAPY

Although music and the treatment of illness have been associated since the beginning of recorded history, modern music therapy has its roots in the Veterans Administration (VA) Hospitals. After World War II, volunteer musicians calmed, comforted and entertained wounded soldiers and found music to be an effective way to reach patients when other strategies had been unsuccessful (Rosenfeld, 1985). From the VA Hospitals, music therapy expanded to other settings. In the mid to late 1940s, music therapy courses and curricula were developed at several universities. By 1950 the National Association for Music Therapy, Inc. was formed, establishing guidelines and standards of practice for the field of music therapy.

Currently there are approximately 75 undergraduate and 20 graduate degree programs in music therapy across the United States. The undergraduate curriculum consists of coursework in "music therapy, psychology, music, biological, social and behavioral sciences, disabling conditions and general studies" (NAMT, 1993). In addition to coursework, students practice music therapy techniques through field work in a variety of facilities. After coursework is completed, a six-month internship is required "in an approved mental health, special education, or health care facility" (NAMT, 1993).

Following completion of academic and clinical training, students are eligible for registration as a Registered Music Therapist (RMT) by the National Association for Music Therapy, Inc., or as a Certified Music Therapist (CMT) by the American Association for Music Therapy. A CMT or RMT is then eligible for the board certification examination which is administered by the Certification Board for Music Therapists, Inc. As of 1990, there were approximately 3,650 music therapists practicing in the United States (Davis, Gfeller, and Thaut, 1992).

RATIONALE AND BENEFITS GAINED FROM USING MUSIC AS A THERAPEUTIC TOOL

Music can be a powerful force in changing our emotions. Goldstein (1980) found the most common way in which people have sudden changes in emotion or "thrills" is in response to music. People described chills, goosebumps, a lump in the throat, tingling and weeping as responses to certain favorite music. Other thrills mentioned less often than music were: a scene in a movie, play, ballet or book, great beauty in nature or art, physical contact with another person, sexual activity, and other various stimuli (Rosenfeld, 1985). Because music can change emotions, it can be used with chemically dependent clients to demonstrate a non-chemical way to help them feel differently. Examples of specific techniques for using music to alter mood are given in the following section.

Certain music can also be a trigger for relapse. If clients used their drug of choice listening to a particular song or style of music, when it is used in a music therapy session, strong reactions can occur. The music therapist has observed clients shaking, sweating, and displaying other outward signs of anxiety in response to certain music. Clients state that they are "jonesin" or really wanting to use their drug of choice. When asked what they can do when this happens, at times they reply, "I don't know." A discussion takes place and feedback is given by peers about ways to get through a craving. In this way, clients are actually experiencing a trigger, problem solving and receiving support and assistance instead of merely talking about what may be a trigger after discharge.

This is one example of the effectiveness of music with chemically dependent clients, who may tend to intellectualize as a way of avoidance. Again, music has a way of getting down to the feeling level and helps the client to speak from the heart, not the head. Music therapy can help clients experience painful feelings and emotions which have been suppressed. Many times these feelings are just too painful, so the client pushes them down so far that he or she may just feel numb. Music can help intensify these feelings and bring them to the surface to be identified. Frequently clients display tears, nervousness, blushing, or even laughter in response to music. This expression of feelings is encouraged in treatment, but clients also discover it is socially acceptable to release feelings to music.

Another benefit of music is its versatility. Almost everyone relates to some type of music at some time in his or her life. Music can be enjoyed by being an active music maker or by passively listening. Since music is also social in nature, clients are encouraged to interact with each other in a variety of ways. They may sing or play instruments together, work together in a songwriting project, compare memories to certain music, self-disclose thoughts and feelings to music, move or dance to music, or actively listen to a song someone has written about sobriety. Clients are also encouraged to continue enjoyable, sober musical leisure events after discharge. Attending AA dances or free concerts, learning to play a social instrument or listening to music for pleasure or to change mood are all positive uses of leisure time. In addition, the versatility of musical styles is incorporated in music therapy groups, since no one type of music will please a group of people. In this way, clients are asked to keep an open mind. They may dislike the music itself, but they are encouraged to take something meaningful away with them such as the words, a phrase or message, feedback from a peer, or a memory.

SPECIFIC MUSIC THERAPY TECHNIQUES
TO ASSIST WITH SPIRITUALITY ISSUES

Spirituality

Although there are many definitions of spirituality, here it will be viewed broadly as "one's relationship in three areas: (1) with the universe, (2) with other people, and (3) with one's self" (Whitfield, 1984 p. 14). The concept of "Higher Power" is incorporated into the relationship with the universe. Spirituality encompasses "both solitude and corporate life, including the way one thinks, acts, and feels in every circumstance. In essence, it has to do with the whole of our lives"(Nagai-Jacobson and Burkhardt, 1989, p. 19).

Because spirituality includes how we think, act and feel, for the chemically dependent client this may include many negative characteristics as well as other blocks to recovery. Egocentricity, grandiosity, low frustration tolerance, the inability to listen to others, rigidity, problems with interpersonal skills, low self-esteem, denial, demand for control and general resistance may block the path to spiritual growth (Carroll, 1991; Milliken, 1990; Whitfield, 1984).

POSITIVE ATTITUDE, OPEN MIND,
AND WILLINGNESS TO LEARN OR GROW

Because of these blocks and resistance, it is necessary for the clients to begin each music therapy group with a positive attitude, an open mind and a willingness to learn or to grow. Whitfield (1984) believes, "Of all the spiritual practices available to us, one of the most powerful is thinking positively" (p. 14). According to Alcoholics Anonymous (1976), willingness and open-mindedness are essential to recovery, and "a positive attitude opens vast possibilities for healing" (Stuart, Deckro and Mandle, 1989).

It is helpful for the clients to remember these concepts by using a mnemonic device: "POW." The letter "P" is for positive, the letter "O" is for open mind, and the letter "W" is for willingness. Using "POW" makes it easier to remember and put into practice for patients who are having short term memory problems related to their drug use. If a client tends to look at "POW" as meaning prisoner of war, other peers or the music therapist will check to see if the client is using a positive attitude or an open mind, etc. In addition to "POW," Carroll (1991) believes spiritual growth begins with "an emphasis upon self-honesty, patience, tolerance, kindness and humility" (p. 298). Utilizing "POW" with these concepts during discussions and actually experiencing and practicing the concepts in music therapy help the clients generalize behavior to other situations. Examples are explained in the next section.

USING MOVEMENT TO CHANGE MOOD AND REINFORCE OPEN-MINDEDNESS

Many times in music therapy sessions the clients are unwilling to try new things. This may be due to low self-esteem, or the need for perfectionism or control, or merely resistive behavior. However, when the music therapist asks the clients to form a circle and stand, many are genuinely threatened by the possibility of "having to dance" even though the word "dance" is never used. When clients are standing and waiting, not knowing what they will be required to do, they each must describe how they are feeling and this is written on the board. Common feelings expressed by the clients are: confusion, curiosity, nervousness, apprehensiveness, wondering, tiredness, numbness, uneasiness, tension, and fear.

Next, each client is asked to think of a small, appropriate movement that everyone in the group will be able to do. For example, someone may snap their fingers, another person might turn around, another might swing their hips. Everyone will have a different movement, and we will go around the circle and everyone will do each person's movement for a short time. Clients are able to be quite creative with their movements. Music with a steady, up tempo beat such as Phil Collins' *I Can't Dance* or Boyz II Men's *Motown-philly* is then added. Next, we will do each person's movement for eight beats to the music and go around the circle two times, followed by the same for only four beats, then two beats. By this time, people are having to concentrate and think about the movements they are trying to do, making mistakes and laughing with each other. People are warmed up and the group is generally quite cohesive. After this, other music movement games are played, or props are added to make moving easier for the clients. This may last for approximately twenty minutes and may be quite aerobic. Everyone sits down and again describes how they are feeling. Common feelings expressed post-movement include: energized, better, good, fun, silly, not tired, relaxed, calm, pumped, more positive, relieved, and ready to try it again.

A discussion follows the description of feelings. The clients are asked to compare the two lists of feelings on the board. Usually they say that after the movement the feelings are better or more upbeat and positive. Next, they are asked what contributed to the change of feelings and mood. Common answers listed are: the music, moving around, laughing, everyone participating, working together, having fun, getting our minds off our problems, and physical exercise. We discuss what types of activities the clients are going to do for fun in their leisure time post-discharge, along with problem-solving how to actually follow through and do leisure activities.

This leads to a discussion of the blocks clients may have for attending AA or NA meetings. Often it seems that actually getting to the meeting appears to be the difficulty. After the meeting they feel better, just as they did after the movement was over. The clients discover that before any new activity or meeting that the feelings of fear, confusion, nervousness and curiosity are normal. If they follow through and go to a meeting or activity, they will likely feel the more positive feelings and generally feel better. They encourage each other to participate and work together to get to meetings just as they worked together during the movement activity. Clients will often say, "I thought that music therapy was going to be stupid and I didn't want to go. But it was fun and you helped me change my outlook. Now I will give things a chance before making a judgment."

One client named Rob recently made a negative call to his girlfriend right before the music therapy movement group. He initially stated he was in a "lousy mood" and had fought with his girlfriend about nothing that mattered, and he had "tried to make her feel bad and guilty." After moving around with the group, during the discussion he talked about the angry phone call and stated, "I wish I could make that phone call now, because it would be a lot different." He stated he saw how he could change his mood by using music or physical exercise, talking with others, or doing something enjoyable instead of trying to "make everyone else feel as bad as I do."

MUSIC AND RELAXATION

Just as music can help clients become energized and feel better, it can also be used to help calm them down and relax. This is extremely important for clients because the beginning of recovery is particularly stressful. Whitfield (1984) states in the first 30 days of abstention from chemicals the "person often feels no relief from feeling stressed" (p. 11).

Although no one style of music will work for every person, generally slow, soft instrumental music tends to lower heart rate, blood pressure and respiration (Hodges, 1980). There are many recordings which are marketed to help people relax, such as environmental sounds paired with classical music, or specific New Age recordings geared toward relaxation.

Combining progressive muscle relaxation with guided imagery and music is a technique which has been successful with chemically dependent clients. After clients have tensed and relaxed muscle groups and have slowed their breathing, music is played, and then the music therapist may verbally guide the clients with soothing suggestions such as: "continue to concentrate on your breathing, your hands and feet are feeling very heavy, if any thoughts or worries come to your mind let them float back away from you, but remember them and talk with your counselor later, use this time to feel free and let all tensions go."

After finishing the procedure, the clients process what has taken place. Some clients are able to really feel relaxed, others may have been close to sleeping, and others may have had a spiritual experience. Rew (1989) states, "To become receptive to spiritual and intuitive truths, a person must first clear a pathway or channel for these truths to travel into conscious awareness" (p. 61). This pathway may become clear to a client while being in a non-chemical altered state of consciousness in music therapy relaxation techniques sessions.

Again, the actual experience of altering mood is processed in the group and clients appear receptive to practicing the technique. They discuss using relaxation techniques to get through cravings or especially tough times in relationships and also to help those who have difficulty with getting to sleep or insomnia. It is important for clients to actually experience non-chemical ways to change mood.

LYRIC ANALYSIS

Lyric analysis is a technique used in music therapy to stimulate thoughts and feelings. It works quite well with the chemically dependent population because clients can identify with stories and feelings demonstrated through song lyrics. Clients are also familiar with a lot of music because most bars and lounges have a juke box, live music or karaoke, and music usually has a large role in "partying." Not all clients relate to the *same* type of music, but most relate to *some* type of music. Thus in order for clients to be able to relate their thoughts and feelings about themselves to the group, a wide variety of music is used for lyric analysis. The goal of lyric analysis is not to intellectualize or interpret what the song is about, but to stimulate and help intensify and identify feelings of the clients so they are able to express themselves, possibly in a way they would be unable to do in a more traditional verbal therapy situation.

Music and lyrics can help stimulate memories of painful and joyful past events that clients have forgotten due to denial or use of chemicals. Because music is often associated with meaningful life events, it can take us right back to the moment and help us feel the emotions we felt at that time. Most people have songs from their youth which are associated with first love, graduations, wedding ceremonies, funerals or other social or spiritual activities.

Some clients relate to the actual music itself, while others concentrate on the lyrics. Feelings are intensified with the music, which makes them easier for the clients to identify and then discuss. Lyric analysis also gives the clients something concrete from which to base their thoughts. They can hold the song lyrics in their hands while listening to the music. Less confident or shy clients may feel more comfortable contributing to the discussion when they can relate their feelings to actual lyrics on paper.

A music therapist will select a song for lyric analysis for specific reasons. For example, clients may need education or help with certain issues such as anger management, assertiveness training, emotional needs or self-esteem. A song will gain the interest of the clients, a discussion will take place, specific steps are reviewed to help deal with the issues, and then something experiential will take place to reinforce concepts gained from the session.

Examples of Lyric Analysis

1. If the topic for discussion is anger management, music such as *The Living Years* by Mike Rutherford and B. A. Robertson, performed by Mike and the Mechanics, might be used to stimulate client's contributions. This song can elicit sadness as well as feelings of anger or "unfinished business" in personal relationships. One client talked about this song being played at his young son's funeral, another discussed how his best friend died in his arms after a drug related accident, and this song was also used at his funeral. Many clients relate to this song because they cannot seem to resolve continuous conflicts with a significant other in their lives.

A portion of *The Living Years* follows (used by permission):

> You say you just don't see it he says it's perfect sense
> You just can't get agreement in this present tense
> We all talk a different language talking in defense
>
> Say it loud say it clear you can listen as well as you hear
> It's too late when we die to admit we don't see eye to eye
>
> So we open up a quarrel between the present and the past
> We only sacrifice the future it's the bitterness that lasts . . .
>
> I wasn't there that morning when my father passed away
> I didn't get to tell him all the things I had to say
> I think I caught his spirit later that same year
> I'm sure I heard his echo in my baby's new born tears
> I just wish I could have told him in the living years

After discussing our feelings, specific steps to help deal with anger are introduced by the music therapist. Clients are asked to role play situations, and are asked to practice concepts learned before the next session. Frequently clients practice the following four questions (Rosellini and Worden, 1985, p.74).

1. What am I feeling?
2. Why am I feeling this way?
3. What can I do about it?
4. What am I *going* to do about it?

2. Another song which has proven useful for discussing how to "fight fairly" or become more assertive, instead of aggressive, is Garth Brooks' *We Bury the Hatchet.* The lyrics depict how people tend to continue to bring up issues from past unfinished arguments when they may be having a dispute about some unrelated issue in the present moment. Clients can discuss how to stay in the now while leaving the past and future out of disagreements. Other methods of "fair fighting" are introduced as found in Whitfield (1984) and Rosellini and Worden (1985).

3. If a session involves gaining insight into self-esteem, music such as *Big Shot* by Billy Joel, *Let Her Cry* by Hootie and the Blowfish, or Kris Kristofferson's *Sunday Morning Coming Down* might be employed. The clients or therapist would sing this song, or a recording might be used. A discussion would follow about self-esteem, and specific steps would again be practiced and talked about in subsequent sessions.

4. Another pertinent issue with clients is neglect of psychological needs. Kathy Mattea sings *Whole Lotta Holes* by Jon Vezner and Don Henry:

> I gotta whole lotta holes in my life I gotta whole lotta holes in my life
> If you stacked 'em all together you could fall in there forever
> Got a whole lotta holes in my life[1]

---

1. "TIME PASSES BY" Written by Jon Vezner and Susan Ruth Longacre Copyright© 1990 Sheddhouse Music (and as designated by co-publisher). Used by permission. All rights reserved.

A variety of "holes" are described in the lyrics, but we concentrate on plugging up the "holes" with the five emotional needs described in *Loosening the Grip* (Kinney and Leaton, 1983): (1) love and affection, (2) belonging, (3) achievement, (4) pleasure, and (5) acceptance and understanding. Clients problem-solve ways to obtain these needs and work toward spiritual growth. For example, a discussion about pleasure would involve talking about the little things clients enjoy, all the pleasures relished through the five senses. Clients are encouraged to appreciate these small pleasures because they will not have the huge swings between highs and lows as a result of chemicals. The discussion might end with the Huey Lewis song *I Want A New Drug*, or *I Will Not Take These Things for Granted* by Toad the Wet Sprocket, and clients will discuss how to be high on life or how to get the natural highs life has to offer.

SONGWRITING

Songwriting is an effective way for clients to express their feelings (Ficken, 1976; Freed, 1987). Clients are able to write their thoughts and feelings in place of lyrics to familiar music and are able to receive validation and support from peers and staff. After completing a songwriting task, one which initially clients feel they will be unable to do, they feel a sense of accomplishment. This may help the clients become more confident as well as improve self-esteem. Songwriting techniques vary, but a structured approach and a less structured method will be explained.

The Cloze Procedure (Fill in the Blank)

The cloze method of songwriting begins with a framework, and the clients fill in the places where there are blanks in the lyrics. The music therapist will write parts of the lyrics to "encourage people to describe themselves, identify feelings and needs, and reinforce knowledge gained in treatment" (Freed, 1987, p. 15). This is a structured approach which can be used with individuals or groups. In the following example, the italicized words were written by clients who filled in the blanks with their own ideas. The original

song, *Heart of Gold,* was written by Neil Young; the original lyrics
are not included below.

> I've been *a junkie* and I've been *a drunkard*
> I've always *been selfish in every way*
> I felt *confusion* whenever I *use*
> But now I'm *looking for a better way*
> 'Cause *life's a challenge*
> I want *to live a positive life*
> I'll have to *keep on working for sobriety*
>
> I need *ambition* I need *acceptance*
> I know I *have a long way to go*
> When I think back *the pain is plenty*
> But now I feel *though* it's the time to *try*
> I hope to *stay straight with my higher power*
> When I leave here I'll *be on my way*
> I'll use my time to *enjoy each and every day*

Changing Lyrics to Pre-Existing Melodies

Another approach to songwriting which is less structured
involves writing new verses to pre-existing melodies. This works
well with small groups of clients who need to interact and share
ideas and feelings. Working toward a common goal also promotes
unity and cohesiveness among group members. After clients have
written their songs, they may perform or the music therapist will
sing it. The lyrics are typed after the group, and during the next
session the songs will be sung and the lyrics will be discussed. The
following songs, *Edelweiss* from Rodgers and Hammerstein's musical *The Sound of Music,* and *You've Got a Friend* by Carole King,
were each written by four clients in approximately fifteen minutes.
The originals are not included.

Endless Lines (sung to the tune of *Edelweiss*)

Endless lines, endless lines
Every morning you greet me
Chunks of white big and bright

You seem happy to kill me
Flakes of snow may you forever
   go
And let me grow forever
Higher power, higher power
Bless my sobriety forever

You've Got a Friend (sung to the tune of *You've Got a Friend*)

When you're sick and troubled
And you feel like giving up

And there's no one, oh no one
   there to help
Close your bottle smash your pipe
And give your life to me
I'll be there to fulfill your every
   need

You just hold out your hand
And you know wherever I am
I'll come running and I'll
   understand
Anytime night or day
All you have to do is pray
And I'll be there yeah
   you got a friend

Writing Raps

Another less structured method of writing lyrics is to have the clients compose raps. This may be easier for the professional who is unable to sing or play an instrument to use in group sessions. Using an instrumental beat found on portable keyboards as an accompaniment, or having the clients make their own background sounds helps set the mood for rapping. Small groups of clients may write any number of lines of poetry, and then they may decide how to perform them. Clients are encouraged to create a "hook" for their rap–some short, catchy pattern which can be used as an introduction or background for someone rapping solo. For example, in the following rap the hook was, "I got my hearse in reverse."

> I got my hearse in reverse, I got my hearse in reverse
> Drinking, smoking, hitting the pipe trying to get out to find a
> new life
> I been through money, women, fancy cars if I don't get out I'll
> be behind bars
> Now I've got a new objective trying for a new perspective
> Every second, minute, every hour working with my higher
> power
> I got my hearse in reverse, I got my hearse in reverse

In addition to having a hook, another idea to make writing raps more effective is to have all clients participate with some pre-existing raps either written by former clients or the group leader. It is important for clients to see a concrete example before they begin interacting and composing their raps. Clients are encouraged to be as creative as possible, and many also add movements or sounds to their raps. Videotaping small groups of clients performing their raps helps to get the groups motivated and also gives the clients feedback on their body images and behaviors.

USING CREATIVITY TO ENHANCE TREATMENT

There are many references to the link between creativity and spirituality and the healing process (Burkhardt, 1989; Fisher, 1990; Nagai-Jacobson and Burkhardt, 1989; Whitfield, 1984). "If the creative process is defined as 'the process of change, of development, of evolution, in the organization of life' (Ghiselin, 1954), we can call the commitment to the First Step a creative process" (Fisher, 1990, p. 327). When we are creating, Ghiselin (1954) states that we tap into our unconscious.

Clients are able to see the importance of creativity when they try to problem-solve. They realize that talking to other people helps them eliminate tunnel vision, and helps them think of and open up to new ideas. For example, if a client was asked to write a song or do a movement by him or herself, it would be more threatening and harder to do than in a small group of peers. Clients become aware that trusting and relying on others for support is healthy and isolating themselves is counterproductive to sobriety.

Many clients feel they are not creative in any way. However, when they begin to think about what they actually do in their lives as creative, they often change their minds. Many clients fix motors without having the necessary parts, improvise new recipes when ingredients are unavailable, wear their clothing or hair a certain way, change their furniture around, etc. They also realize how they formerly used their creativity to manipulate other people, to make up excuses for being late or not showing up for work, to make drug paraphernalia out of everyday materials, and other negative ways of behaving. They say, "If we will only use one-hundredth of this creativity for the good, we will live so much better lives."

Playing Instruments, Making Tapes or Doing Variety Shows

Some other ways in which music therapy encourages creativity are: playing instruments, making music videos, making interview tapes and having a variety show. Clients are encouraged to play an instrument such as guitar or piano for relaxation and improvement of self-esteem, as long as it does not interfere with their treatment in any way. The music therapist will set up guitars and keyboards so that clients can play them successfully right away, and a group session may consist of playing and singing a song together, and then doing a lyric analysis on it.

Clients can also make music videos to songs which are treatment-related. These can become quite involved, as small groups of clients make props and costumes to add to their videos. After some rehearsal, each group is videotaped, and then the whole group comes together and watches the videos. These are sometimes a good indication of where the clients are in treatment, for some videos concentrate on the drug use itself, while others focus on positive or treatment issues.

Another way to foster creativity is to have the clients interview each other about treatment, only instead of having a peer answer a question, a part of a song is played for the answer. The questions are audiotaped by the client, and then the answers are recorded from familiar songs. For example:

Ken, what do you think about treatment?	*"Stairway to heaven"* . . . (Led Zeppelin)
Randy, what's your reaction to sobriety?	*"Joy to the world"* . . . (Three Dog Night)
Jack, how do you feel when you're drinking?	*"You had to be a big shot last night, oh"* . . . (Billy Joel)
What has drinking got you, Steve?	*"I ain't got nothin' but the blues"* . . . (Duke Ellington)
How do you feel about the AA steps, Gary?	*"Good, good, good, good vibrations"* . . . (The Beach Boys)
Sandy, what have your last five years been like?	*"Time in a bottle"* . . . (Jim Croce)
Kathy, what do you think AA and NA will do for you?	*"Give me something to believe in, that there's a Lord above, give me something to believe in"* . . . (Poison)

Again, what the focus of the questions include is an indication of how the clients are doing in treatment. Some clients refer to using drugs in the present or future, or are negative, arrogant or grandiose, or belittle others or treatment itself. Others are more positive as in the previous examples.

Another way to encourage clients to be creative is with a variety show. The word "talent" is not used at all. All clients have to participate in some way. Some clients read from the Big Book, others read poetry they have written, some tell jokes, clients may just tell their stories or why they are in treatment, others sing or play an instrument, put on skits, puppet shows, air bands, lip sync or do other appropriate things. Clients may get extremely creative with making props, such as instruments for an air band (a band of people playing imaginary or improvised instruments to recorded music). Clients have used garbage cans, lampshades, boxes and paper to construct elaborate trap sets for the drummers in air bands, and cardboard for saxophones, guitars or puppets for the show. The variety show is videotaped so the clients as well as the staff are able to watch. The clients say they "feel good" when they are able to create something like a song, a video or audio tape, an instrumental piece, a movement or something for the variety show.

RECOMMENDATIONS FOR OTHER PROFESSIONALS

A Process-Oriented Approach

Music therapy can help clients discover and deal with feelings as well as assist them with their spiritual growth. The emphasis in music therapy is on the word therapy, and music is used as a way to work toward a goal. Although the products in music therapy can be quite good as well as reinforcing, the most important part is actually the process the clients have gone through.

For example, if the clients have written a song, they may receive positive reinforcement for it and have something tangible that they can keep with them. However, the process they went through to finish the product is significant. The clients had to decide as a small group which song they would use as well as whose ideas to use on which lyrics, interact with each other without letting one person dominate or another be passive, be honest with each other when they did not like something, overcome fears and do something they didn't think they could do, bring up painful memories and feelings, be creative, and be able to discuss their finished product with other peers.

In other words, they had to make decisions, cooperate, be assertive and honest, take a risk, identify feelings, be creative and be ready to discuss issues in a large group, all qualities which clients will need in order to grow spiritually and work their AA or NA program. Thus, emphasis is placed on the process that the clients go through, not on the final product.

Entertaining and Showcasing

Music therapists must be able to perform songs for lyric analysis or sing or play for some of the products created by the patients.

However, talented clients and staff need to be aware of "showcasing." Although they may be great entertainers, the focus is on the program itself, and musicianship should not be a way to defocus off treatment.

Interpreting

Although there are music therapists who adopt a psychoanalytical approach when working with clients, most professionals who use music should let the clients interpret for themselves. For example, when a famous song is used for lyric analysis, each client will have his or her own reactions and feelings associated with the song. Differences of opinion need to be encouraged. The goal is **not** to actually interpret a song, but to intensify, identify and express our feelings in reaction to the music. Group leaders should set the tone for a session by encouraging everyone to remain open and by stating there is no one right or wrong way to look at the lyrics (unless the lyricist is sitting in the group). In this way, the leader helps to nurture choice, creativity and dignity with the clients.

Using a Variety of Music

A variety of music must be used in the sessions in order to hold the clients' interest. The style of music preferred by the group leader may not be the same held by most of the clients. The leader must be prepared to use music that he or she does not like. The clients are often good sources for ideas about music which is treatment-related and will offer a wide range of styles and subjects from which to choose.

Using Music to Enhance Sessions

Although one needs a degree to practice "music therapy," music can be used by other health professionals to enhance therapy sessions. Music can be used as described above or as a background for learning, for meditation, or for other tasks such as completing art therapy projects. Since music is versatile, flexible, familiar and social in nature, it can be adapted to many therapeutic situations.

Other health professionals may enhance their sessions with live or recorded music and may find strong emotional responses from clients. Clients who may have difficulty verbalizing their thoughts and feelings may be able to express themselves by playing an instrument or by reacting to music. Certainly music can intensify feelings, and can help clients and therapists identify what the feelings are so that they can be expressed and discussed.

In conclusion, just as music has been identified as the stimulus that gives us the most thrills (Goldstein, 1980), it is also the most common trigger for being "very close to a powerful, spiritual force that seemed to lift you out of yourself" (quoted in Wein, 1987, p. 73). Forty-nine percent of respondents in a survey by Father Andrew M. Greeley mentioned music as the most common trigger for this spiritual connection, followed by prayer at 48% and the beauty of nature at 45% (Wein, 1987). Therefore, the bond between music, emotions and spirituality is a strong one that can be utilized by helping professionals to assist chemically dependent clients find fulfillment in their journey toward spiritual growth.

REFERENCES

Alcoholics Anonymous. (1976). *Alcoholics Anonymous* (3rd ed.). New York: A.A. World Services.

Burkhardt, M. A. (1989). Spirituality: An analysis of the concept. *Holistic Nursing Practice, 3*(3), 69-77.

Carroll, S. (1991). Spirituality and purpose in life in alcoholism recovery. *Journal of Studies on Alcohol, 5*, 297-301.

Davis, W. B., Gfeller, K. E., & Thaut, M. H. (1992). *An introduction to music therapy theory and practice.* Dubuque, IA: Wm. C. Brown.

Ficken, T. (1976). The use of songwriting in a psychiatric setting. *Journal of Music Therapy, 13*, 161-171.

Fisher, B. (1990). Dance/movement therapy: Its use in a 28-day substance abuse program. *The Arts in Psychotherapy, 17*, 325-331.

Freed, B. S. (1987). Songwriting with the chemically dependent. *Music Therapy Perspectives, 4*, 13-18.

Ghiselin, B. (1954). The creative process: A symposium. Berkeley: University of California Press.

Goldstein, A. (1980). Thrills in response to music and other stimuli. *Physiological Psychology, 8*(1), 126-129.

Hodges, D. A. (Ed.). (1980). *Handbook of Music Psychology.* National Association for Music Therapy, Inc.: Lawrence, KS.

Kinney, J., & Leaton, G. (1983). Loosening the grip: A handbook of alcohol information. (2nd ed.) St. Louis, MO: C. V. Mosby.

Milliken, R. (1990). Dance/movement therapy with the substance abuser. *The Arts in Psychotherapy, 17,* 309-317.

Nagai-Jacobson, M., & Burkhardt, M. A. (1989). Spirituality: Cornerstone of holistic nursing practice. *Holistic Nursing Practice, 3*(3), 18-26.

National Association for Music Therapy, (1993). *Music therapy as a career.* Silver Spring, MD.

Rew, L. (1989). Intuition: Nursing knowledge and the spiritual dimension of persons. *Holistic Nursing Practice, 3*(3), 56-68.

Rosellini G., & Worden, M. (1985). *Of course you're angry: A guide to dealing with the emotions of chemical dependence.* Center City, MN: Hazelden.

Rosenfeld, A. H. (1985). Music, the beautiful disturber. *Psychology Today, 19*(12), 48-56.

Stuart, E. M., Deckro, J. P. & Mandle, C. L. (1989). Spirituality in health and healing: A clinical program. *Holistic Nursing Practice, 3*(3), 35-46.

Wein, B. (1987, April). Body and soul music. *American Health,* pp. 67-73.

Whitfield, C. L. (1984). Stress Management and spirituality during recovery: A transpersonal approach, Part 1: Becoming. *Alcoholism Treatment Quarterly, 1*(1), 3-54.

Whitfield, C. L. (1984). Stress Management and spirituality during recovery: A transpersonal approach, Part II: Being. *Alcoholism Treatment Quarterly, 1*(2), 1-50.

Never Too Late:
The Spiritual Recovery of an Alcoholic
with HIV

Anonymous

SUMMARY. In this article, a gay recovering alcoholic man who is also HIV+ shares his story in the hope that it will be beneficial for clinicians faced with advising recovering chemically dependent persons who are also HIV+. In addition to sharing what it is like to be HIV+, the author shares some of the positive literature available to HIV+ persons in recovery. Finally, the author provides some clinical implications based on his own life experience. Because he is a member of AA and has a profound respect for the Traditions of AA, including Tradition 11 which advocates personal anonymity of AA members in the printed word, he has chosen to remain anonymous in this article. *[Single or multiple copies of this article are available from The Haworth Document Delivery Service: 1-800-342-9678, 9:00 a.m. - 5:00 p.m. (EST).]*

BACKGROUND

The fabric of the Alcoholics Anonymous recovery community is a coat of many colors, whose threads patch together a diverse com-

Anonymous is a gay, recovering alcoholic man from Iowa who is also HIV+. Because he is very active in Alcoholics Anonymous and respects the Traditions of AA, he remains anonymous here, the level of the printed word. Anonymous is a college administrator, poet, and writer.

[Haworth co-indexing entry note]: "Never Too Late: The Spiritual Recovery of an Alcoholic with HIV." Anonymous. Co-published simultaneously in *Journal of Chemical Dependency Treatment* (The Haworth Press, Inc.) Vol. 5, No. 2, 1995, pp. 167-178; and: *Spirituality and Chemical Dependency* (ed: Robert J. Kus) The Haworth Press, Inc., 1995, pp. 167-178; and: *Spirituality and Chemical Dependency* (ed: Robert J. Kus) Harrington Park Press, an imprint of The Haworth Press, Inc., 1995, pp. 167-178. Single or multiple copies of this article are available from The Haworth Document Delivery Service [1-800-342-9678, 9:00 a.m. - 5:00 p.m. (EST)].

© 1995 by The Haworth Press, Inc. All rights reserved.

munity of special interest groups. The purpose of these groups is to welcome members who seem to have special needs (Kus and Latcovich, 1995). These include men's groups, women's groups, gay groups, lesbian groups, gay/lesbian groups, groups for the hearing-impaired, non-English language groups, beginners' groups, and a variety of groups for people with special professional affiliations such as doctors, lawyers, judges. Much has been written on the subject of these special groups (Kus, 1988; Kus, 1992; Kus and Latcovich, 1995), and this author does not intend to review the literature as a whole. I attend such groups regularly, including a weekly men's group of AA and a weekly gay men's group of Alcoholics Anonymous. Among the many positive features of such groups cited in the literature and generally acknowledged, perhaps the most important is their creation of a safe setting for the skittish newcomer to recovery. Providing a common ground for recovery and a common language in which to discuss it, these groups are an important point of entry especially for people who perceive themselves as marginalized by society as a whole. In these groups, alcoholics who have functioned up till now as loners can begin to turn over their recovery to the care of fellow members and to surrender to the healing dynamic of the group. Once this is accomplished, they can enter the larger recovery community and function well in less narrowly defined groups, conceding to them the same power in recovery that they have yielded to the special interest group.

AWAY BUT NOT ALONE

Traveling on business in a distant city, I was fortunate, soon after learning of my HIV status, to encounter Positively Sober, a special interest AA group for alcoholics who are also dealing with HIV and AIDS. At my first Positively Sober meeting, I found a group of over 40 men and women, gay and straight, with this special issue in common. I had felt terribly alone, even among good friends in my home town and home groups, because I didn't know others in recovery who were dealing with the issues around HIV and I was doubly aware of my special need for confidentiality. Abundant messages had reached me that cautioned me to keep my HIV status to myself, because of dangers to my job, my insurance, my ability to rent an apartment. I felt a little like a leper, and because the experience was not unlike that of being "in the closet," I knew instinctively that this secrecy was very dangerous to my continuing recovery from alcoholism. In Positively Sober, I felt instantly at home. Here was a group of fellow travelers who wouldn't ask me how I got my HIV any more than they would think of asking me how I acquired my alcoholism, who welcomed me unconditionally and without judging me. Here was a place where I could voice my fears and name them, and where I was to learn that in the naming there was victory over these devils. As I continued to travel on business and on vacations, I began to make it a point, in each larger city, to seek out such groups. I often found them under the name Positively Sober in local AA schedules of meetings.

REPRIEVE, NOT TRANSFORMATION; RECOVERY, NOT CURE

In Alcoholics Anonymous, we are never cured of our alcoholism; rather, we are relieved of it by the daily application of the principles of AA recovery. We get a reprieve from the obsession with alcohol but we are never transformed into non-alcoholics. This is one of the mysteries most difficult for our non-alcoholic friends and families to understand. The second half of the Twelfth Step of AA—"to practice these principles in all our affairs" (AA, 1976)—leads us to apply AA's Twelve Steps in every aspect of our lives, admitting our own powerlessness, seeking help from a power greater than ourselves, aligning ourselves with the will of that higher power, asking for removal of our character defects, practicing good works, righting past wrongs, leading an examined life, and sharing our recovery with others who still suffer. If we truly believe that these principles do work in all our affairs, are relevant in our everyday lives, it should come as no surprise that our suffering as a result of potentially terminal disease also can find relief.

When I first learned about my HIV, I was devastated. Death, which had been an acknowledged reality all along, now seemed frighteningly immediate. In the second, very entertaining volume of his autobiography, the British composer and author Anthony Burgess wrote, "Life itself is lethal but, we hope, not yet" (Burgess, 1990). What happens when we receive a diagnosis is that what had seemed distant now appears right before our eyes, and we realize we're not ready. I began immediately to imagine drawn-out and painful hospitalizations, blindness, rejection, isolation, poverty, and death. I lived these scenarios through in my mind and felt paralyzed by fear and unable to act. I began to toy with the dangerous notion that now my recovery from chemical dependency wasn't important, since AIDS would surely kill me before the alcoholism would. In fact, it crossed my mind that I might find some relief from my illness by resorting to my good old reliable drugs and alcohol.

I was very fortunate to have just completed a Fourth and Fifth Step in AA–a moral inventory followed by admitting the nature of my wrongs as I understood them. I had gotten immediate relief through these steps, and I received strong spiritual support from the man with whom I did my Fifth Step, a Benedictine monk experienced in the twelve-step recovery process. Although a non-Catholic and not a particularly religious person, I found myself repeating the Third and Seventh Step prayers of Alcoholics Anonymous (AA, 1976) and the prayer of St. Francis, which figures prominently in AA's Eleventh Step (AA, 1981). I realized that in repeating these prayers, I was asking, first and foremost, to be made useful, both to my higher power and to my fellows in recovery. I certainly wouldn't be of much use drunk.

SPIRITUAL CHANGES: UNCOVERING THE PURPOSE

I was also fortunate that a friend from my gay AA group, in whom I had confided my HIV status, gave me a copy of Perry Tilleraas's *The Color of Light* (1988), a book of meditations for people with HIV and AIDS. From time to time as I pick up this book and open it to the current date, I am reminded how the power of meditation and prayer can work in my daily life. The following is one of Tilleraas's meditations:

> ... When we identify only with our body, the condition of our body determines our feelings and attitudes–whether we are happy, peaceful, anxious, fearful, angry, or depressed. When

we identify only with our body, we walk in a small, narrow world.

Is it possible that we have made a mistake in our identity? Perhaps, in addition to our body, we are also a powerful field of energy connected to other powerful fields of energy, connected to the source of all energy.

Perhaps, inside each of us is a vast pool of love, an ocean of memory, and a space big enough to include the world. If this is true, we no longer need to feel lonely, shameful, or afraid.

A Guide to Self-Care for HIV Infection (APLA, 1991) also emphasizes the spiritual aspect of dealing with HIV in a section on spiritual health.

The spiritual journey of facing life-threatening illness can be described as a quest for connectedness with the universe, taking time with yourself to ponder the universe and your place in it. Often the questions for the journey are: "What has the purpose of my life so far been?" "What do I want the meaning of my life to be?" (p. 15)

In answer to these questions, and relating them to chemical dependency, let's return to Tilleraas (1988):

. . . The point now is to find a good reason to be sober. And that reason is simple: we decide that we want to live. Every day that we are clean and sober we renew our affirmation for life. Whether or not we have a problem with alcohol or other drugs, we can all understand what it means to say, "Yes, I want to live." It is the heart of our relationship with ourselves. If we affirm this decision in our lives, we are more loving to ourselves and to the people around us.

At the end of my drinking, I had looked forward to death. I had wished for it. I believe I would have welcomed it, had it come. Every morning as I woke, I regretted not having died the night before. Ahead of me lay only more unhappiness, more depression, more senseless, aimless spiritual void. Now, after three years of recovery in AA and with the devastating news of my HIV, I realized that I didn't want to die, yet. In those three years I had seen loneliness and despair fade away, to be replaced by a wealth of friendships and abundant hopes for a useful and meaningful life. Most importantly, I had seen others around me recovering, and in small ways I had participated in their recovery, and I wanted to see more years of their recovery unfold and their lives grow and prosper in sobriety.

Soon the phone would ring and someone would need a ride to a meeting. A person I sponsored would want help interpreting the instructions for preparing a Fourth Step. There would be an AA dance to be planned or a workshop or a trip to the international convention with other sober friends, gay and straight. The more I began to see myself as part of the world and not isolated from it by my disease, the more rapidly my fear and despair fell aside, to be replaced by a sense of renewed purpose. My usefulness in the scheme of things was reaffirmed, and although I still knew I would die, I was living in the present. Those horrifying scenarios of disease and debilitation had lost their power over me. Whenever they return to haunt me—and they do—all that is necessary is for me to repeat again those faithful standards—the Third, Seventh, and Eleventh Step prayers. If I repeat them enough, I return to the present and to a life of happy usefulness.

Through working the Twelve Steps of the Alcoholics Anonymous program as well and as regularly as I can in all aspects of my life, I am gradually overcoming fear and growing spiritually. I know of no other way better to achieve this spiritual growth. Working the steps as suggested in *Alcoholics Anonymous* (AA, 1976) and *Twelve Steps and Twelve Traditions* (AA, 1981), attending meetings regularly, doing spiritual reading, meditating and praying, sharing myself with others, recalling and applying common AA slogans, living my life the best I can, and frequently reaching out to help the newcomer to recovery—these are the characteristics of a successful AA program. Success is life. It is staying sober. As a good friend of mine is fond of remarking, this is a highly improbable event for the alcoholics we were.

Beyond the AA community, there is much that the gay person in recovery can do to help other gays develop healthy attitudes about their homosexuality, seeing it as a gift rather than a curse to be hidden or a handicap to be overcome. Volunteering on gay outreach telephone services, staffing gay community organization offices, fundraising for a local AIDS coalition, joining an AIDS buddy program, delivering hot meals to the bedridden, engaging in AIDS/ HIV outreach, speaking to local business and professional groups about issues related to AIDS in the workplace, speaking in schools and churches–there are so many ways in which we can turn our personal experience to the benefit of our communities. Rather than being isolated by our alcoholism or our HIV, rather than withdrawing from the world and being bitter that it has abused or neglected us, we can be part of the conduit that delivers love and support and understanding to our fellow sufferers.

CLINICAL IMPLICATIONS

Although I am not a clinician, I do feel my experience can help the counseling professional meet the needs of alcoholic clients who are dealing with HIV infection and AIDS.

First and foremost, I think it is essential that counseling professionals read and absorb as much literature as possible about gay recovery issues. A good source of information is *Gay Men of Alcoholics Anonymous: First-Hand Accounts* (Kus, 1990). It is particularly important that you get all the information you can about HIV disease. Some good sources of information are *The Guide to Living with HIV Infection* (Bartlett and Finkbeiner, 1993); *A Guide to Self-Care for HIV Infection* (APLA, 1991); and *POZ* (April/May, 1994), a magazine specifically targeted at people with HIV/AIDS. Keep abreast of current developments by reading the newspapers regularly. HIV-positive clients will receive medical advice from their increasingly frequent contact with physicians and may know more than you do about the medical aspects of their condition. It may be beneficial to them, reaffirming their sense of participation in their recovery process, to instruct you in this area. The more the counselor knows, however, the more he or she will be able to understand what the client is going through and talking about. The less you know, the less the client may think you care.

Second, people with HIV are very sensitive to rejection. They expect to encounter it and frequently this expectation is borne out in reality. Like me, many people with HIV are gay and have encountered homophobia all their lives from family, friends, work associates and others. Thus we are primed for rejection from the start. When a dreaded, fatal disease about which most people are deplorably ignorant, is added to the equation, the situation seems even worse. Alcoholic and other chemically-dependent clients need reassurance of your acceptance. They need you as an ally in overcoming their own ignorance and confronting the ignorance and fear they are encountering in the world around them. They may need you as an advocate, so be ready to take up their cause.

Third, physical contact is important. It is not dangerous to you, since HIV is not passed from person to person by casual contact. This may include reaching out to take the hands, hugging, or other simple signs of affection and support. Physical contact can help to overcome the client's expectation of rejection and build trust.

Fourth, be aware that people with HIV/AIDS are frequently treated as though they are already dead. Many of my friends have recounted instances in which they felt compelled to remind somebody–even a family member, close friend, or health care provider–that "I'm not dead meat yet." Relate to your HIV-positive clients as you would to any other clients who face difficulties, as living fellow travelers on this planet who need positive reinforcement in their recovery process.

Fifth, learn what resources are available in your community for people with HIV. Keep asking until you find them. The American Red Cross, United Way, county and state health departments, crisis centers, gay community centers, hospitals, Alcoholics Anonymous, Narcotics Anonymous, and many other community groups may be able to direct you to local AIDS coalitions and other organizations that are directly concerned with HIV/AIDS issues. Bartlett and Finkbeiner (1993) include a brief but information-packed chapter entitled "Resources: Where to Go for Help." If there are important resources missing in your community, then do what you can to establish them. Sooner or later, you'll need them for your clients.

Sixth, establish and maintain contact with gay community service organizations locally and on nearby college campuses. Make a point of meeting leaders in these organizations personally and keeping in touch with them and their colleagues and volunteers. If you want to refer clients to one of these organizations for more information or assistance, it will be much better to have a specific person to refer them to. We with HIV encounter enough nameless, faceless bureaucracies in our daily dealings with the health system, insurance companies and social services. It is nice to have the name of a real person when we walk in the door. Although HIV is not a gay-specific disease, the fact remains that the vast majority of Americans with HIV are gay. Gay service organizations have been dealing with the AIDS pandemic longer than any other groups, and they have the most information and experience.

Seventh, if your client is gay, don't assume he or she is "out." Many gay people are deeply buried in their closets and have never encountered gay community organizations. Even when these exist nearby, your clients may have very little knowledge of the resources available to them from their gay peers. If internalized homophobia (gay self-loathing) has played a part in their chemical dependency problems (Kus, 1988), it may well have been involved in their infection with HIV. They may need some coaxing before they'll walk into a gay community center or an AIDS/HIV support group for help. Just be patient and supportive and assume nothing until you know it.

Eighth, keep abreast of new literature that may be helpful to your clients. Keep a library of it at hand in your office. This may include clipping files, meditation books, self-care guides, and information on alternative therapies. Be careful not to be judgmental about these alternative treatments (including exercise, therapeutic massage, dietary and vitamin therapies, herbal medicines, etc.), as they may do a world of good for clients. Above all, keep an open mind about these measures. If you imply that you think them quaint or ineffective, clients may lose trust in you or be reluctant to talk about this aspect of their treatment process.

Ninth, if there are Twelve Step groups locally that specifically cater to HIV-positive individuals, locate all the information you can about their meeting times and locations and try to get a contact telephone number where clients can get preliminary information. Without the powerful presence of AA's Twelve Steps in my life, I would almost certainly have died of my alcoholism long before now. The power of Twelve Step recovery can be applied to any number of difficulties, and I can firmly attest that it works to counter the despair and hopelessness that plague the HIV-infected. The national AIDS hotline (800/342-AIDS) and local AIDS service organizations can help with information about such groups, and local central offices of Alcoholics Anonymous and Narcotics Anonymous can provide meeting information about their groups.

Tenth, assist and encourage your clients to identify the things that they have in common with others who are facing terminal or potentially terminal illness. For example, a friend with terminal cancer once told me that his family was withdrawing from him in small ways that even they perhaps didn't recognize (hugs had been replaced by tentative pats on the head, and finally with a little wave upon arrival or parting). I myself have noticed that I have many medical problems in common with my generally healthy but elderly mother. We are sort of growing old together, in ways I had never anticipated. I have much more appreciation of what she is going through (lessened mobility and stamina, shortness of breath, morning's generalized aches and pains, the sense that all systems are gradually wearing out). I am discovering new bonds of understanding between myself and my family and friends in this way, and I am learning that I share many experiences and many life and health concerns with older AA members in my regular groups.

Eleventh, be prepared to fail some of the time. Some people, no matter how desperately they need it, are never able to get sober. People with HIV/AIDS are no exception in this regard. Many people get their first information about their HIV status before they get sober. Many have been worrying about it throughout the last years of their drinking, knowing that they have indulged in high-risk behaviors, but have avoided having the antibody test for fear of the likely results. Some get the news while they are in treatment. These people do not have the advantage I had of a significant period of recovery prior to getting the test results. They haven't seen their lives improve with sobriety. They have been lost in a semi-stupor for years and wake from it to discover that they have a terrifying and mysterious infectious disease that will surely kill them if something else doesn't do so first. It may seem to them that there is no point in getting sober. Why bother? In fact, why not party all the harder while they can? With such people, it may or may not help gently to remind them that the despair and hopelessness that brought them to the counselor or to AA in the first place will almost certainly return when they resume drinking.

Twelfth, remind your clients, once they have made an earnest beginning in their recovery, that nothing so protects that recovery as work with fellow-sufferers who turn to us for help. Carrying the message of hope to our brothers and sisters, being of service to them and to our community as a whole, is the basis of a sound program of growth.

CONCLUSION

It may be late, but it is never *too* late to find happiness and peace. Just as spiritual growth is the key element in recovery from alcoholism and other chemical dependencies, it can be central to our recovery from the terror and despair so often associated with HIV infection and AIDS.

Serenity is not a monopoly of the physically healthy. If indeed those of us who are HIV-infected now must face the end of our lives–and for most of us this is not imminent–then there is all the more reason to stretch for spiritual meaning in the time we have remaining. Using all the tools of meditation and prayer at our disposal and working with others as opportunities present themselves, we can hope to achieve a sense of unity and purpose, the deep and abiding knowledge that has been buried within us all along: that at the end we are all connected with each other, and that in discovering this connection we recover from fear.

REFERENCES

Alcoholics Anonymous. (1976). *Alcoholics Anonymous,* (3rd Edition.) New York: Alcoholics Anonymous World Services, Inc.

Alcoholics Anonymous. (1981). *Twelve Steps and Twelve Traditions.* New York: Alcoholics Anonymous World Services, Inc.

APLA. (1991). *Living with AIDS: A self-care guide.* Los Angeles: AIDS Project Los Angeles.

Bartlett, J.G., & Finkbeiner, A.K. (1993). *The guide to living with HIV infection,* (Rev. Ed.). Baltimore: The Johns Hopkins University Press.

Burgess, A. (1990). *You've had your time*. New York: Grove Press.

Kus, R.J. (Ed.) (1990). *Gay Men of Alcoholics Anonymous: First-Hand Accounts.* North Liberty, IA: WinterStar Press.

Kus, R.J. (1992). Spirituality in everyday life: Experiences of gay men of Alcoholics Anonymous. *Journal of Chemical Dependency Treatment, 5*(1): 49-66.

Kus, R.J. (1988). "Working the program": The Alcoholics Anonymous experience and gay American men. *Holistic Nursing Practice, 2*(4): 62-74.

Kus, R.J. and Latcovich, M.A. (1995). Special interest groups in Alcoholics Anonymous: A focus on gay men's groups. *Journal of Gay & Lesbian Social Services,* 67-82.

Tilleraas, P. (1988). *The Color of Light.* Center City, MN: Hazelden.

Spiritual Exiles in Their Own Homelands:
Gays, Lesbians, and Native Americans

Terry Tafoya, PhD
Kevin R. Roeder, MSW, CICSW

SUMMARY. Clinical considerations and comparisons are explored in direct relationship to the role of spirituality in recovery for gays, lesbians, and Native Americans with an emphasis on American Indians and Alaskan Natives. Considered are the development stages of identity, common prejudices experienced by these minority groups, the influence of Christianity and the role of the church and synagogue, alcohol incidence rates, and the historical context of 'exile' from homeland. Comparisons occur among these groups which could aid the worker in a greater understanding of this clientele, thus directly impacting the success of client/worker contact in the recovery and healing process. *[Single or multiple copies of this article are available from The Haworth Document Delivery Service: 1-800-342-9678, 9:00 a.m. - 5:00 p.m. (EST).]*

Terry Tafoya is a traditional Native American Storyteller who uses American Indian ritual and ceremony in his work in family therapy at the University of Washington School of Medicine in Seattle. Dr. Tafoya is a national consultant with the U.S. Center for Substance Abuse Prevention and a frequent convention speaker. Kevin Roeder is Director of Life Care Services for three HIV/AIDS human services agencies in Green Bay, has a part-time psychotherapy practice, and teaches at the University of Wisconsin-Green Bay.

Address correspondence to: Mr. Kevin Roeder, MSW, CICSW, University of Wisconsin-Green Bay, Social Work Program, Green Bay, WI 54311-7001, USA or to Dr. Terry Tafoya, Tamanawit Unlimited, 1202 E. Pike Street, Seattle, WA 98122 USA.

[Haworth co-indexing entry note]: "Spiritual Exiles in Their Own Homelands: Gays, Lesbians, and Native Americans." Tafoya, Terry, and Kevin R. Roeder. Co-published simultaneously in *Journal of Chemical Dependency Treatment* (The Haworth Press, Inc.) Vol. 5, No. 2, 1995, pp. 179-197; and: *Spirituality and Chemical Dependency* (ed: Robert J. Kus) The Haworth Press, Inc., 1995, pp. 179-197; and: *Spirituality and Chemical Dependency* (ed: Robert J. Kus) Harrington Park Press, an imprint of The Haworth Press, Inc., 1995, pp. 179-197. Single or multiple copies of this article are available from The Haworth Document Delivery Service [1-800-342-9678, 9:00 a.m. - 5:00 p.m. (EST)].

© 1995 by The Haworth Press, Inc. All rights reserved.

When we were originally asked to contribute an article that combined the issues of Native American spirituality and the spiritual concerns of lesbians and gays in dealing with treatment, we must admit we experienced a moment of confusion as to the connections between these groups. After thinking things through, however, we began to see more parallels in developmental stages of identity, prejudices experienced common to oppressed minorities, the influence of Christianity, an incidence rate of alcohol abuse higher than a number of other groups, and a prevalent history of "exile" from home and homeland. Another connecting pattern is the similar way in which Native Americans, lesbians, and gay people have been able to utilize spirituality as a way of life and survival, especially as a creative and powerful component in recovery.

A COMMON HISTORY

Although there is some controversy as to the precise percentage of same-sex orientation (7-10% is the most likely figure), there is no question that lesbian and gay people cut across all ethnicities and generations. Cross-cultural and historical research clearly show the existence of same-sex love in the vast majority of groups studied (Tripp, 1975; Reinisch and Beasley, 1990). Cultures have varied as to their responses to same-sex love–from reverence, to indifference, to condemnation.

Interestingly enough, the original tenets of Christianity did not seem to condemn homosexuality. Indeed, there is some evidence that until the 4th Century, the marriage vow as we recognize it was used as a pledge among same-sex couples in the Christian Church (Boswell 1980). The work of St. Augustine and later writers seem to have altered the course of Christianity to one more homonegative, i.e., anti-gay. Nelson (1985) states:

> No gay or lesbian person in our society can escape responding in some manner to the ways in which the Judeo-Christian tradition has dealt with homosexuality. Likewise, it is predictable that numerous gay and lesbian clients will be working on issues of self-worth and self-esteem stemming from preconceived condemnation by organized religion. Whether the bibli-

cal and theological arguments are of personal interest to the therapist (or counselor) is beside the point. They do matter to many gay and lesbian clients. (p. 165)

More recent biblical studies have led to significant changes in current interpretations of passages often quoted to justify homophobic oppression against lesbian and gay people (Hasbany, 1989). For example, one of the major "gay-bashing" scriptures, Leviticus 18:22 ("You shall not lie with a male as with a woman; it is an abomination"):

> is enclosed by jabs at foreign cult practice. S. R. Driver links Leviticus 18:22 therefore to his discussion of the precept against cultic prostitution in Deuteronomy 23:17f., concluding that "Leviticus 18:22 (cf. 20:13), though general in its wording, is aimed probably at the same practice." In addressing Leviticus 18:22 Norman Snaith does not hesitate to say: "Thus homosexuality (sic) here is condemned on account of its association with idolatry." . . . there is increasing awareness that male sacral prostitution–the absence of reference to homosexual acts among women in the sex laws of the Holiness Code illustrates the patriarchal perspective–is morally irrelevant to private, consensual, nonsacral homosexuality [sic] . . . . (Edwards, 1984, pp. 64-65)

It should be noted that "homosexuality" was never condemned in the Bible. In fact, the term was not even coined until the 19th Century. Biblical writers condemned same-sex sexual behavior among men, not homosexuality. Homosexuality may be defined as "an unchosen, lifelong, irreversible state of being in which the individual is attracted sexually to one's own sex, rather than to the opposite sex" (Kus, 1990b, p. 10). In summary, being gay or lesbian is something one is, not something one does.

As an aside, it is sometimes pointed out that even if one fully and literally accepts male same-sex sexual behavior as an abomination within a biblical context (recalling that there is no specific condemnation for lesbian sex), "abominations" also included in the "biblical laws" forbid "eating rare meat, having marital intercourse during menstruation, and wearing clothing of mixed fabrics" (Nelson, 1985, p. 166).

With the advent of the AIDS pandemic, the extreme Christian fundamentalist belief of the disease as "God's punishment against homosexuals" became widespread even though the rate of AIDS among lesbians was significantly lower than among heterosexuals. Even before AIDS, many gay and lesbian people felt alienated from the churches and synagogues of their families of origin.

Native Americans were also condemned as pagans by Europeans who first arrived in the so-called New World. There was even a running debate as to the "humanness" of American Indians, until Pope Julius II proclaimed Native people of the Americas to have a soul in 1512 (Gattuso, 1992). The impact of the Europeans on Native Americans is difficult to comprehend. As Gattuso (1992) relates:

> Epidemics alone wiped out 25 to 50% of the population, warfare another 10%. In places like the Caribbean or Central America, only about 1 person in 10 survived, possibly less. In the U.S., a pre-contact population of approximately 1.5 million (a very rough estimate) dropped to less than 250,000 between 1890 and 1910. Then as now, religion and politics made a potent combination. In the twisted rhetoric of conquest, "saving" the Indians was usually equated with subjugating them. (pp. 35-36)

Native American people were informed by missionaries that their traditional spirituality and practices were of the Devil and that civilization by European standards was by definition related to becoming Christian. For example, in 1769,

> ... The San Diego mission was established, the first in a series of 21 religious agrarian settlements to be built approximately a day's journey apart along El Camino Real, the Spanish land route from San Diego to San Francisco. Completed by 1823, the mission supported two Franciscan friars as overseers, a protective military garrison, and hundreds of "Christianized" Indians (neophytes), who were impressed for mission work

and religious conversion. Tribal ties were suppressed. (California Department of Education, 1991, p. 69)

The United States government was even more oppressive in its effort to formally eliminate Native religious and spiritual practices. For example:

Charles H. Burke, Commissioner of Indian Affairs in 1924, directed that propaganda be carried out against Indian religions. He circulated documents to churchmen, members of Congress, and newspaper editors, asserting that Indian religious observances were sadistic and obscene. He expressed the belief that Native religion was a crutch preventing the useful assimilation of the Indian into white society . . . [At a meeting in 1926,] Burke told the Taos Pueblo Council that they were "half-animals," because of their "pagan religion." Even before this speech, Burke had issued orders to Indian Bureau personnel directing them to tell the Pueblo people to rid themselves of their Native religion "within a year." (Sando, 1992, p. 92)

As we enter the twenty-first century, Christian and Jewish clergy are often addressing the inequity and oppression of earlier efforts in dealing with alternative sexuality and spirituality of gay, lesbian, and Native peoples. Indeed, in the 1980s, a coalition of church leaders offered formal apologies to Native Americans for the devastation experienced by Native people as a direct result of Christian missionaries. Just so, many church and synagogue leaders have been exploring the acceptance of gay and lesbian members of their congregations. For example:

there is a significant and increasing pluralism within organized Christianity with regard to these issues. Theologians and churches, both Protestant and Catholic, simply do not have a unified mind, and the client needs to know this. In spite of the official Vatican position, there are distinguished Catholic theologians who publicly proclaim homosexuality as Christianly valid, and there are creative and affirming Catholic ministries to gay and lesbian communities. Within Protestantism, the spectrum is even greater. Here, too, one can find an increasing number of significant theological voices giving full affirmation to lesbians and gay men–not only among "liberal" theologians but now also among those who identify themselves as "evangelical". . . . The point is this: Particularly within the last dozen years there has been a vigorous ferment about homosexual issues within American church life. In every case except the most conservative and fundamentalist groups, this ferment has produced new openness toward and affirmation of lesbians and gay men. (Nelson, 1985, pp. 169-170)

In part, this may reflect changing modern attitudes that include the removal of homosexuality as a mental illness category in 1973 by the American Psychiatric Association and by the World Health Organization in 1990. Homosexuality is now considered scientifically as being simply a normal variation of human sexuality. Earlier theories of the development of homosexuality as being the result of an absent father and an overprotective mother or being an "arrested" stage of psychosexual development have not been substantiated as accurate. Previous studies that indicated gays and lesbians had a higher rate of mental illness were clearly biased studies with a truncated range–i.e., they had focused on gay and lesbian people already in therapy and compared them to the general population. More recent research indicates that gay and lesbian people as a whole have no more significant degree of mental illness than any other group. There is no scientific evidence that sexual orientation can be changed; previous attempts to "convert" gays and lesbians (almost always in connection with a fundamental Christian extremist group) are now seen as unethical, since being gay or lesbian is no longer seen as a "disease" to be "fixed."

Considering the similarity of historical experience with condemnation by virtually all formal social agencies, it should hardly be surprising that Native Americans as well as lesbian and gay people have internalized a great deal of the hostility expressed against them, as reflected in a higher rate of alcohol and other substance abuse than most other ethnic and social groups. For example, with Native American young people, "the available findings indicate that more Indian youth use virtually every type of drug with greater frequency than non-Indian Youth" (Beauvais and

LaBoueff, 1985; Beauvais et al., 1985a, 1985b; Oetting et al., 1988). Within the gay and lesbian communities, the incidence of alcoholism is very high (Kus, 1990a). In reviewing incidence studies of gay and/or lesbian persons, Bickelhaupt (1995) found that between 20-35 percent of gay and lesbian persons are alcoholic or problem drinkers.

Kus (1992) states:

> It is particularly important for helping professionals who work with gay men [and lesbians] to be clear about spirituality for two reasons. First, gay American men [and lesbians] are afflicted with alcoholism and other forms of chemical dependency at a very high rate. . . Second, many gay men [and lesbians] have been alienated by anti-gay religious persons. Failing to distinguish religion from spirituality may be an obstacle for a man [or woman] who has been hurt by such bigotry. (p. 51)

This distinction between spirituality and religion may be a difficult one for some clinicians who were reared in a conventional American family where the church or temple was by definition the formal place of worship and spirituality. Perhaps it would be useful to more closely examine Native American concepts of spiritual expression. Many Native languages have no word that translates as "religion." A better way of understanding spirituality is how one lives, how one conducts oneself on a daily basis, three hundred and sixty-five days a year. Beck et al. (1992) suggest that:

> Classic tribal sacred ways do not try to explain or control all *phenomena* in the universe. They do not, as organizations, seek to dominate people's thoughts or ways of personal worship. This is what makes these sacred ways distinct–from "schools" of philosophy in the history of ideas, of "denominations" in the history of religion. One concept held by the elders to be very important is *respect*. Great respect is held for those who protect sacred ways and help them grow. A human being's spiritual life is his/her most important expression of his/her humanity. To respect this is something the elders teach

in almost every tribal community in North America. Native American sacred ways were not, classically, incorporated, sectarian, or evangelical. They were just ways of seeking life. (pp. 4-5)

In the Sahaptin language, the closest one can get to discussing traditional "religion" is to see it within the spiritual context of the words "Washut," and "Tamanawit." Washut literally translates into English as "Dance," implying not only the worship dancing that is a principle part of the culture, but on a metaphorical level, the Dance of Life–the interactional patterns of being in relationships with others. Tamanawit means "The Road" or "The Way," a manner of speaking about one's life. In both instances, the emphasis is on an active involvement, rather than a passive one–that one is moving and changing within the context of time. In this way, healing is always possible.

Considering the historically unwelcoming attitude of organized religions, it should hardly seem unusual that gay and lesbian people would often seek non-conventional sources of spiritual comfort, looking to Native American traditions, Eastern philosophy, and certain "New Age" approaches that offer respect and acceptance of difference rather than condemnation. Tilleraas (1988), a gay man and person with AIDS, stated:

We don't need to be religious to pray or meditate. In fact, for many of us, religion got in the way of our prayer and mediation. Now, as we reclaim our spirituality, we can develop a form of prayer and meditation that suits us. We can become more familiar with our Higher Power, or however we understand God. (p. 19)

Perhaps a strong connective element within the gay and lesbian communities is the necessity to construct their own reality. In other words, the heterosexist American society provides a "script" for white, middle-class, "straight" men and women. For people of color, and for gay and lesbian people, there is no such existing "script" for being part of American society. While "scripts" exist for Native Americans to be appropriately native, gay men and lesbians must "create" themselves. Downing (1991) says:

That *we* choose to call ourselves lesbians, that we decide what this designation means to us, is itself a challenge to how same-sex loving has most often been defined in our culture. For by and large, we have been the defined, not the self-definers, the object of others' mythmaking rather than the creators of our own mythology. (p. 3)

It should seem clear to the clinician that this creative principle could be an excellent resource in therapy for Native Americans as well as gay and lesbian people. Perhaps one of the most difficult issues in working with substance abusing patients is a tendency they often have of seeing the world in a binary way–right/wrong; good/bad; drunk/sober; gay/straight, rather than being able to perceive shades of difference. The spiritual approach of many Native people emphasizes "Looking Twice," to see beyond the surface of things to deeper and more significant levels of understanding. Native American tradition tends to place things and actions within a context of "appropriate" or "inappropriate" rather than good or bad. For example, in the Yurok language, the word "skuyeni" which is usually translated as "good," may be more accurately rendered as "successful" just as the word "kimoleni" or "bad" may be better translated as "unsuccessful" (Buckley, 1989, p. 38). Thus, "failure" in treatment can be reframed as an "unsuccessful" attempt, and re-examined for a more appropriate approach.

SEXUAL ORIENTATION

The clinician should be aware that it is common for *all* clients to experience homosexual fantasies, and these do not necessarily indicate a gay or lesbian orientation. In a study published in the *American Journal of Psychiatry,* sexual encounters with men were the fourth most reported sexual fantasy among heterosexual men, and the third most common sexual fantasy among lesbian women–sexual encounters with women were the third most reported sexual fantasy among gay men, and the fifth most common fantasy among heterosexual women (Schwartz and Masters, 1984). As we have become more sophisticated as a scientific society, we are also experiencing a growing recognition of transsexual and transgendered concerns that go beyond the focus of this article.

The client or patient the clinician may encounter will potentially range across a complex continuum of identity. The term gay or lesbian may not be the preferred one for some clients, who may identify themselves as "homosexuals," "dykes," "queers," "radical fairies," "fems," "fags," "butch daggers," etc. There is no question that the words used to define oneself are both age-related and regional. For example, much younger and urban clients may primarily identify with "queer," while older clients may be deeply resentful of such a term. Within the gay and lesbian communities, there may be an attitude or evolutionary process of moving from a "homosexual" to a "gay" or "lesbian." This linear progression model may not at all reflect the cultural reality of various ethnic groups. For example, for some Native American groups and Latinos, the gender of one's sexual partner has no relevance to one's sexual orientation–sexual orientation is defined by one's behavior. In other words, as long as a man is in the "active" insertive role, he will still be seen within his community as "heterosexual." The only "homosexual" involved would be the male sexual partner who "passively" received. This should be noted by the clinician who otherwise might judge such an individual as being "in denial" about his sexual orientation.

IDENTITY FORMATION

It has been suggested by Cass (1983/1984) that there are at least three levels of identity formation: self-identity (what I think I am); perceived identity (what others think I am); and presented identity (what I tell you I am). While this was originally formulated around gay/lesbian identity, it can also be applied to Native American identity. If American Indians and Alaskan Native people are not dressed in stereotypical Native dress and have surnames like Gonzales or McDonald, clinicians may not recognize them as Native at all. Even though the self-identity of the client or patient may be Native, the clinician may perceive him/her as Euro-American, Latino, Asian-American, or African-American, especially if the client or patient is of "mixed" heritage. It is then up to the client or patient to disclose or "present" his/her true identity.

In the same way, a gay or lesbian client or patient may have an "invisible" identity to heterosexist clinicians who assume automatically that all clients and patients are "straight." For clinicians who expect gay and lesbians to be recognizable by cultural stereotypes, including gender non-conforming appearance and behavior, they will find "that as few as 15 percent of the homosexual population fit these stereotypes" (Rathus et al., 1993, p. 278).

Depending on the comfort level and feelings of safety, as well as his/her own stage of identity development, a gay or lesbian may choose to "come out" to the therapist or counselor. Members of the "Queer Movement" and other gays and lesbians who are "loud and proud" in their identity and see the political necessity of not being invisible may not be the ones seen in one's practice, especially in rural communities. The perceived need to remain "closeted" and thereby invisible in one's sexual identity in order to escape overt homophobic prejudice and the possibility of being fired from his/ her job, evicted from his/her home, or having a child removed (all three instances a sadly common reality for many gay and lesbian people), may maintain a systemic condition of denial of many aspects of the client/patient's life, including substance use and abuse.

Gay and lesbian clients who remain extremely closeted are forced to continually monitor their behaviors and statements in therapy, support groups, and AA. It should be clearly understood by clinicians that AA and group therapy will most likely reflect American society as a whole, including homophobic attitudes. One can imagine the effect on a closeted gay man starting to feel safe within a group and then suddenly hearing another group member making a pejorative remark about "those damn faggots." The availability of gay and lesbian AA meetings or support groups are a reality in specific urban areas, but not in many rural communities.

In the same way, Native American people may remain "closeted" about their ethnic identity, especially if they are engaged in traditional approaches of worship and healing, fearful that this might be seen as "crazy" behavior by non-Native clinicians (Tafoya, 1990). While there are no real statistics regarding this factor concerning treatment issues, it has been shown that the rate of AIDS diagnosis among Native Americans has been reported at a rate two to four times too low, precisely because of mis-identification of the ethnicity by health care professionals (perceived identity) and the refusal of Native people to "reveal" themselves (presented identity) (Data files, National Native American AIDS Prevention Center, 1993).

GENERATIONAL DIFFERENCES

There are a number of significant generational differences related to Native American as well as gay and lesbian substance abuse important for clinicians to know. For older gays and lesbians, for example, who became active prior to Stonewall, when homosexual acts could be grounds for imprisonment (several states still outlaw sodomy, for example), gay and lesbian bars were some of the very few places where people could come without fear of prejudice or arrest. As a result, gay and lesbian culture often revolved around "The Bars" and the use of alcohol. By the 1970s, bar culture and the growing number of gay discos as gathering places added "poppers" and recreational drug use to the consumption of alcohol (Lauritsen, 1993).

Even today, "bar culture" remains a prominent factor in rural communities. In the same way, Native American bars in urban areas are often gathering places for American Indians and Alaskan Natives who may not otherwise know how to come into contact with other Native people. Unlike most other ethnic groups, Native Americans do not tend to move into specific "neighborhoods" or barrios, but scatter throughout cities. This may be related to the fact that American Indians and Alaskan Natives tend to be tribally oriented. That is, a Navajo will most likely primarily identify as a Navajo, rather than as an American Indian. Urban populations of Native Americans actually represent over 500 tribal entities, some of whom may have a historical reality of being enemies.

At any rate, in both instances, a great deal of the socialization process may be related to bars and drinking. In the recovery process for Native Americans, as well as for lesbian and gay people, there may be a strong sense of loss of a social network that had been bar-centered. It is therefore a major issue for clinicians to work with clients and patients to insure that a supportive network exists. For

Native Americans especially, there has been an increasing role of the Children of Alcoholics (COA) movement in providing a social support network outside of the bars (c.f. Middleton-Moz, 1993). The COA movement for Native Americans has had a major focus on spirituality and revitalization of traditional culture and values, in a way that is healing generational gaps.

These Native generational gaps were the direct result of the federal creation of residential boarding schools that forcibly removed school-age American Indian and Alaskan Native children from their homes in an attempt to eradicate Native languages and cultures. The early boarding schools also had a missionary focus for Christian conversion. There are some Native families that literally have no living memory of how to parent children of a certain age, since for at least three generations, children would have been attending boarding schools (Attneave and Dill, 1980). Tragically, these boarding schools were often the source of extensive sexual abuse of Native children in a manner that is only now being exposed. The clinician working with Native clients would be well advised to examine the possibility of sexual abuse and its connection to alcohol and substance abuse (Tafoya, in press).

There has been a corresponding healing process within the gay and lesbian community, but it would seem its origins are more related to the AIDS crisis. Various "healing circles" that permit an integration of members of different generations, sexual orientations, and genders are supplementing drug and alcohol free social environments for many gays and lesbians. These healing circles will almost always have a spiritual emphasis and may also be affiliated with organized church groups.

It should be remembered that this article's topic fosters an artificial division between gay and lesbian people and Native Americans, leaving out the concept of Native Americans who are gay or lesbian. There has been an increasing number of "out" Native American gays and lesbians who are identifying themselves as "Two-Spirits," a term that encompasses aspects of being gay and lesbian, or bisexual, but represents a more traditional concept of such people having both a male and a female spirit (Tafoya, 1992).

It should be apparent by now the powerful resource that a supportive spiritual background can provide to clients in their recovery process, as well as to their lives in general. It should be equally obvious how those clients who do not have the "tools" and resources discussed to work with, are at a tremendous disadvantage. Spirituality as a way of life can provide the structure and guidelines in making sense of dealing with crisis as well as success. Again, it is important to emphasize the distinction we are making between spirituality and organized religion. Even though many gays, lesbians, and Native Americans have found tremendous comfort in their churches and synagogues, and many more have learned to compartmentalize and accommodate the discrepancies between their lives and their religion (for example, in the more liberal groups, the acceptance may be of the lesbian or gay person, but not his/her sexual behavior), there are many others who have been so brutalized that the clinician would do well to deal directly with how the client or patient him/herself understands these terms. A client who has not had direct contact with a specific church or synagogue for many years may be quite surprised by the recent acceptance that has become part of several American religions. There are churches, such as the Metropolitan Community Church, that were created to do outreach to the gay and lesbian communities, as well as church-affiliated groups like Dignity (Catholic), Integrity (Espiscopal) or Lutherans Concerned. Within the Jewish community, the 1987 Union of American Hebrew Congregations General Assembly endorsed a resolution that sexual

> orientation should not be a criterion for membership or participation in an activity of any synagogue. [This reflects the prophecy of Isaiah, that states] "Let My house be called a house of prayer for all people. . . ." Each of us, created in God's image, has a unique talent which can contribute to that high moral purpose (tikkun olam); and to exclude any Jew from the community of Israel lessens our chances of achieving that goal. (Kahn, 1989, p. 64)

FINAL CLINICAL CONSIDERATIONS

As religious institutions slowly move to make amends for their often oppressive patterns of the past towards Native Americans, gays, and lesbians (oppression which ironically is contradictory to biblical teachings of love and acceptance), and as other societal institutions also make movements toward unconditional acceptance, increased tolerance, and respect for the human rights of all people, clinicians need to remember that these three populations may need to deal with the many unfortunate historical influences prior to the client achieving a feeling of comfort in his/her environment which could promote and enhance recovery and spiritual awareness.

Gay and lesbian youth may also present additional dilemmas for the clinician. Hetrick and Martin state that "at a time when heterosexual adolescents are learning how to socialize, (young gay and lesbian people) are learning to hide" (Hetrick and Martin, 1983, p. 6). This isolation, whether societally or individually imposed, whether adult or child, means the clinician needs to take the time necessary to build a rapport with the client which fosters trust and respect in a nonjudgmental and unconditionally supportive environment. The clinician should see gay and lesbian youth as human beings, regardless of ethnicity, and attempting to overcome problems, rather than being a problem themselves because of their orientation:

> Denied better environments in which to meet other gay and lesbian people, unable to find adults who do not respond with contempt and hostility, such youth may perceive the streets as their only choice. Drugs and alcohol may appear to be the best way of blotting out emotional pain; drug trafficking or prostitution may become essential for survival. The potential for sexual abuse or assault is very high in street life; even where sex is consensual, the vulnerabilities of lesbian and gay street youth make them ready targets for sexual exploitation by adult men–many of whom are heterosexual. (Whitlock and Kamel, 1988, p. 80)

Therapists and counselors must remember that, at the onset for clients, a clinical environment may seem to emanate many of those institutional, Euro-American, heterosexist issues already discussed. It is critical that the patient/client be empowered to explore and claim his/her experience and identity, with the awareness on the part of the clinician that client-imposed terms and definitions may change over the course of therapy/recovery.

Additionally, clinicians should also consider other aspects of spirituality which do not evolve from contemporary Christianity or Judaism. Native Americans, gays and lesbians often believe in higher powers, utilize herbs, crystals, music, oils, readings, chants, meditation, homeopathic techniques, etc., which may not be common or usual to some people's notion of the religious or spiritual community. Spirituality does not necessarily equal religion, but because so many people new to recovery define spirituality as religion, we have thus given it the degree of attention found within this article. Clinicians usually have to address the historical notion of institutionalized religion prior to a greater definition of spirituality being developed by the client. Once this is done, many Native American, gays and lesbians will then blend these spiritual methods or beliefs into their recovery.

For many Native people, ceremonies, rituals, and teachings have focused on the need for wholeness. Indeed, the origin of the word "heal" is linguistically related to the word "whole," which is itself related to the word "holy," or sacred. Perhaps one definition of pathology is the state of being disconnected, to have lost that sense of wholeness. For the individual coping with substance abuse, addiction can become the center for his or her life, severing the "ties that bind"–the lines of the web of life that include family, work, and happiness.

For Native Americans, as well as for gays and lesbians, the experience of American society has been one of disconnection. In the older versions of the Cinderella fairytale, the two wicked stepsisters are unable to fit their feet into the glass slipper. Two force the fit, one sister cuts off her toe and the other sister cuts off her heel. Just so, gay and lesbian people, Native Americans, and others who are "different," have been told that if they wish to fit into "the real world," they must do so by cutting off a part of themselves. The price of acceptance is the slicing off of one's sexuality, one's language, one's culture, one's spirituality. For some this has been a cost that is far too great for the expected benefits of being accepted. Especially since it is not a true acceptance as one is not being accepted for one's self. As a result, there is an awareness that one is only provisionally admitted–and membership can always be revoked when one does not act like a "middle-class, white, straight" person.

For some, alcohol and other drugs are the anesthetic that has allowed the attempted amputation of sexuality, language, culture, or spirituality. The true purpose of spirituality is to allow the process of reclaiming one's wholeness–realizing that the glass slipper was never created for most of us in the first place.

Havey states that:

> To be lesbian or gay is to be given one of life's most complex and most inspiring challenges. To be gay or lesbian is a gift and a paradox: from the difference and alienation emerge the hope and possibility of accepting who we are in spite of rejection by others. (Havey, 1990, p. 278)

Native Americans proudly developed this celebratory notion of self in the face of oppression long before gays and lesbians did. However, this philosophical and realistic notion is one each of us would do well to partake of. Let us celebrate the spirituality and spirit of all those who walk this earth and to continue to understand and to demonstrate why we truly need to do so.

REFERENCES

Attneave, C.L., & Dill, A. (1980). Indian boarding schools and Indian women: Blessing or curse? In programs on teaching and learning (Eds.), *Conference on the education and occupational needs of American Indian women,* (pp. 211-230). National Institute of Education (NIE).

Beauvais, F., & Laboueff, S. (1985). Drug and alcohol abuse intervention in American Indian communities. *The International Journal of the Addictions, 20*(1):139-171.

Beauvais, F., Oetting, E.R., & Edwards, R.W. (1985a). Trends in drug use of Indian adolescents living on reservations: 1975-1983. *American Journal of Drug and Alcohol Abuse, 11*(4):209-229.

Beauvais, F., Oetting, E.R., & Edwards, R.W. (1985b). Trends in the use of inhalants among American Indian adolescents. *White Cloud Journal, 3*:3-11.

Beck, P.V., Walters, A.L., & Francisco, N. (1992). *The sacred: Ways of knowledge, sources of life.* Tsaile, AZ: Navajo Community College Press.

Bickelhaupt, E. (1995). Alcoholism and drug abuse in gay and lesbian persons: A review of incidence studies. *Journal of Gay & Lesbian Social Services. 2*(1): 5-14.

Boswell, J. (1980). *Christianity, social tolerance and homosexuality.* Chicago: University of Chicago Press.

Buckley, T. (1989). Doing your thinking. In D.M. Dooling & P. Jordon-Smith (Eds.), *I become part of it: Sacred dimensions in Native American life.* (pp. 36-52). San Francisco, CA: Harper.

California Department of Education. (1991). *The American Indian: Yesterday, today, and tomorrow.* Sacramento, CA: California Department of Education.

Cass, V. C. (1983/1984). "Homosexual identity: A concept in need of definition." *Journal of Homosexuality, 9*(2/3): 105-26.

DeCecco, J.P., & Elia, J.P. (1993). *If you seduce a straight person, can you make them gay? Issues in biological essentialism versus social constructionism in gay and lesbian identities.* Binghamton, NY: Harrington Park Press.

Downing, C. (1991). *Myths and mysteries of same-sex love.* New York, NY: The Continuum Publishing Company.

Edwards, G. R. (1984). *Gay/lesbian liberation.* New York, NY: The Pilgrim Press.

Gattuso, J. (1992). *Native America.* (1st ed.). Singapore: Hofer Press Pte. Ltd.

Havey, B. (1990). Gay and lesbian Protestants. In R.J. Kus (Ed.), *Keys to caring.* (pp. 271-279). Boston, MA: Alyson Publishing.

Hetrick, E., & Martin, D. (1983). Ego-dystonic homosexuality: A developmental view. In E. Hetrick & T. Stein (Eds.), *Psychotherapy with homosexuals.* Washington, DC: American Psychiatric Press.

Kahn, Y. H. (1989). Judaism and homosexuality: The traditionalist/progressive debate. In R. Husbany (Ed.), *Homosexuality and religion.* Boston, MA: Alyson Pub., Inc.

Kus, R.J. (1990a). Alcoholism in the gay and lesbian communities. In R. J. Kus (Ed.), *Keys to caring: Assisting your gay and lesbian clients.* (pp. 66-81). Boston, MA: Alyson Pub., Inc.

Kus, R.J. (1990b). Introduction. In R.J. Kus (Ed.), *Keys to caring: Assisting your gay and lesbian clients.* (pp. 7-10). Boston: Alyson Pub., Inc.

Kus, R.J. (1992). Spirituality in everyday life: Experiences of gay men in Alcoholics Anonymous. *Journal of Chemical Dependency Treatment, 5*(1), pp. 49-66.

Lasswell, M. & Lasswell, T. (1991). *Marriage and the family.* (3rd Ed.) Belmont, CA: Wadsworth Publishing Company.

Lauristen, J. (1993). Political-economic construction of gay male clone identity. In DeCecco, J.P. & Elia, J.P. (Eds.), *If you seduce a straight person, can you make them gay? Issues in biological essentialism versus social constructionism in gay and lesbian identities.* (pp. 221-232). Binghamton, NY: Harrington Park Press.

Middleton-Moz, J. (1993). *From nightmare to vision: A training manual for Native American adult children of alcoholics.* Seattle, WA: Seattle Indian Health Board.

National Native American AIDS Prevention Center. (1993). Data files.

Nelson, J.B. (1985). Religious and moral issues in working with homosexual clients. In J.C. Gonsiorek (Ed.), *A guide to psychotherapy with gay and lesbian clients.* (pp. 163-175). Binghamton, NY: Harrington Park Press.

Oetting, E., Beauvais, F., & Edwards, R. W. (1988). Alcohol and Indian youth: Social and psychological correlates and prevention. *Journal of Drug Issues, 18*:87-101.

Rathus, S.A., Nevid, J.S., & Fichner-Rathus, L. (1993). *Human sexuality in a world of diversity.* Needham Heights, MA: Allyn and Bacon.

Reinisch, J.M., & Beasley, R. (1990). *The Kinsey Institute's new report on sex: What you must know to be sexually literate.* New York, NY: St. Martin Press.

Sando, J.S. (1992). *Pueblo nations: Eight centuries of Pueblo Indian history.* Santa Fe, NM: Clear Light Publishers.

Schwartz, M., & Masters, W. (1984). The Masters and Johnson treatment program for dissatisfied homosexual men. *American Journal of Psychiatry,* 173-81.

Tafoya, T. (in press). Epistemology of Native American healing. *Journal of Family Psychology.*

Tafoya, T. (1992). Native gay and lesbian issues: The two-spirited. In B. Berzon (Ed.), *Positively gay: New approaches to gay and lesbian life.* (pp. 253-60). Berkeley, CA: Celestial Arts.

Tafoya, T. (1990). Circles and cedar: Native Americans and family therapy. In G. Saba, B. Karrer, & K. Hardy, (Eds.), *Minorities and family therapy,* pp. 71-98.

Tilleraas, P. (1988). *The color of light.* Center City, MN: Hazelden.

Tripp, C.A. (1975). *The homosexual matrix.* New York, NY: Signet.

Whitlock, K. (1988). Bridges of respect. In R. Kemel (Ed.), *Creating support for lesbian and gay youth.* Philadelphia, PA: American Friends Service Committee.

ABOUT THE CONTRIBUTORS

Rojann R. Alpers, PhD, RN, is currently Assistant Professor at Texas Christian University in the Harris College of Nursing. Dr. Alpers, who specializes in public and maternal/child health, received her BSN and MS degrees from Arizona State University. She received her doctorate in education at The University of Iowa where she taught in the College of Nursing for ten years. An active researcher, Dr. Alpers has presented her findings in maternal-child and alcohol studies research in Europe and the United States, and she is becoming known in her fields through her writings. Currently, Dr. Alpers is studying health education participation with pregnant and parenting teens. She is also an active member of Sigma Theta Tau International, having held both regional and international positions.

Anonymous is a gay, recovering alcoholic man in his early fifties. He's a very active member of Alcoholics Anonymous who has been sober since 1988 and who tested positive for HIV in 1991. He is employed as a college administrator in Iowa. In addition, he is a poet whose current works deal with gay identity and experience and the physical and spiritual consequences of HIV infection. Because of his great respect for A.A. and its traditions, he remains anonymous here in keeping with Tradition 11, which advocates anonymity for A.A. members at the level of the printed word as well as in radio and films. Although not a counselor, Anonymous shares his story from a personal level in the hope that it will be helpful to professionals faced with advising recovering chemically dependent clients who are also HIV+.

© 1995 by The Haworth Press, Inc. All rights reserved.

Fr. Leo Booth, MTh, CAC, CEDC, for over 15 years has pioneered in the field of spirituality and recovery from depression, addictions and low self-esteem. An Episcopal priest and recovering alcoholic, he challenges unhealthy and disempowering beliefs and messages wherever he finds them: in religion, psychology, and even recovery support groups. He has developed a dynamic new spiritual model based on connecting body, mind and emotions in order to become positive, creative and empowered to change. An addictions and eating disorders consultant, Father Leo is a national workshop facilitator and spiritual motivator. Father Leo is Parish Priest of St. George's Episcopal Church in Hawthorne, California, outside Los Angeles. His latest book is *The God Game–It's Your Move: Reclaim Your Spiritual Power*, Stillpoint, 1994. To reach Father Leo, call Spiritual Concepts, (310) 434-4813.

Sr. Letitia Marie Close, BVM, NCAC II [See Sr. Mary Gene Kinney].

Dana G. Finnegan, PhD, CAC, is a certified alcoholism counselor in private practice. She is Co-Director of Discovery Counseling Center, Millburn, New Jersey and New York City; Co-Founder and current board member of the National Association of Lesbian and Gay Alcoholism Professionals; a faculty member of the Rutgers Summer Schools of Alcohol and Drug Studies; and Co-Author (with E. McNally) of *Dual identities: Counseling chemically dependent gay men and lesbians* (Hazelden, 1987).

Rev. Andrew M. Greeley, PhD, is Professor of social science at the University of Chicago and at the University of Arizona and has been a visiting professor at the University of Cologne. His most recent sociology books are *Religion as Poetry* (Transaction Press) and *Sex: The Catholic Experience* (Thomas More Press). His most recent novel is *Irish Gold* (Tor Books).

Douglas J. King, MArch, is currently an architect specializing in the design of large-scale, high-rise, health care facilities. In addition to assisting the founding of many urban and rural AA groups, Mr. King is Co-founder of the Lambda Service Group in Chicago, an organization which conducts outreach and education regarding alcoholism in the gay and lesbian communities. In addition to assisting in a research study on gay men of Alcoholics Anonymous at The University of Iowa, Mr. King has given several presentations in the United States and Europe on such topics as the special needs of the rural gay and lesbian alcoholic, founding special interest groups of A.A., spirituality in recovery, coming out in recovery, and educational and outreach needs of special populations. In addition to his many presentations, he has also written in this field and continues to be active in assisting many persons on their path to recovery. Doug currently resides in Chicago with his partner, Bob, and their teenager, Pedro.

Sr. Mary Gene Kinney, BVM, MA, NCAC II, is a Catholic nun currently working as a certified addictions counselor who specializes in the assessment and counseling of persons charged with driving under the influence (DUI) of alcohol or other drugs. In 1979, along with Sr. Letitia Close, also a nun and addictions counselor, she established the Intercongregational Alcoholism Program (ICAP) in Chicago, Illinois. ICAP is operated exclusively for nuns. Through it, Srs. Kinney and Close conduct assessments, interventions, referrals to treatment, and a national support network for nuns with alcoholism/chemical dependency. **Sr. Letitia Marie Close, BVM, NCAC II,** currently administers Education & Intervention, Inc. under which the ICAP and DUI programs function in Oak Park, IL. Sr. Close was an incorporator of Education & Intervention, Inc. in 1976 in Minnesota to address a need for student assistance activities in high schools. As an assignment from their own religious congregation, The Sisters of Charity of The Blessed Virgin Mary (BVMs) in 1977, Srs. Kinney and Close developed a program to bring chemical dependency education into every local community of their congregation and are still involved in this work. Motivated by that work, Sisters Close and Kinney developed and implemented ICAP as an outreach to alcoholic/chemically dependent nuns of other communities. ICAP operates from Oak Park, IL, but its outreach beyond Illinois is accomplished through the personal travel, telephone, and mail networking of Srs. Kinney and Close.

Robert J. Kus, RN, PhD, is a nurse-sociologist who specializes in gay men's studies and alcohol studies. In addition to a Diploma in nursing, he has a B.A. in sociology from Cleveland State University, an M.S. in psychiatric-mental health nursing from the University of Oklahoma, and a Ph.D. in sociology from the University of Montana. Besides studying sobriety in gay American men, Dr. Kus has been conducting cross-cultural gay men's studies in Europe where he has presented over 25 workshops and papers. In addition to 30 book chapters and journal articles, Dr. Kus has edited *Keys to caring: Assisting your gay and lesbian clients* (Alyson, 1990), *Gay men of Alcoholics Anonymous: First-hand accounts* (WinterStar Press, 1990), and *Addiction and recovery in gay and lesbian persons* (The Haworth Press, Inc., 1995). After teaching for ten years at The University of Iowa, Bob moved to Ohio in 1992 where he is currently studying to become a Roman Catholic priest while practicing nursing at Laurelwood Hospital in Willoughby, Ohio.

Rev. Mark A. Latcovich, MDiv, PhD, is a priest for the Diocese of Cleveland and teaches both pastoral and systematic theology at St. Mary Seminary, Wickliffe, Ohio. He is currently completing his doctorate in Sociology at Case Western Reserve University in Cleveland. Rev. Latcovich has served as parochial vicar for nine years in various parishes in the Cleveland area and has served as a "soulfriend" in the Fifth Step process.

Emily B. McNally, PhD, CAC, is a licensed psychologist in private practice. She is Co-Director of Discovery Counseling Center, Millburn, New Jersey and New York City; Co-Founder and current board member of the National Association of Lesbian and Gay Alcoholism Professionals (NALGAP); and Co-Author (with D. Finnegan) of *Dual identities: Counseling chemically dependent gay men and lesbians* (Hazelden, 1987).

Mary Ann Miller, RN, CARN, BLS, is currently the head nurse of the Chemical Dependency Center at The University of Iowa Hospitals and Clinics where she has worked for the past fourteen years. In addition to being a Certified Addictions Registered Nurse, Ms. Miller has been conducting art therapy groups at the Chemical Dependency Center for the past ten years under the supervision of her teacher and mentor, Janie Rhyne, PhD, ATR. Ms. Miller is a member of the American Art Therapy Association and has made presentations of her art therapy work with chemically dependent clients in the United States and Europe. Mary Ann has also published some of her work in nursing and chemical dependency literature. She makes her home in Iowa City.

Kevin R. Roeder, MSW, CICSW, is Director of Life Care Services for a network of three Northeastern Wisconsin HIV/AIDS human service organizations based out of Green Bay. He is also in private part-time psychotherapy practice for Edward Johnson, M.D. and Associates and teaches part-time as adjunct instructor for the social work professional program at the University of Wisconsin-Green Bay. Kevin received his B. S.W. degree from the University of Wisconsin-Green Bay and his M.S.W. degree from the University of Wisconsin-Milwaukee. He was certified in 1994 as an Independent Clinical Social Worker in the State of Wisconsin.

Rev. James E. Royce, SJ, PhD, a Jesuit priest, is Professor Emeritus of psychology and founding professor of addiction studies at Seattle University. His doctorate in psychology is from Loyola University in Chicago; he also has graduate degrees in philosophy and theology. His *Alcohol Problems and Alcoholism* won two national awards and is the leading textbook in the field. Rev. Royce was honored by the American Psychological Association for his work on psychology and religion and by the National Association of Alcoholism Counselors (now NAADAC) and by the National Council on Alcoholism (now NCADD) for his contributions to alcohol education.

Terry Tafoya, PhD, was trained as a traditional Native American Storyteller. Dr. Tafoya, who is a Taos Pueblo and Warm Springs Indian, has used American Indian ritual and ceremony in his work as a Family Therapist at the Interpersonal Psychotherapy Clinic, part of the University of Washington's School of Medicine in Seattle. While serving as Clinical Faculty and Senior Staff at the Interpersonal Psychotherapy Clinic, Dr. Tafoya was Professor of psychology at Evergreen State College where he directed transcultural counseling. In 1988, Dr. Tafoya co-founded the National Native American AIDS Prevention Center, a CDC-funded Minority AIDS Project, and in 1989 he created Tamanawit Unlimited, an international counseling firm for training and educating in mental health, human sexuality, HIV/AIDS, substance abuse prevention, and bilingual education. Dr. Tafoya serves as a National Consultant with the U.S. Center for Substance Abuse Prevention and is the Chief Curriculum Writer for the Gathering of Native Americans, a national project for Native American Substance Abuse Prevention. Dr. Tafoya has presented over a thousand keynotes, lectures, and workshops throughout the United States, Canada, Mexico, and Europe.

Joey Walker, MA, RMT-BC, is currently a music therapist at The University of Iowa Hospitals and Clinics. She is a former music educator who received her bachelor's degree in music education and psychology from William Penn College, and her equivalency in music therapy and her M.A. in music education/music therapy at The University of Iowa. In addition to working with chemically dependent clients, she also sees patients in the general hospital as well as in adult and child psychiatry.

Index

Adoration, prayers of, 104
Adult children of dysfunctional
    families, spirituality of, 7
African Americans
    AA whiteness and, 45
    church communities of, 47
Alaskan Natives
    "bar culture" of, 190
    self- vs. perceived identity of, 188
Alcoholics Anonymous (AA)
    historical perspective of, 120-122
    maleness of, 44-45,47
    "power greater than ourselves"
        concept of, 43-44
    Serenity Prayer of, 106-107
    special interest groups of, 45,
        167-168,189
    spiritual reading and, 49-50
    See also Applied spirituality;
        individual Steps
Alcoholism
    effects of on faith, 41-42
    "ism" phenomenon of, 131
    pre-alcoholism stage: context of
        addiction and, 41
    religion vs. spirituality in, 7-8
    trauma prior to, 39-40
    See also individual Steps;
        Spiritual recovery of an
        alcoholic with HIV
*Alcoholism: A Merry-Go-Round
    Named Denial* (Kellerman),
    21
Alcoholism effects on spirituality
    counseling's spiritual dimensions
        and, 21-22
    denial and, 19-21
    spiritual disease concept and,
        22-29

distortion of concept of God
    and, 26-27
incapacity to relate to the
    Infinite, 23
rejected by and rejecting God,
    28-29
seeking vs. escaping in, 28
sickness as a lack of health
    and, 22
spiritual progression chart, 24-25
    downward spiral, 26-29
    hitting bottom, 29,30
    spiritual recovery, 29-36
Alienation, spiritual disease
    symptom, 27
Amends, making of in Step Nine, 98
American Association for Music
    Therapy, 148
American Psychiatric Association,
    homosexuality as an illness
    and, 184
American Red Cross, 174
Anger management, music therapy
    lyric analysis for, 155-156
Applied spirituality
    achieving balance to, 131
    activities which manifest
        day-to-day activities, 122-123
        in everyday life, 124
        requiring greater commitment
        activities, 123
    barriers and misunderstandings of
        to newcomers, 124-126
    counters to, 126-128
    clinical implications of, 133
    examples of, 117-118
        case examples of, 118-120
        historical perspective of, 120-122

© 1995 by The Haworth Press, Inc. All rights reserved.

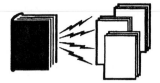

Haworth
DOCUMENT DELIVERY
SERVICE

This valuable service provides a single-article order form for any article from a Haworth journal.

- *Time Saving:* No running around from library to library to find a specific article.
- *Cost Effective:* All costs are kept down to a minimum.
- *Fast Delivery:* Choose from several options, including same-day FAX.
- *No Copyright Hassles:* You will be supplied by the original publisher.
- *Easy Payment:* Choose from several easy payment methods.

Open Accounts Welcome for ...
- Library Interlibrary Loan Departments
- Library Network/Consortia Wishing to Provide Single-Article Services
- Indexing/Abstracting Services with Single Article Provision Services
- Document Provision Brokers and Freelance Information Service Providers

---

MAIL or *FAX* THIS ENTIRE ORDER FORM TO:

Haworth Document Delivery Service
The Haworth Press, Inc.
10 Alice Street
Binghamton, NY 13904-1580

or FAX: 1-800-895-0582
or CALL: 1-800-342-9678
9am-5pm EST

PLEASE SEND ME PHOTOCOPIES OF THE FOLLOWING SINGLE ARTICLES:

1) Journal Title: _____

    Vol/Issue/Year:_____ Starting & Ending Pages:_____

    Article Title:_____

2) Journal Title: _____

    Vol/Issue/Year:_____ Starting & Ending Pages:_____

    Article Title:_____

3) Journal Title: _____

    Vol/Issue/Year:_____ Starting & Ending Pages:_____

    Article Title:_____

4) Journal Title: _____

    Vol/Issue/Year:_____ Starting & Ending Pages:_____

    Article Title:_____

(See other side for Costs and Payment Information)

COSTS: Please figure your cost to order quality copies of an article.

1. Set-up charge per article: $8.00

    ($8.00 × number of separate articles) _____

2. Photocopying charge for each article:

    1-10 pages: $1.00 _____

    11-19 pages: $3.00 _____

    20-29 pages: $5.00 _____

    30+ pages: $2.00/10 pages _____

3. Flexicover (optional): $2.00/article _____

4. Postage & Handling: US: $1.00 for the first article/

    $.50 each additional article _____

    Federal Express: $25.00 _____

    Outside US: $2.00 for first article/

    $.50 each additional article _____

5. Same-day FAX service: $.35 per page _____

GRAND TOTAL: _____

METHOD OF PAYMENT: (please check one)

❑ Check enclosed   ❑ Please ship and bill. PO # _____

(sorry we can ship and bill to bookstores only! All others must pre-pay)

❑ Charge to my credit card: ❑ Visa; ❑ MasterCard; ❑ Discover;

❑ American Express;

Account Number: _____ Expiration date: _____

Signature: *X* _____

Name: _____ Institution: _____

Address: _____

_____

City: _____ State: _____ Zip: _____

Phone Number: _____ FAX Number: _____

MAIL or *FAX* THIS ENTIRE ORDER FORM TO:

Haworth Document Delivery Service	**or FAX:** 1-800-895-0582
The Haworth Press, Inc.	**or CALL:** 1-800-342-9678
10 Alice Street	9am-5pm EST)
Binghamton, NY 13904-1580	